DAVID GRAEBER

Bullshit Jobs

A Theory

ALLEN LANE
an imprint of
PENGUIN BOOKS

ALLEN LANE

UK | USA | Canada | Ireland | Australia
India | New Zealand | South Africa

Penguin Books is part of the Penguin Random House group of companies
whose addresses can be found at global.penguinrandomhouse.com.

First published in the United States of America by Simon & Schuster, Inc. 2018
First published in Great Britain by Allen Lane 2018
002

Printed in Great Britain by Clays Ltd, St Ives plc

A CIP catalogue record for this book is available from the British Library

ISBN: 978–0–241–26388–4

www.greenpenguin.co.uk

MIX
Paper from
responsible sources
FSC® C018179

Penguin Random House is committed to a
sustainable future for our business, our readers
and our planet. This book is made from Forest
Stewardship Council® certified paper.

Bullshit Jobs

To anyone who would rather be doing something useful with themselves.

Contents

Chapter 1

What Is a Bullshit Job?   1

Why a Mafia Hit Man Is Not a Good Example of a Bullshit Job | On the
Importance of the Subjective Element, and Also, Why It Can Be Assumed
That Those Who Believe They Have Bullshit Jobs Are Generally Correct | On
the Common Misconception That Bullshit Jobs Are Confined Largely to the
Public Sector | Why Hairdressers Are a Poor Example of a Bullshit Job | On
the Difference Between Partly Bullshit Jobs, Mostly Bullshit Jobs, and Purely
and Entirely Bullshit Jobs

Chapter 2

What Sorts of Bullshit Jobs Are There?   27

The Five Major Varieties of Bullshit Jobs | 1. What Flunkies Do | 2. What
Goons Do | 3. What Duct Tapers Do | 4. What Box Tickers Do | 5. What
Taskmasters Do | On Complex Multiform Bullshit Jobs | A Word on Second-
Order Bullshit Jobs | A Final Note, with a Brief Return to the Question: Is It
Possible to Have a Bullshit Job and Not Know It?

Chapter 3

Why Do Those in Bullshit Jobs Regularly Report Themselves Unhappy? 67
(On Spiritual Violence, Part 1)

About One Young Man Apparently Handed a Sinecure Who Nonetheless
Found Himself Unable to Handle the Situation | Concerning the Experience of
Falseness and Purposelessness at the Core of Bullshit Jobs, and the Importance
Now Felt of Conveying the Experience of Falseness and Purposelessness to

Contents

Youth | Why Many of Our Fundamental Assumptions on Human Motivation Appear to Be Incorrect | A Brief Excursus on the History of Make-Work, and Particularly of the Concept of Buying Other People's Time | Concerning the Clash Between the Morality of Time and Natural Work Rhythms, and the Resentment It Creates

Chapter 4
What Is It Like to Have a Bullshit Job?

(On Spiritual Violence, Part 2)

Why Having a Bullshit Job Is Not Always Necessarily That Bad | On the Misery of Ambiguity and Forced Pretense | On the Misery of Not Being a Cause | On the Misery of Not Feeling Entitled to One's Misery | On the Misery of Knowing That One Is Doing Harm | Coda: On the Effects of Bullshit Jobs on Human Creativity, and On Why Attempts to Assert Oneself Creatively or Politically Against Pointless Employment Might Be Considered a Form of Spiritual Warfare

Chapter 5
Why Are Bullshit Jobs Proliferating?

A Brief Excursus on Causality and the Nature of Sociological Explanation | Sundry Notes on the Role of Government in Creating and Maintaining Bullshit Jobs | Concerning Some False Explanations for the Rise of Bullshit Jobs | Why the Financial Industry Might Be Considered a Paradigm for Bullshit Job Creation | On Some Ways in Which the Current Form of Managerial Feudalism Resembles Classical Feudalism, and Other Ways in Which It Does Not | How Managerial Feudalism Manifests Itself in the Creative Industries through an Endless Multiplication of Intermediary Executive Ranks | Conclusion, with a Brief Return to the Question of Three Levels of Causation

Chapter 6
Why Do We as a Society Not Object to the
Growth of Pointless Employment?

On the Impossibility of Developing an Absolute Measure of Value | How Most People in Contemporary Society Do Accept the Notion of a Social Value That Can Be Distinguished from Economic Value, Even If It Is Very Difficult

Contents

to Pin Down What It Is | Concerning the Inverse Relationship Between the Social Value of Work and the Amount of Money One Is Likely to Be Paid for It | On the Theological Roots of Our Attitudes Toward Labor | On the Origins of the Northern European Notion of Paid Labor as Necessary to the Full Formation of an Adult Human Being | How, with the Advent of Capitalism, Work Came to Be Seen in Many Quarters Either as a Means of Social Reform or Ultimately as a Virtue in Its Own Right, and How Laborers Countered by Embracing the Labor Theory of Value | Concerning the Key Flaw in the Labor Theory of Value as It Became Popular in the Nineteenth Century, and How the Owners of Capital Exploited That Flaw | How, over the Course of the Twentieth Century, Work Came to Be Increasingly Valued Primarily as a Form of Discipline and Self-Sacrifice

Chapter 7
What Are the Political Effects of Bullshit Jobs, and Is There Anything That Can Be Done About This Situation?   245

On How the Political Culture under Managerial Feudalism Comes to Be Maintained by a Balance of Resentments | How the Current Crisis over Robotization Relates to the Larger Problem of Bullshit Jobs | On the Political Ramifications of Bullshitization and Consequent Decline of Productivity in the Caring Sector as It Relates to the Possibility of a Revolt of the Caring Classes | On Universal Basic Income as an Example of a Program That Might Begin to Detach Work from Compensation and Put an End to the Dilemmas Described in This Book

BULLSHIT JOBS

Preface:

On the Phenomenon of Bullshit Jobs

In the spring of 2013, I unwittingly set off a very minor international sensation.

It all began when I was asked to write an essay for a new radical magazine called *Strike!* The editor asked if I had anything provocative that no one else would be likely to publish. I usually have one or two essay ideas like that stewing around, so I drafted one up and presented him with a brief piece entitled "On the Phenomenon of Bullshit Jobs."

The essay was based on a hunch. Everyone is familiar with those sort of jobs that don't seem, to the outsider, to really do much of anything: HR consultants, communications coordinators, PR researchers, financial strategists, corporate lawyers, or the sort of people (very familiar in academic contexts) who spend their time staffing committees that discuss the problem of unnecessary committees. The list was seemingly endless. What, I wondered, if these jobs really *are* useless, and those who hold them are aware of it? Certainly you meet people now and then who seem to feel their jobs are pointless and unnecessary. Could there be anything more demoralizing than having to wake up in the morning five out of seven days of one's adult life to perform a task that one secretly believed did not need to be performed—that was simply a waste of time or resources, or that even made the world worse? Would this not be a terrible psychic wound running across our society? Yet if so, it was one that no one ever seemed to talk about. There were plenty of surveys over whether people were happy at work. There were none, as far as I knew, about whether or not they felt their jobs had any good reason to exist.

This possibility that our society is riddled with useless jobs that no one wants to talk about did not seem inherently implausible. The subject of work is riddled with taboos. Even the fact that most people don't like their jobs and would relish an excuse not to go to work is considered something that can't really be admitted on TV—certainly not on the TV news, even if it might occasionally be alluded to in documentaries and stand-up comedy. I had experienced these taboos myself: I had once acted as the media liaison for an activist group that, rumor had it, was planning a civil disobedience campaign to shut down the Washington, DC, transport system as part of a protest against a global economic summit. In the days leading up to it, you could hardly go anywhere looking like an anarchist without some cheerful civil servant walking up to you and asking whether it was really true he or she wouldn't have to go to work on Monday. Yet at the same time, TV crews managed dutifully to interview city employees—and I wouldn't be surprised if some of them were the *same* city employees—commenting on how terribly tragic it would be if they wouldn't be able to get to work, since they knew that's what it would take to get them on TV. No one seems to feel free to say what they really feel about such matters—at least in public.

It was plausible, but I didn't really know. In a way, I wrote the piece as a kind of experiment. I was interested to see what sort of response it would elicit.

This is what I wrote for the August 2013 issue:

On the Phenomenon of Bullshit Jobs

In the year 1930, John Maynard Keynes predicted that, by century's end, technology would have advanced sufficiently that countries like Great Britain or the United States would have achieved a fifteen-hour work week. There's every reason to believe he was right. In technological terms, we are quite capable of this. And yet it didn't happen. Instead, technology has been marshaled, if anything, to figure out ways to make us all work more. In order to achieve this, jobs have had to be created that are, effectively, pointless. Huge swathes of people, in Europe and North America in particular, spend their entire working lives performing tasks they secretly believe do not really need to be performed. The moral and spiritual damage that comes from this situation is profound. It is a scar across our collective soul. Yet virtually no one talks about it.

Why did Keynes's promised utopia—still being eagerly awaited in the sixties—never materialize? The standard line today is that he didn't figure in the massive increase in consumerism. Given the choice between less hours and more toys and pleasures, we've collectively chosen the latter. This presents a nice morality tale, but even a moment's reflection shows it can't really be true. Yes, we have witnessed the creation of an endless variety of new jobs and industries since the twenties, but very few have anything to do with the production and distribution of sushi, iPhones, or fancy sneakers.

So what are these new jobs, precisely? A recent report comparing employment in the US between 1910 and 2000 gives us a clear picture (and I note, one pretty much exactly echoed in the UK). Over the course of the last century, the number of workers employed as domestic servants, in industry, and in the farm sector has collapsed dramatically. At the same time, "professional, managerial, clerical, sales, and service workers" tripled, growing "from one-quarter to three-quarters of total employment." In other words, productive jobs have, just as predicted, been largely automated away. (Even if you count industrial workers globally, including the toiling masses in India and China, such workers are still not nearly so large a percentage of the world population as they used to be.)

But rather than allowing a massive reduction of working hours to free the world's population to pursue their own projects, pleasures, visions, and ideas, we have seen the ballooning not even so much of the "service" sector as of the administrative sector, up to and including the creation of whole new industries like financial services or tele-marketing, or the unprecedented expansion of sectors like corporate law, academic and health administration, human resources, and public relations. And these numbers do not even reflect all those people whose job is to provide administrative, technical, or security support for these industries, or, for that matter, the whole host of ancillary industries (dog washers, all-night pizza deliverymen) that only exist because everyone else is spending so much of their time working in all the other ones.

These are what I propose to call "bullshit jobs."

It's as if someone were out there making up pointless jobs just for the sake of keeping us all working. And here, precisely, lies the mystery. In capitalism, this is precisely what is *not* supposed to happen. Sure, in the old inefficient Socialist states like the Soviet Union, where employment was considered both a right and a sacred duty, the system made up as many jobs as it had to. (This is why in Soviet department stores it took three clerks to sell a piece of meat.) But, of course, this is the very sort of problem market competition is supposed to fix. According to economic theory, at least, the last thing a profit-seeking firm is going to do is shell out money to workers they don't really need to employ. Still, somehow, it happens.

While corporations may engage in ruthless downsizing, the lay-offs and speed-ups invariably fall on that class of people who are actually making, moving, fixing, and maintaining things. Through some strange alchemy no one can quite explain, the number of salaried paper pushers ultimately seems to expand, and more and more employees find themselves—not unlike Soviet workers, actually—working forty- or even fifty-hour weeks on paper but effectively working fifteen hours just as Keynes predicted, since the rest of their time is spent organizing or attending motivational seminars, updating their Facebook profiles, or downloading TV box sets.

The answer clearly isn't economic: it's moral and political. The ruling class has figured out that a happy and productive population with free time on their hands is a mortal danger. (Think of what started to happen when this even began to be approximated in the sixties.) And, on the other hand, the feeling that work is a moral value in itself, and that anyone not willing to submit themselves to some kind of intense work discipline for most of their waking hours deserves nothing, is extraordinarily convenient for them.

Once, when contemplating the apparently endless growth of administrative responsibilities in British academic departments, I came up with one possible vision of hell. Hell is a collection of individuals who are spending the bulk of their time working on a task they don't like and are not especially good at. Say they were hired because they were excellent cabinetmakers, and then discover they are expected to spend a great deal of their time frying fish. Nor does the task really need to be done—at least, there's only a very limited number of fish that need to be fried. Yet somehow they all become so obsessed with resentment at the thought that some of their coworkers might be spending more time making cabinets and not doing their fair share of the fish-frying responsibilities that before long, there's endless piles of useless, badly cooked fish piling up all over the workshop, and it's all that anyone really does.

I think this is actually a pretty accurate description of the moral dynamics of our own economy.

Now, I realize any such argument is going to run into immediate objections: "Who are you to say what jobs are really 'necessary'? What's 'necessary,' anyway? You're an anthropology professor—what's the 'need' for that?" (And, indeed, a lot of tabloid readers would take the existence of my job as the very definition of wasteful social expenditure.) And on one level, this is obviously true. There can be no objective measure of social value.

I would not presume to tell someone who is convinced they are making a meaningful contribution to the world that, really, they are not. But what about those people who are themselves convinced their jobs are meaningless? Not long ago, I got back in touch with a school friend whom I hadn't seen since I was fifteen. I was amazed to discover that in the interim, he had become first a poet, then the front man in an indie rock band. I'd heard some of his songs on the radio, having no idea the singer was someone I actually knew. He was obviously brilliant, innovative, and his work had unquestionably brightened and improved the lives of people all over the world. Yet, after a couple of unsuccessful albums, he'd lost his contract, and, plagued with debts and a newborn daughter, ended up, as he put it, "taking the default choice of so many directionless folk: law school." Now he's a corporate lawyer working in a prominent New York firm. He was the first to admit that his job was utterly meaningless, contributed nothing to the world, and, in his own estimation, should not really exist.

There's a lot of questions one could ask here, starting with, What does it say about our society that it seems to generate an extremely limited demand for talented poet-musicians but an apparently infinite demand for specialists in corporate law? (Answer: If 1 percent of the population controls most of the disposable wealth, what we call "the market" reflects what *they* think is useful or important, not anybody else.) But even more, it shows that most people in pointless jobs are ultimately aware of it. In fact, I'm not sure I've ever met a corporate lawyer who didn't think their job was bullshit. The same goes for almost all the new industries outlined above. There is a whole class of salaried professionals that, should you meet them at parties and admit that you do something that might be considered interesting (an anthropologist, for example), will want to avoid even discussing their line of work entirely. Give them a few drinks, and they will launch into tirades about how pointless and stupid their job really is.

This is a profound psychological violence here. How can one even begin to speak of dignity in labor when one secretly feels one's job should not exist? How can it not create a sense of deep rage and resentment? Yet it is the peculiar genius of our society that its rulers have figured out a way, as in the case of the fish fryers, to ensure that rage is directed precisely against those who actually do get to do meaningful work. For instance: in our society, there seems to be a general rule that, the more obviously one's work benefits other people, the less one is likely to be paid for it. Again, an objective measure is hard to find, but one easy way to get a sense is to ask: What would happen were this entire class of people to simply disappear? Say what you like about nurses, garbage collectors, or mechanics, it's obvious that were they to vanish in a puff of smoke, the results would be immediate and catastrophic. A world without teachers or dockworkers would soon be in trouble, and even one without science-fiction writers or ska musicians would clearly be a lesser place. It's not entirely clear how humanity would suffer were all private equity CEOs, lobbyists, PR researchers, actuaries, telemarketers, bailiffs, or legal consultants to similarly vanish.[1] (Many suspect it might improve markedly.) Yet apart from a handful of well-touted exceptions (doctors), the rule holds surprisingly well.

Even more perverse, there seems to be a broad sense that this is the way things should be. This is one of the secret strengths of right-wing populism. You can see it when tabloids whip up resentment against tube workers for paralyzing London during contract disputes: the very fact that tube workers can paralyze London shows that their work is actually necessary, but this seems to be precisely what annoys people. It's even clearer in the United States, where Republicans have had remarkable success mobilizing resentment against schoolteachers and autoworkers (and not, significantly, against the school administrators or auto industry executives who actually cause the problems) for their supposedly bloated wages and benefits. It's as if they are being told "But you get to teach children! Or make cars! You get to have real jobs! And on top of that, you have the nerve to also expect middle-class pensions and health care?"

If someone had designed a work regime perfectly suited to maintaining the power of finance capital, it's hard to see how he or she could have done a better job. Real, productive workers are relentlessly squeezed and exploited. The remainder are divided between a terrorized stratum of the universally reviled unemployed and a larger stratum who are basically paid to do nothing, in positions designed to make them identify with the perspectives and sensibilities of the ruling class (managers, administrators, etc.)—and particularly its financial avatars—but, at the same time, foster a simmering resentment against anyone whose work has clear and undeniable social value. Clearly, the system was never consciously designed. It emerged from almost a century of trial and error. But it is the only explanation for why, despite our technological capacities, we are not all working three- to four-hour days.

If ever an essay's hypothesis was confirmed by its reception, this was it. "On the Phenomenon of Bullshit Jobs" produced an explosion.

The irony was that the two weeks after the piece came out were the same two weeks that my partner and I had decided to spend with a basket of books, and each other, in a cabin in rural Quebec. We'd made a point of finding a location with no wireless. This left me in the awkward position of having to observe the results only on my mobile phone. The essay went viral almost immediately. Within weeks, it had been translated into at least a dozen languages, including German, Norwegian, Swedish, French, Czech, Romanian, Russian, Turkish, Latvian, Polish, Greek, Estonian, Catalan, and Korean, and was reprinted in newspapers from Switzerland to Australia. The original *Strike!* page received more than a million hits and crashed repeatedly from too much traffic. Blogs sprouted. Comments sections filled up with confessions from white-collar professionals; people wrote me asking for guidance or to tell me I had inspired them to quit their jobs to find something more meaningful. Here is one enthusiastic response (I've collected hundreds) from the comments section of Australia's *Canberra Times*:

> Wow! Nail on the head! I am a corporate lawyer (tax litigator, to be specific). I contribute nothing to this world and am utterly miserable all of the time. I don't like it when people have the nerve to say "Why do it, then?" because it is so clearly not that simple. It so happens to be the only way right now for me to contribute to the 1 percent in such a significant way so as to reward me with a house in Sydney to raise my future kids . . . Thanks to technology, we are probably as productive in two days as we previously were in five. But thanks to greed and some busy-bee syndrome of productivity, we are still asked to slave away

for the profit of others ahead of our own nonremunerated ambitions. Whether you believe in intelligent design or evolution, humans were not made to work—so to me, this is all just greed propped up by inflated prices of necessities.[2]

At one point, I got a message from one anonymous fan who said that he was part of an impromptu group circulating the piece within the financial services community; he'd received five emails containing the essay just that day (certainly one sign that many in financial services don't have much to do). None of this answered the question of how many people really felt that way about their jobs—as opposed to, say, passing on the piece as a way to drop subtle hints to others—but before long, statistical evidence did indeed surface.

On January 5, 2015, a little more than a year after the article came out, on the first Monday of the new year—that is, the day most Londoners were returning to work from their winter holidays—someone took several hundred ads in London Underground cars and replaced them with a series of guerrilla posters consisting of quotes from the original essay. These were the ones they chose:

- Huge swathes of people spend their days performing tasks they secretly believe do not really need to be performed.
- It's as if someone were out there making up pointless jobs for the sake of keeping us all working.
- The moral and spiritual damage that comes from this situation is profound. It is a scar across our collective soul. Yet virtually no one talks about it.
- How can one even begin to speak of dignity in labor when one secretly feels one's job should not exist?

The response to the poster campaign was another spate of discussion in the media (I appeared briefly on *Russia Today*), as a result of which the polling agency YouGov took it upon itself to test the hypothesis and conducted a poll of Britons using language taken directly from the essay: for example, Does your job "make a meaningful contribution to the world"? Astonishingly, more than a third—37 percent—said they believed that it did not (whereas 50 percent said it did, and 13 percent were uncertain).

This was almost twice what I had anticipated—I'd imagined the percentage of bullshit jobs was probably around 20 percent. What's more, a later poll in Holland came up with almost exactly the same results: in fact, a little higher, as 40 percent of Dutch workers reported that their jobs had no good reason to exist.

So not only has the hypothesis been confirmed by public reaction, it has now been overwhelmingly confirmed by statistical research.

■ ■ ■

Clearly, then, we have an important social phenomenon that has received almost no systematic attention.[3] Simply opening up a way to talk about it became, for many, cathartic. It was obvious that a larger exploration was in order.

What I want to do here is a bit more systematic than the original essay. The 2013 piece was for a magazine about revolutionary politics, and it emphasized the political implications of the problem. In fact, the essay was just one of a series of arguments I was developing at the time that the neoliberal ("free market") ideology that had dominated the world since the days of Thatcher and Reagan was really the opposite of what it claimed to be; it was really a political project dressed up as an economic one.

I had come to this conclusion because it seemed to be the only way to explain how those in power actually behaved. While neoliberal rhetoric was always all about unleashing the magic of the marketplace and placing economic efficiency over all other values, the overall effect of free market policies has been that rates of economic growth have slowed pretty much everywhere except India and China; scientific and technological advance has stagnated; and in most wealthy countries, the younger generations can, for the first time in centuries, expect to lead less prosperous lives than their parents did. Yet on observing these effects, proponents of market ideology always reply with calls for even stronger doses of the same medicine, and politicians duly enact them. This struck me as odd. If a private company hired a consultant to come up with a business plan, and it resulted in a sharp decline in profits, that consultant would be fired. At the very least, he'd be asked to come up with a different plan. With free market reforms, this never seemed to happen. The more they failed, the more they were enacted. The only logical conclusion was that economic imperatives weren't really driving the project.

What was? It seemed to me the answer had to lie in the mind-set of the political class. Almost all of those making the key decisions had attended college in the 1960s, when campuses were at the very epicenter of political ferment, and they felt strongly that such things must never happen again. As a result, while they might have been concerned with declining economic indicators, they were also quite delighted to note that the combination of globalization, gutting the power of unions, and creating an insecure and overworked workforce—along with aggressively paying lip service to sixties calls to hedonistic personal liberation (what came to be known as "lifestyle liberalism, fiscal conservativism")—had the effect of simultaneously shifting more and more wealth and power to the wealthy and almost completely destroying the basis for organized challenges to their power. It might not have worked very well economically, but politically it worked like a dream. If nothing else, they had little incentive to abandon such policies. All I did in the essay was to pursue this insight: whenever you find someone doing something in the name of economic efficiency that seems completely economically irrational (like, say, paying people good money to do nothing all day), one had best start by asking, as the ancient Romans did, *"Qui bono?"*—"Who benefits?"—and how.

This is less a conspiracy theory approach than it is an *anti*conspiracy theory. I was asking why action *wasn't* taken. Economic trends happen for all sorts of reasons, but if they cause problems for the rich and powerful, those rich and powerful people will pressure institutions to step in and do something about the matter. This is why after the financial crisis of 2008–09, large investment banks were bailed out but ordinary mortgage holders weren't. The proliferation of bullshit jobs, as we'll see, happened for a variety of reasons. The real question I was asking is why no one intervened ("conspired," if you like) to do something about the matter.

■ ■ ■

In this book I want to do considerably more than that.

I believe that the phenomenon of bullshit employment can provide us with a window on much deeper social problems. We need to ask ourselves, not just how did such a large proportion of our workforce find themselves laboring at tasks that they themselves consider pointless, but also why do so many people believe this state of affairs to be normal, inevitable—even desirable? More oddly still, why, despite the fact that they hold these opinions in the abstract, and even believe that it is entirely appropriate that those who labor at pointless jobs should be paid more and receive more honor and recognition than those who do something they consider to be useful, do they nonetheless find themselves depressed and miserable if they themselves end up in positions where they are being paid to do nothing, or nothing that they feel benefits others in any way? There is clearly a jumble of contradictory ideas and impulses at play here. One thing I want to do in this book is begin to sort them out. This will mean asking practical questions such as: How do bullshit jobs actually happen? It will also mean asking deep historical questions, like, When and how did we come to believe that creativity was supposed to be painful, or, how did we ever come up with the notion that it would be possible to sell one's time? And finally, it will mean asking fundamental questions about human nature.

Writing this book also serves a political purpose.

I would like this book to be an arrow aimed at the heart of our civilization. There is something very wrong with what we have made ourselves. We have become a civilization based on work—not even "productive work" but work as an end and meaning in itself. We have come to believe that men and women who do not work harder than they wish at jobs they do not particularly enjoy are bad people unworthy of love, care, or assistance from their communities. It is as if we have collectively acquiesced to our own enslavement. The main political reaction to our awareness that half the time we are engaged in utterly meaningless or even counterproductive activities—usually under the orders of a person we dislike—is to rankle with resentment over the fact there might be others out there who are not in the same trap. As a result, hatred, resentment, and suspicion have become the glue that holds society together. This is a disastrous state of affairs. I wish it to end.

If this book can in any way contribute to that end, it will have been worth writing.

Chapter 1

What Is a Bullshit Job?

Let us begin with what might be considered a paradigmatic example of a bullshit job.

Kurt works for a subcontractor for the German military. Or . . . actually, he is employed by a subcontractor of a subcontractor of a subcontractor for the German military. Here is how he describes his work:

> The German military has a subcontractor that does their IT work.
>
> The IT firm has a subcontractor that does their logistics.
>
> The logistics firm has a subcontractor that does their personnel management, and I work for that company.
>
> Let's say soldier A moves to an office two rooms farther down the hall. Instead of just carrying his computer over there, he has to fill out a form.
>
> The IT subcontractor will get the form, people will read it and approve it, and forward it to the logistics firm.
>
> The logistics firm will then have to approve the moving down the hall and will request personnel from us.
>
> The office people in my company will then do whatever they do, and now I come in.
>
> I get an email: "Be at barracks B at time C." Usually these barracks

are one hundred to five hundred kilometers [62–310 miles] away from my home, so I will get a rental car. I take the rental car, drive to the barracks, let dispatch know that I arrived, fill out a form, unhook the computer, load the computer into a box, seal the box, have a guy from the logistics firm carry the box to the next room, where I unseal the box, fill out another form, hook up the computer, call dispatch to tell them how long I took, get a couple of signatures, take my rental car back home, send dispatch a letter with all of the paperwork and then get paid.

So instead of the soldier carrying his computer for five meters, two people drive for a combined six to ten hours, fill out around fifteen pages of paperwork, and waste a good four hundred euros of taxpayers' money.[1]

This might sound like a classic example of ridiculous military red tape of the sort Joseph Heller made famous in his 1961 novel *Catch-22*, except for one key element: almost nobody in this story actually works for the military. Technically, they're all part of the private sector. There was a time, of course, when any national army also had its own communications, logistics, and personnel departments, but nowadays it all has to be done through multiple layers of private outsourcing.

Kurt's job might be considered a paradigmatic example of a bullshit job for one simple reason: if the position were eliminated, it would make no discernible difference in the world. Likely as not, things would improve, since German military bases would presumably have to come up with a more reasonable way to move equipment. Crucially, not only is Kurt's job absurd, but Kurt himself is perfectly well aware of this. (In fact, on the blog where he posted this story, he ended up defending the claim that the job served no purpose against a host of free market enthusiasts who popped up instantly—as free market enthusiasts tend to do on internet forums—to insist that since his job was created by the private sector, it by definition had to serve a legitimate purpose.)

This I consider the defining feature of a bullshit job: one so completely pointless that even the person who has to perform it every day cannot convince himself there's a good reason for him to be doing it. He might not be able to admit this to his coworkers—often there are very good reasons not to do so. But he is convinced the job is pointless nonetheless.

So let this stand as an initial provisional definition:

> Provisional Definition: a bullshit job is a form of employment that is so completely pointless, unnecessary, or pernicious that even the employee cannot justify its existence.

Some jobs are so pointless that no one even notices if the person who has the job vanishes. This usually happens in the public sector:

Spanish Civil Servant Skips Work for Six Years to Study Spinoza

—*Jewish Times*, February 26, 2016

A Spanish civil servant who collected a salary for at least six years without working used the time to become an expert on the writings of Jewish philosopher Baruch Spinoza, Spanish media reported.

A court in Cadiz in southern Spain last month ordered Joaquin Garcia, sixty-nine, to pay approximately $30,000 in fines for failing to show up for work at the water board, Agua de Cadiz, where Garcia was employed as an engineer since 1996, the news site euronews.com reported last week.

His absence was first noticed in 2010, when Garcia was due to receive a medal for long service. Deputy Mayor Jorge Blas Fernandez began making inquiries that led him to discover that Garcia had not been seen at his office in six years.

Reached by the newspaper *El Mundo*, unnamed sources close to Garcia said he devoted himself in the years before 2010 to studying the writings of Spinoza, a seventeenth-century heretic Jew from Amsterdam. One source interviewed by *El Mundo* said Garcia became an expert on Spinoza but denied claims Garcia never showed up for work, saying he came in at irregular times.[2]

This story made headlines in Spain. At a time when the country was undergoing severe austerity and high unemployment, it seemed outrageous that there were civil servants who could skip work for years without anybody noticing. Garcia's defense, however, is not without merit. He explained that while he had worked for many years dutifully monitoring the city's water treatment plant, the water board eventually came under the control of higher-ups who loathed him for his Socialist politics and refused to assign him any responsibilities. He found this situation so demoralizing that he was eventually obliged to seek clinical help for depression. Finally, and with the concurrence of his therapist, he decided that rather than just continue to sit around all day pretending to look busy, he would convince the water board he was being supervised by the municipality, and the municipality that he was being supervised by the water board, check in if there was a problem, but otherwise just go home and do something useful with his life.[3]

Similar stories about the public sector appear at regular intervals. One popular one is about postal carriers who decide that rather than delivering the mail, they prefer to dump it in closets, sheds, or Dumpsters—with the result that tons of letters and packages pile up for years without anyone figuring it out.[4] David Foster Wallace's novel *The Pale King*, about life inside an Internal Revenue Service office in Peoria, Illinois, goes even further: it culminates in an auditor dying at his desk and remaining propped in his chair for days before anyone notices. This seems pure absurdist caricature, but in 2002, something almost exactly like this did happen in Helsinki. A Finnish tax auditor working in a closed office sat dead at his desk for more than forty-eight hours while thirty colleagues carried on around him. "People thought he wanted to work in peace, and no one disturbed him," remarked his supervisor—which, if you think about it, is actually rather thoughtful.[5]

It's stories like these, of course, that inspire politicians all over the world to call for a larger role for the private sector—where, it is always claimed, such abuses would not occur. And while it is true so far that we have not heard any stories of FedEx or UPS employees stowing their parcels in garden sheds, privatization generates its own, often much less genteel, varieties of madness—as Kurt's story shows. I need hardly point out the irony in the fact that Kurt was, ultimately, working for the German military. The German military has been accused of many things over the years, but inefficiency was rarely one of them. Still, a rising tide of bullshit soils all boats. In the twenty-first century, even panzer divisions have come to be surrounded by a vast penumbra of sub-, sub-sub-, and sub-sub-subcontractors; tank commanders are obliged to perform complex and exotic bureaucratic rituals in order to move equipment from one room to another, even as those providing the paperwork secretly post elaborate complaints to blogs about how idiotic the whole thing is.

If these cases are anything to go by, the main difference between the public and private sectors is not that either is more, or less, likely to generate pointless work. It does not even necessarily lie in the kind of pointless work each tends to generate. The main difference is that pointless work in the private sector is likely to be far more closely supervised. This is not always the case. As we'll learn, the number of employees of banks, pharmaceutical companies, and engineering firms allowed to spend most of their time updating their Facebook profiles is surprisingly high. Still, in the private sector, there are limits. If Kurt were to simply walk off the job to take up the study of his favorite seventeenth-century Jewish philosopher, he would be swiftly relieved of his position. If the Cadiz Water Board had been privatized, Joaquin Garcia might well still have been deprived of responsibilities by managers who disliked him, but he would have been expected to sit at his desk and pretend to work every day anyway, or find alternate employment.

I will leave readers to decide for themselves whether such a state of affairs should be considered an improvement.

why a mafia hit man is not a good example of a bullshit job

To recap: what I am calling "bullshit jobs" are jobs that are primarily or entirely made up of tasks that the person doing that job considers to be pointless, unnecessary, or even pernicious. Jobs that, were they to disappear, would make no difference whatsoever. Above all, these are jobs that the holders themselves feel should not exist.

Contemporary capitalism seems riddled with such jobs. As I mentioned in the preface, a YouGov poll found that in the United Kingdom only 50 percent of those who had full-time jobs were entirely sure their job made any sort of meaningful contribution to the world, and 37 percent were quite sure it did not. A poll by the firm Schouten & Nelissen carried out in Holland put the latter number as high as 40 percent.[6] If you think about it, these are staggering statistics. After all, a very large percentage of jobs involves doing things that no one could possibly see as pointless. One must assume that the percentage of nurses, bus drivers, dentists, street cleaners, farmers, music teachers, repairmen, gardeners, firefighters, set designers, plumbers, journalists, safety inspectors, musicians, tailors, and school crossing guards who checked "no" to the question "Does your job make any meaningful difference in the world?" was approximately zero. My own research suggests that store clerks, restaurant workers, and other low-level service providers rarely see themselves as having bullshit jobs, either. Many service workers hate their jobs; but even those who do are aware that what they do does make some sort of meaningful difference in the world.[7]

So if 37 percent to 40 percent of a country's working population insist their work makes no difference whatsoever, and another substantial chunk suspects that it might not, one can only conclude that any office worker who one might suspect secretly believes themselves to have a bullshit job does, indeed, believe this.

■ ■ ■

The main thing I would like to do in this first chapter is to define what I mean by bullshit jobs; in the next chapter I will lay out a typology of what I believe the main varieties of bullshit jobs to be. This will open the way, in later chapters, to considering how bullshit jobs come about, why they have come to be so prevalent, and to considering their psychological, social, and political effects. I am convinced these effects are deeply insidious. We have created societies where much of the population, trapped in useless employment, have come to resent and despise equally those who do the most useful work in society, and those who do no paid work at all. But before we can analyze this situation, it will be necessary to address some potential objections.

The reader may have noticed a certain ambiguity in my initial definition. I describe bullshit jobs as involving tasks the holder considers to be "pointless, unnecessary, or even pernicious." But, of course, jobs that have no significant effect on the world and jobs that have pernicious effects on the world are hardly the same thing. Most of us would agree that a Mafia hit man does more harm than good in the world, overall; but could you really call Mafia hit man a bullshit job? That just feels somehow wrong.

As Socrates teaches us, when this happens—when our own definitions produce results that seem intuitively wrong to us—it's because we're not aware of what we really think. (Hence, he suggests that the true role of philosophers is to tell people what they already know but don't realize that they know. One could argue that anthropologists like myself do something similar.) The phrase "bullshit jobs" clearly strikes a chord with many people. It makes sense to them in some way. This means they have, at least on some sort of tacit intuitive level, criteria in their minds that allow them to say "That was such a bullshit job" or "That one was bad, but I wouldn't say it was exactly bullshit." Many people with pernicious jobs feel the phrase fits them; others clearly don't. The best way to tease out what those criteria are is to examine borderline cases.

So, why does it feel wrong to say a hit man has a bullshit job?[8]

I suspect there are multiple reasons, but one is that the Mafia hit man (unlike, say, a foreign currency speculator or a brand marketing researcher) is unlikely to make false claims. True, a mafioso will usually claim he is merely a "businessman." But insofar as he is willing to own up to the nature of his actual occupation at all, he will tend to be pretty up front about what he does. He is unlikely to pretend his work is in any way beneficial to society, even to the extent of insisting it contributes to the success of a team that's providing some useful product or service (drugs, prostitution, and so on), or if he does, the pretense is likely to be paper thin.

This allows us to refine our definition. Bullshit jobs are not just jobs that are useless or pernicious; typically, there has to be some degree of pretense and fraud involved as well. The jobholder must feel obliged to pretend that there is, in fact, a good reason why her job exists, even if, privately, she finds such claims ridiculous. There has to be some kind of gap between pretense and reality. (This makes sense etymologically[9]: "bullshitting" is, after all, a form of dishonesty.[10])

So we might make a second pass:

Provisional Definition 2: a bullshit job is a form of employment that is so completely pointless, unnecessary, or pernicious that even the employee cannot justify its existence even though the employee feels obliged to pretend that this is not the case.

Of course, there is another reason why hit man should not be considered a bullshit job. The hit man is not personally convinced his job should not exist. Most mafiosi believe they are part of an ancient and honorable tradition that is a value in its own right, whether or not it contributes to the larger social good. This is, incidentally, the reason why "feudal overlord" is not a bullshit job, either. Kings, earls, emperors, pashas, emirs, squires, zamindars, landlords, and the like might, arguably, be useless people; many of us would insist (and I would be inclined to agree) that they play pernicious roles in human affairs. But *they* don't think so. So unless the king is secretly a Marxist, or a Republican, one can say confidently that "king" is not a bullshit job.

This is a useful point to bear in mind because most people who do a great deal of harm in the world are protected against the knowledge that they do so. Or they allow themselves to believe the endless accretion of paid flunkies and yes-men that inevitably assemble around them to come up with reasons why they are really doing good. (Nowadays, these are sometimes referred to as think tanks.) This is just as true of financial-speculating investment bank CEOs as it is of military strongmen in countries such as North Korea and Azerbaijan. Mafiosi families are unusual perhaps because they make few such pretensions—but in the end, they are just miniature, illicit versions of the same feudal tradition, being originally enforcers for local landlords in Sicily who have over time come to operate on their own hook.[11]

There is one final reason why hit man cannot be considered a bullshit job: it's not entirely clear that hit man is a "job" in the first place. True, the hit man might well be employed by the local crime boss in some capacity or other. Perhaps the crime boss makes up some dummy security job for him in his casino. In that case, we can definitely say *that* job is a bullshit job. But he is not receiving a paycheck in his capacity as a hit man.

■ ■ ■

This point allows us to refine our definition even further. When people speak of bullshit jobs, they are generally referring to employment that involves being paid to work for someone else, either on a waged or salaried basis (most would also include paid consultancies). Obviously, there are many self-employed people who manage to get money from others by means of falsely pretending to provide them with some benefit or service (normally we call them grifters, scam artists, charlatans, or frauds), just as there are self-employed people who get money off others by doing or threatening to do them harm (normally we refer to them as muggers, burglars, extortionists, or thieves). In the first case, at least, we can definitely speak of bullshit, but not of bullshit jobs, because these aren't "jobs," properly speaking. A con job is an act, not a profession. So is a Brink's job. People do sometimes speak of professional burglars, but this is just a way of saying that theft is the burglar's primary source of income.[12] No one is actually paying the burglar regular wages or a salary to break into people's homes. For this reason, one cannot say that burglar is, precisely, a job, either.[13]

These considerations allow us to formulate what I think can serve as a final working definition:

Final Working Definition: a bullshit job is a form of paid employment that is so completely pointless, unnecessary, or pernicious that even the employee cannot justify its existence even though, as part of the conditions of employment, the employee feels obliged to pretend that this is not the case.

on the importance of the subjective element, and also, why it can be assumed that those who believe they have bullshit jobs are generally correct

This, I think, is a serviceable definition; good enough, anyway, for the purposes of this book.

The attentive reader may have noticed one remaining ambiguity. The definition is mainly subjective. I define a bullshit job as one that the worker considers to be pointless, unnecessary, or pernicious—but I also suggest that the worker is correct.[14] I'm assuming there is an underlying reality here. One really has to make this assumption because otherwise we'd be stuck with accepting that the exact same job could be bullshit one day and nonbullshit the next, depending on the vagaries of some fickle worker's mood. All I'm really saying here is that since there is such a thing as social value, as apart from mere market value, but since no one has ever figured out an adequate way to measure it, the worker's perspective is about as close as one is likely to get to an accurate assessment of the situation.[15]

Often it's pretty obvious why this should be the case: if an office worker is really spending 80 percent of her time designing cat memes, her coworkers in the next cubicle may or may not be aware of what's going on, but there's no way that she is going to be under any illusions about what she's doing. But even in more complicated cases, where it's a question of how much the worker really contributes to an organization, I think it's safe to assume the worker knows best. I'm aware this position will be taken as controversial in certain quarters. Executives and other bigwigs will often insist that most people who work for a large corporation don't fully understand their contributions, since the big picture can be seen only from the top. I am not saying this is entirely untrue: frequently there are some parts of the larger context that lower-level workers cannot see or simply aren't told about. This is especially true if the company is up to anything illegal.[16] But it's been my experience that any underling who works for the same outfit for any length of time—say, a year or two—will normally be taken aside and let in on the company secrets.

True, there are exceptions. Sometimes managers intentionally break up tasks in such a way that the workers don't really understand how their efforts contribute to the overall enterprise. Banks will often do this. I've even heard examples of factories in America where many of the line workers were unaware of what the plant was actually making; though in such cases, it almost always turned out to be because the owners had intentionally hired people who didn't speak English. Still, in those cases, workers tend to assume that their jobs are useful; they just don't know how. Generally speaking, I think employees can be expected to know what's going on in an office or on a shop floor, and, certainly, to understand how their work does, or does not, contribute to the enterprise—at least, better than anybody else.[17] With the higher-ups, that's not always clear. One frequent theme I encountered in my research was of underlings wondering in effect, "Does my supervisor actually *know* that I spend eighty percent of my time designing cat memes? Are they just pretending not to notice, or are they actually unaware?" And since the higher up the chain of command you are, the more reason people have to hide things from you, the worse this situation tends to become.

The real sticky problem comes in when it's a question of whether certain *kinds* of work (say, telemarketing, market research, consulting) are bullshit—that is, whether they can be said to produce any sort of positive social value. Here, all I'm saying is that it's best to defer to the judgment of those who do that kind of work. Social value, after all, is largely just what people think it is. In which case, who else is in a better position to judge? In this instance, I'd say: if the preponderance of those engaged in a certain occupation privately believe their work is of no social value, one should proceed along the assumption they are right.[18]

Sticklers will no doubt raise objections here too. They might ask: How can one actually know for sure what the majority of people working in an industry secretly think? And the answer is that obviously, you can't.

11

Even if it were possible to conduct a poll of lobbyists or financial consultants, it's not clear how many would give honest answers. When I spoke in broad strokes about useless industries in the original essay, I did so on the assumption that lobbyists and financial consultants are, in fact, largely aware of their uselessness—indeed, that many if not most of them are haunted by the knowledge that nothing of value would be lost to the world were their jobs simply to disappear.

I could be wrong. It is possible that corporate lobbyists or financial consultants genuinely subscribe to a theory of social value that holds their work to be essential to the health and prosperity of the nation. It is possible they therefore sleep securely in their beds, confident that their work is a blessing for everyone around them. I don't know, but I suspect this is more likely to be true as one moves up the food chain, since it would appear to be a general truth that the more harm a category of powerful people do in the world, the more yes-men and propagandists will tend to accumulate around them, coming up with reasons why they are really doing good—and the more likely it is that at least some of those powerful people will believe them.[19] Corporate lobbyists and financial consultants certainly do seem responsible for a disproportionately large share of the harm done in the world (at least, harm carried out as part of one's professional duties). Perhaps they really do have to force themselves to believe in what they do.

In that case, finance and lobbying wouldn't be bullshit jobs at all; they'd actually be more like hit men. At the very, very top of the food chain, this does appear to be the case. I remarked in the original 2013 piece, for instance, that I'd never known a corporate lawyer who didn't think his or her job was bullshit. But, of course, that's also a reflection of the sort of corporate lawyers that I'm likely to know: the sort who used to be poet-musicians. But even more significantly: the sort who are not particularly high ranking. It's my impression that genuinely powerful corporate lawyers think their roles are entirely legitimate. Or perhaps they simply don't care whether they're doing good or harm.

At the very top of the financial food chain, that's certainly the case. In April 2013, by a strange coincidence, I happened to be present at a conference on "Fixing the Banking System for Good" held inside the Philadelphia Federal Reserve, where Jeffrey Sachs, the Columbia University economist most famous for having designed the "shock therapy" reforms applied to the former Soviet Union, had a live-on-video-link session in which he startled everyone by presenting what careful journalists might describe as an "unusually candid" assessment of those in charge of America's financial institutions. Sachs's testimony is especially valuable because, as he kept emphasizing, many of these people were quite up front with him because they assumed (not entirely without reason) that he was on their side:

> Look, I meet a lot of these people on Wall Street on a regular basis right now . . . I know them. These are the people I have lunch with. And I am going to put it very bluntly: I regard the moral environment as pathological. [These people] have no responsibility to pay taxes; they have no responsibility to their clients; they have no responsibility to counterparties in transactions. They are tough, greedy, aggressive, and feel absolutely out of control in a quite literal sense, and they have gamed the system to a remarkable extent. They genuinely believe they have a God-given right to take as much money as they possibly can in any way that they can get it, legal or otherwise.
>
> If you look at the campaign contributions, which I happened to do yesterday for another purpose, the financial markets are the number one campaign contributors in the US system now. We have a corrupt politics to the core . . . both parties are up to their necks in this.
>
> But what it's led to is this sense of impunity that is really stunning, and you feel it on the individual level right now. And it's very, very unhealthy, I have waited for four years . . . five years now to see one figure on Wall Street speak in a moral language. And I've have not seen it once.[20]

So there you have it. If Sachs was right—and honestly, who is in a better position to know?—then at the commanding heights of the financial system, we're not actually talking about bullshit jobs. We're not even talking about people who have come to believe their own propagandists. Really we're just talking about a bunch of crooks.

Another distinction that's important to bear in mind is between jobs that are pointless and jobs that are merely bad. I will refer to the latter as "shit jobs," since people often do.

The only reason I bring up the matter is because the two are so often confused—which is odd, because they're in no way similar. In fact, they might almost be considered opposites. Bullshit jobs often pay quite well and tend to offer excellent working conditions. They're just pointless. Shit jobs are usually not at all bullshit; they typically involve work that needs to be done and is clearly of benefit to society; it's just that the workers who do them are paid and treated badly.

Some jobs, of course, are intrinsically unpleasant but fulfilling in other ways. (There's an old joke about the man whose job it was to clean up elephant dung after the circus. No matter what he did, he couldn't get the smell off his body. He'd change his clothes, wash his hair, scrub himself endlessly, but he still reeked, and women tended to avoid him. An old friend finally asked him, "Why do you do this to yourself? There are so many other jobs you could do." The man answered, "What? And give up show business!?") These jobs can be considered neither shit nor bullshit, whatever the content of the work. Other jobs—ordinary cleaning, for example—are in no sense inherently degrading, but they can easily be made so.

The cleaners at my current university, for instance, are treated very badly. As in most universities these days, their work has been outsourced. They are employed not directly by the school but by an agency, the name of which is emblazoned on the purple uniforms they wear. They are paid little, obliged to work with dangerous chemicals that often damage their hands or otherwise force them to have to take time off to recover (for which time they are not compensated), and generally treated with arbitrariness and disrespect. There is no particular reason that cleaners have to be treated in such an abusive fashion. But at the very least, they take some pride in knowing—and, in fact, I can attest, for the most part do take pride in knowing—that buildings do need to be cleaned, and, therefore, without them, the business of the university could not go on.[21]

Shit jobs tend to be blue collar and pay by the hour, whereas bullshit jobs tend to be white collar and salaried. Those who work shit jobs tend to be the object of indignities; they not only work hard but also are held in low esteem for that very reason. But at least they know they're doing something useful. Those who work bullshit jobs are often surrounded by honor and prestige; they are respected as professionals, well paid, and treated as high achievers—as the sort of people who can be justly proud of what they do. Yet secretly they are aware that they have achieved nothing; they feel they have done nothing to earn the consumer toys with which they fill their lives; they feel it's all based on a lie—as, indeed, it is.

These are two profoundly different forms of oppression. I certainly wouldn't want to equate them; few people I know would trade in a pointless middle-management position for a job as a ditchdigger, even if they knew that the ditches really did need to be dug. (I do know people who quit such jobs to become cleaners, though, and are quite happy that they did.) All I wish to emphasize here is that each is indeed oppressive in its own way.[22]

It is also theoretically possible to have a job that is both shit *and* bullshit. I think it's fair to say that if one is trying to imagine the worst type of job one could possibly have, it would have to be some kind of combination of the two. Once, while serving time in exile at a Siberian prison camp, Dostoyevsky developed the theory that the worst torture one could possibly devise would be to force someone to endlessly perform an obviously pointless task. Even though convicts sent to Siberia had theoretically been sentenced to "hard labor," he observed, the work wasn't actually all that hard. Most peasants worked far harder. But peasants were working at least partly for themselves. In prison camps, the "hardness" of the labor was the fact that the laborer got nothing out of it:

It once came into my head that if it were desired to reduce a man to nothing—to punish him atrociously, to crush him in such a manner that the most hardened murderer would tremble before such a punishment, and take fright beforehand—it would only be necessary to give to his work a character of complete uselessness, even to absurdity.

Hard labor, as it is now carried on, presents no interest to the convict; but it has its utility. The convict makes bricks, digs the earth, builds; and all his occupations have a meaning and an end. Sometimes the prisoner may even take an interest in what he is doing. He then wishes to work more skillfully, more advantageously. But let him be constrained to pour water from one vessel into another, to pound sand, to move a heap of earth from one place to another, and then immediately move it back again, then I am persuaded that at the end of a few days, the prisoner would hang himself or commit a thousand capital crimes, preferring rather to die than endure such humiliation, shame, and torture.[23]

on the common misconception that bullshit jobs are confined largely to the public sector

So far, we have established three broad categories of jobs: useful jobs (which may or may not be shit jobs), bullshit jobs, and a small but ugly penumbra of jobs such as gangsters, slumlords, top corporate lawyers, or hedge fund CEOs, made up of people who are basically just selfish bastards and don't really pretend to be anything else.[24] In each case, I think it's fair to trust that those who have these jobs know best which category they belong to. What I'd like to do next, before turning to the typology, is to clear up a few common misconceptions. If you toss out the notion of bullshit jobs to someone who hasn't heard the term before, that person may assume you're really talking about shit jobs. But if you clarify, he is likely to fall back on one of two common stereotypes: he may assume you're talking about government bureaucrats. Or, if he's a fan of Douglas Adams's *The Hitchhiker's Guide to the Galaxy*, he may assume you're talking about hairdressers.

Let me deal with the bureaucrats first, since it's the easiest to address. I doubt anyone would deny that there are plenty of useless bureaucrats in the world. What's significant to me, though, is that nowadays, useless bureaucrats seem just as rife in the private sector as in the public sector. You are as likely to encounter an exasperating little man in a suit reading out incomprehensible rules and regulations in a bank or mobile phone outlet than in the passport office or zoning board. Even more, public and private bureaucracies have become so increasingly entangled that it's often very difficult to tell them apart. That's one reason I started this chapter the way I did, with the story of a man working for a private firm contracting with the German military. Not only did it highlight how wrong it is to assume that bullshit jobs exist largely in government bureaucracies, but also it illustrates how "market reforms" almost invariably create more bureaucracy, not less.[25] As I pointed out in an earlier book, *The Utopia of Rules*, if you complain about getting some bureaucratic run-around from your bank, bank officials are likely to tell you it's all the fault of government regulations; but if you research where those regulations actually come from, you'll likely discover that most of them were written by the bank.

Nonetheless, the assumption that government is necessarily top-heavy with featherbedding and unnecessary levels of administrative hierarchy, while the private sector is lean and mean, is by now so firmly lodged in people's heads that it seems no amount of evidence will dislodge it.

No doubt some of this misconception is due to memories of countries such as the Soviet Union, which had a policy of full employment and was therefore obliged to make up jobs for everyone whether a need existed or not. This is how the USSR ended up with shops where customers had to go through three different clerks to buy a loaf of bread, or road crews where, at any given moment, two-thirds of the workers were drinking, playing cards, or dozing off. This is always represented as exactly what would never happen under capitalism. The last thing a private firm, competing with other private firms, would do is to hire people it doesn't actually need. If anything, the usual complaint about capitalism is that it's *too* efficient, with private workplaces endlessly hounding employees with constant speed-ups, quotas, and surveillance.

Obviously, I'm not going to deny that the latter is often the case. In fact, the pressure on corporations to downsize and increase efficiency has redoubled since the mergers and acquisitions frenzy of the 1980s. But this pressure has been directed almost exclusively at the people at the bottom of the pyramid, the ones who are actually making, maintaining, fixing, or transporting things. Anyone forced to wear a uniform in the exercise of his daily labors, for instance, is likely to be hard-pressed.[26] FedEx and UPS delivery workers have backbreaking schedules designed with "scientific" efficiency. In the upper echelons of those same companies, things are not the same. We can, if we like, trace this back to the key weakness in the managerial cult of efficiency—its Achilles' heel, if you will. When managers began trying to come up with scientific studies of the most time- and energy-efficient ways to deploy human labor, they never applied those same techniques to themselves—or if they did, the effect appears to have been the opposite of what they intended. As a result, the same period that saw the most ruthless application of speed-ups and downsizing in the blue-collar sector also brought a rapid multiplication of meaningless managerial and administrative posts in almost all large firms. It's as if businesses were endlessly trimming the fat on the shop floor and using the resulting savings to acquire even more unnecessary workers in the offices upstairs. (As we'll see, in some companies, this was literally the case.) The end result was that, just as Socialist regimes had created millions of dummy proletarian jobs, capitalist regimes somehow ended up presiding over the creation of millions of dummy white-collar jobs instead.

We'll examine how this happened in detail later in the book. For now, let me just emphasize that almost all the dynamics we will be describing happen equally in the public and private sectors, and that this is hardly surprising, considering that today, the two sectors are almost impossible to tell apart.

why hairdressers are a poor example of a bullshit job

If one common reaction is to blame government, another is, oddly, to blame women. Once you put aside the notion that you're only talking about government bureaucrats, many will assume you must be talking above all about secretaries, receptionists, and various sorts of (typically female) administrative staff. Now, clearly, many such administrative jobs are indeed bullshit by the definition developed here, but the assumption that it's mainly women who end up in bullshit jobs is not only sexist but also represents, to my mind, a profound ignorance of how most offices actually work. It's far more likely that the (female) administrative assistant for a (male) vice dean or "Strategic Network Manager" is the only person doing any real work in that office, and that it's her boss who might as well be lounging around in his office playing World of Warcraft, or very possibly, actually is.

I will return to this dynamic in the next chapter when we examine the role of flunkies; here I will just emphasize that we do have statistical evidence in this regard. While the YouGov survey didn't break down its results by occupation, which is a shame, it did break them down by gender. The result was to reveal that men are far more likely to feel that their jobs are pointless (42 percent) than women do (32 percent). Again, it seems reasonable to assume that they are right.[27]

Finally, the hairdressers. I'm afraid to say that Douglas Adams has a lot to answer for here. Sometimes it seemed to me that whenever I would propose the notion that a large percentage of the work being done in our society was unnecessary, some man (it was always a man) would pop up and say, "Oh, yes, you mean, like, hairdressers?" Then he would usually make it clear that he was referring to Douglas Adams's sci-fi comedic novel *The Restaurant at the End of the Universe*, in which the leaders of a planet called Golgafrincham decide to rid themselves of their most useless inhabitants by claiming, falsely, that the planet is about to be destroyed. To deal with the crisis they create an "Ark Fleet" of three ships, A, B, and C, the first to contain the creative third of the population, the last to include blue-collar workers, and the middle one to contain the useless remainder. All are to be placed in suspended animation and sent to a new world; except that only the B ship is actually built and it is sent on a collision course with the sun. The book's heroes accidentally find themselves on Ship B, investigating a hall full of millions of space sarcophagi, full of such useless people whom they initially assume to be dead. One begins reading off the plaques next to each sarcophagus:

19

"It says 'Golgafrincham Ark Fleet, Ship B, Hold Seven, Telephone Sanitizer, Second Class'—and a serial number."

"A telephone sanitizer?" said Arthur. "A dead telephone sanitizer?"

"Best kind."

"But what's he doing here?"

Ford peered through the top at the figure within.

"Not a lot," he said, and suddenly flashed one of those grins of his which always made people think he'd been overdoing things recently and should try to get some rest.

He scampered over to another sarcophagus. A moment's brisk towel work, and he announced:

"This one's a dead hairdresser. Hoopy!"

The next sarcophagus revealed itself to be the last resting place of an advertising account executive; the one after that contained a secondhand car salesman, third class.[28]

Now, it's obvious why this story might seem relevant to those who first hear of bullshit jobs, but the list is actually quite odd. For one thing, professional telephone sanitizers don't really exist,[29] and while advertising executives and used-car salesmen do—and are indeed professions society could arguably be better off without—for some reason, when Douglas Adams aficionados recall the story, it's always the hairdressers they remember.

I will be honest here. I have no particular bone to pick with Douglas Adams; in fact, I have a fondness for all manifestations of humorous British seventies sci-fi; but nonetheless, I find this particular fantasy alarmingly condescending. First of all, the list is not really a list of useless professions at all. It's a list of the sort of people a middle-class bohemian living in Islington around that time would find mildly annoying. Does that mean that they deserve to die?[30] Myself, I fantasize about eliminating the *jobs*, not the people who have to do them. To justify extermination, Adams seems to have intentionally selected people that he thought were not only useless but also could be thought of as embracing or identifying with what they did.

∎ ∎ ∎

Before moving on, then, let us reflect on the status of hairdressers. Why is a hairdresser not a bullshit job? Well, the most obvious reason is precisely *because* most hairdressers do not believe it to be one. To cut and style hair makes a demonstrable difference in the world, and the notion that it is unnecessary vanity is purely subjective: Who is to say whose judgment of the intrinsic value of hairstyling is correct? Adams's first novel, *The Hitchhiker's Guide to the Galaxy*, which became something of a cultural phenomenon, was published in 1979. I well remember, as a teenager in New York in that year, observing how small crowds would often gather outside the barbershop on Astor Place to watch punk rockers get elaborate purple mohawks. Was Douglas Adams suggesting those giving them the mohawks also deserved to die, or just those hairdressers whose style sense he did not appreciate? In working-class communities, hair parlors often serve as gathering places; women of a certain age and background are known to spend hours at the neighborhood hair parlor, which becomes a place to swap local news and gossip.[31] It's hard to escape the impression, though, that in the minds of those who invoke hairdressers as a prime example of a useless job, this is precisely the problem. They seem to be imagining a gaggle of middle-aged women idly gossiping under their metallic helmets while others fuss about making some marginal attempts at beautification on a person who (it is suggested), being too fat, too old, and too working class, will never be attractive no matter what is done to her. It's basically just snobbery, with a dose of gratuitous sexism thrown in.

Logically, objecting to hairdressers on this basis makes about as much sense as saying running a bowling alley or playing bagpipes is a bullshit job because you personally don't enjoy bowling or bagpipe music and don't much like the sort of people who do.

Now, some might feel I am being unfair. How do you know, they might object, that Douglas Adams wasn't really thinking, not of those who hairdress for the poor, but of those who hairdress for the very rich? What about superposh hairdressers who charge insane amounts of money to make the daughters of financiers or movie executives look odd in some up-to-the-moment fashion? Might they not harbor a secret suspicion that their work is valueless, even pernicious? Would not that then qualify them as having a bullshit job?

In theory, of course, we must allow this could be correct. But let us explore the possibility more deeply. Obviously, there is no objective measure of quality whereby one can say that haircut X is worth $15, haircut Y, $150, and haircut Z, $1,500. In the latter case, most of the time, what the customer is paying for anyway is mainly just the ability to say she paid $1,500 for a haircut, or perhaps that he got his hair done by the same stylist as Kim Kardashian or Tom Cruise. We are speaking of overt displays of wastefulness and extravagance. Now, one could certainly make the argument that there's a deep structural affinity between wasteful extravagance and bullshit, and theorists of economic psychology from Thorstein Veblen, to Sigmund Freud, to Georges Bataille have pointed out that at the very pinnacle of the wealth pyramid—think here of Donald Trump's gilded elevators—there is a very thin line between extreme luxury and total crap. (There's a reason why in dreams, gold is often symbolized by excrement, and vice versa.)

What's more, there is indeed a long literary tradition—starting with the French writer Émile Zola's *Au Bonheur des Dames* (*The Ladies' Delight*) (in 1883) and running through innumerable British comedy routines—celebrating the profound feelings of contempt and loathing that merchants and sales staff in retail outlets often feel for both their clients and the products they sell them. If the retail worker genuinely believes that he provides nothing of value to his customers, can we then say that retail worker does, indeed, have a bullshit job? I would say the technical answer, according to our working definition, would have to be yes; but at least according to my own research, the number of retail workers who feel this way is actually quite small. Purveyors of expensive perfumes might think their products are overpriced and their clients are mostly boorish idiots, but they rarely feel the perfume industry itself should be abolished.

My own research indicated that within the service economy, there were only three significant exceptions to this rule: information technology (IT) providers, telemarketers, and sex workers. Many of the first category, and pretty much all of the second, were convinced they were basically engaged in scams. The final example is more complicated and probably moves us into territory that extends beyond the precise confines of "bullshit job" into something more pernicious, but I think it's worth taking note of nonetheless. While I was conducting research, a number of women wrote to me or told me about their time as pole dancers, Playboy Club bunnies, frequenters of "Sugar Daddy" websites and the like, and suggested that such occupations should be mentioned in my book. The most compelling argument to this effect was from a former exotic dancer, now professor, who made a case that most sex work should be considered a bullshit job because, while she acknowledged that sex work clearly did answer a genuine consumer demand, something was terribly, terribly wrong with any society that effectively tells the vast majority of its female population they are worth more dancing on boxes between the ages of eighteen and twenty-five than they will be at any subsequent point in their lives, whatever their talents or accomplishments. If the same woman can make five times as much money stripping as she could teaching as a world-recognized scholar, could not the stripping job be considered bullshit simply on that basis?[32]

It's hard to deny the power of her argument. (One might add that the mutual contempt between service provider and service user in the sex industry is often far greater than what one might expect to find in even the fanciest boutique.) The only objection I could really raise here is that her argument might not go far enough. It's not so much that stripper is a bullshit job, perhaps, but that this situation shows us to be living in a bullshit society.[33]

on the difference between partly bullshit jobs, mostly bullshit jobs, and purely and entirely bullshit jobs

Finally, I must very briefly address the inevitable question: What about jobs that are just partly bullshit?

This is a tough one because there are very few jobs that don't involve at least a few pointless or idiotic elements. To some degree, this is probably just the inevitable side effect of the workings of any complex organization. Still, it's clear there is a problem and the problem is getting worse. I don't think I know anyone who has had the same job for thirty years or more who doesn't feel that the bullshit quotient has increased over the time he or she has been doing it. I might add that this is certainly true of my own work as a professor. Teachers in higher education spend increasing amounts of time filling out administrative paperwork. This can actually be documented, since one of the pointless tasks we are asked to do (and never used to be asked to do) is to fill out quarterly time allocation surveys in which we record precisely how much time each week we spend on administrative paperwork. All indications suggest that this trend is gathering steam. As the French version of *Slate* magazine noted in 2013, "la bullshitisation de l'économie n'en est qu'à ses débuts." (The bullshitization of the economy has only just begun.)[34]

However inexorable, the process of bullshitization is highly inconsistent. It has, for obvious reasons, affected middle-class employment more than working-class employment, and within the working class, it has been traditionally female, caregiving work that has been the main target of bullshitization: many nurses, for instance, complained to me that as much as 80 percent of their time is now taken up with paperwork, meetings, and the like, while truck drivers and bricklayers still carry on largely unaffected. In this area, we do have some statistics. Figure 1 is excerpted from the US edition of the *2016–2017 State of Enterprise Work Report* (see next page).

According to this survey, the amount of time American office workers say they devoted to their actual duties declined from 46 percent in 2015 to 39 percent in 2016, owing to a proportionate rise in time dealing with emails (up from 12 percent to 16 percent), "wasteful" meetings (8 percent to 10 percent), and administrative tasks (9 percent to 11 percent). Figures that dramatic must be partly the result of random statistical noise—after all, if such trends really continued, in less than a decade, no US office worker would be doing any real work at all—but if nothing else, the survey makes abundantly clear that (1) more than half of working hours in American offices are spent on bullshit, and (2) the problem is getting worse.

As a result, it is indeed possible to say there are partly bullshit jobs, mostly bullshit jobs, and purely and entirely bullshit jobs. This just happens to be a book about the latter (or, to be precise, about entirely or overwhelmingly bullshit jobs—not mostly bullshit jobs, where the meter hovers anywhere near 50 percent).

In no sense am I denying that the bullshitization of all aspects of the economy is a critically important social issue. Simply consider the figures

Figure 1

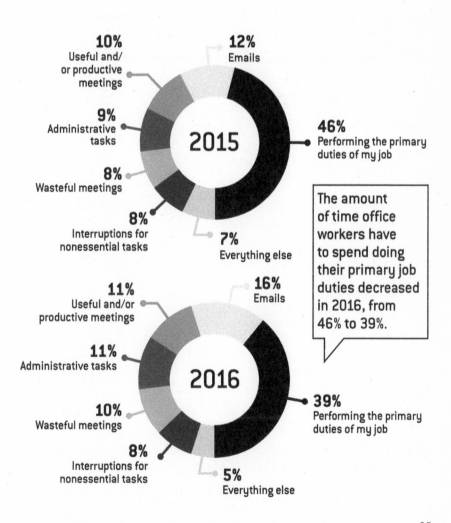

10% Useful and/or productive meetings

12% Emails

9% Administrative tasks

2015

46% Performing the primary duties of my job

8% Wasteful meetings

8% Interruptions for nonessential tasks

7% Everything else

The amount of time office workers have to spend doing their primary job duties decreased in 2016, from 46% to 39%.

11% Useful and/or productive meetings

16% Emails

11% Administrative tasks

2016

10% Wasteful meetings

39% Performing the primary duties of my job

8% Interruptions for nonessential tasks

5% Everything else

cited earlier. If 37 percent to 40 percent of jobs are completely pointless, and at least 50 percent of the work done in nonpointless office jobs is equally pointless, we can probably conclude that at least half of all work being done in our society could be eliminated without making any real difference at all. Actually, the number is almost certainly higher, because this would not even be taking into consideration second-order bullshit jobs: real jobs done in support of those engaged in bullshit. (I'll discuss these in chapter 2.) We could easily become societies of leisure and institute a twenty-hour workweek. Maybe even a fifteen-hour week. Instead, we find ourselves, as a society, condemned to spending most of our time at work, performing tasks that we feel make no difference in the world whatsoever.

In the rest of this book, I will explore how we ended up in this alarming state of affairs.

Chapter 2

What Sorts of Bullshit Jobs Are There?

My research has revealed five basic types of bullshit jobs. In this chapter, I will describe them and outline their essential features.

First, a word about this research. I am drawing on two large bodies of data. In the wake of my original 2013 essay, "On the Phenomenon of Bullshit Jobs," a number of newspapers in different countries ran the essay as an opinion piece, and it was also reproduced on a number of blogs. As a result, there was a great deal of online discussion, over the course of which many participants made references to personal experiences of jobs they considered particularly absurd or pointless. I downloaded 124 of these and spent some time sorting through them.

The second body of data was actively solicited. In the second half of 2016, I created an email account devoted solely to research and used my Twitter account to encourage people who felt they now or once had a bullshit job to send in firsthand testimonies.[1] The response was impressive. I ended up assembling over 250 such testimonies, ranging from single paragraphs to eleven-page essays detailing whole sequences of bullshit jobs, along with speculations about the organizational or social dynamics that produced them, and descriptions of their social and psychological effects. Most of these testimonies were from citizens of English-speaking countries, but I also received testimonies from all over Continental Europe, as well as Mexico, Brazil, Egypt, India, South Africa, and Japan. Some of these were deeply moving, even painful to read. Many were hilarious. Needless to say, almost all respondents insisted their names not be used.[2]

After culling the responses and trimming them of extraneous material, I found myself with a database of more than 110,000 words, which I duly color coded. The results might not be adequate for most forms of statistical analysis, but I have found them an extraordinarily rich source for qualitative analysis, especially since in many cases I've been able to ask follow-up questions and, in some, to engage in long conversations with informants. Some of the key concepts I'll be developing in the book were first suggested in or inspired by such conversations—so, in a way, the book can be seen as a collaborative project. This is particularly true of the following typology, which grew directly from these conversations and which I like to see less as my own creation and more as the product of an ongoing dialogue.[3]

the five major varieties of bullshit jobs

No typology is perfect, and I'm sure there are many ways one could draw the lines, each revealing in its own way,[4] but over the course of my research, I have found it most useful to break down the types of bullshit job into five categories. I will call these: flunkies, goons, duct tapers, box tickers, and taskmasters.

Let us consider each in turn.

1. what flunkies do

Flunky jobs are those that exist only or primarily to make someone else look or feel important.

Another term for this category might be "feudal retainers." Throughout recorded history, rich and powerful men and women have tended to surround themselves with servants, clients, sycophants, and minions of one sort or another. Not all of these are actually employed in the grandee's household, and many of those who are, are expected to do at least some actual work; but especially at the top of the pyramid, there is usually a certain portion whose job it is to basically just stand around and look impressive.[5] You cannot be magnificent without an entourage. And for the truly magnificent, the very uselessness of the uniformed retainers hovering around you is the greatest testimony to your greatness. Well into the Victorian era, for instance, wealthy families in England still employed footmen: liveried servants whose entire purpose was to run alongside carriages checking for bumps in the road.[6]

Servants of this sort are normally given some minor task to justify their existence, but this is really just a pretext: in reality, the whole point is to employ handsome young men in flashy uniforms ready to stand by the door looking regal while you hold court, or to stride gravely in front of you when you enter the room. Often retainers are given military-style costumes and paraphernalia to create the impression that the rich person who employs them has something resembling a palace guard. Such roles tend to multiply in economies based on rent extraction and the subsequent redistribution of the loot.

Just as a thought experiment: imagine you are a feudal class extracting 50 percent of every peasant household's product. If so, you are in possession of an awful lot of food. Enough, in fact, to support a population exactly as large as that of peasant food producers.[7] You have to do something with it—and there are only so many people any given feudal lord can keep around as chefs, wine stewards, scullery maids, harem eunuchs, musicians, jewelers, and the like. Even after you've taken care to ensure you have enough men trained in the use of weapons to suppress any potential rebellion, there's likely to be a great deal left over. As a result, indigents, runaways, orphans, criminals, women in desperate situations, and other dislocated people will inevitably begin to accumulate around your mansion (because, after all, that's where all the food is). You can drive them away, but then they're likely to form a dangerous vagabond class that might become a political threat. The obvious thing to do is to slap a uniform on them and assign them some minor or unnecessary task. It makes you look good, and at least that way, you can keep an eye on them.

Now, later I'm going suggest that a dynamic not entirely different happens under the existing form of capitalism, but for the moment, all I really want to stress is that assigning people minor tasks as an excuse to have them hang around making you look impressive has a long and honorable history.[8]

So, what might the modern equivalent be?

■ ■ ■

Some old-fashioned feudal-style retainer jobs still do exist.[9] Doormen are the most obvious example. They perform the same function in the houses of the very rich that electronic intercoms have performed for everyone else since at least the 1950s. One former concierge complains:

Bill: Another bullshit job—concierge in one of these buildings. Half my time was spent pressing a button to open the front door for residents and saying hello as they passed through the lobby. If I didn't get to that button in time and a resident had to open the door manually, I'd hear about it from my manager.

In some countries, such as Brazil, such buildings still have uniformed elevator operators whose entire job is to push the button for you. There is a continuum from explicit feudal leftovers of this type to receptionists and front-desk personnel at places that obviously don't need them.

Gerte: In 2010 I worked as a receptionist at a Dutch publishing company. The phone rang maybe once a day, so I was given a couple of other tasks:
- Keep candy dish full of mints. (Mints were supplied by someone else at the company; I just had to take a handful out of a drawer next to the candy dish and put them in the candy dish.)
- Once a week, I would go to a conference room and wind a grand-

father clock. (I found this task stressful, actually, because they told me that if I forgot or waited too long, all of the weights would fall, and I would be left with the onerous task of grandfather clock repair.)

- The task that took the most time was managing another receptionist's Avon sales.

Clearly, one call a day could be handled by someone else at the press in the same manner it is in most people's homes: whoever happens to be the closest to the phone and isn't in the middle of something else picks it up and answers. Why shell out a full-time salary and benefits package for a woman—actually, it would seem, in this case, two women—just to sit at the front desk all day doing nothing? The answer is: because not doing so would be shocking and bizarre. No one would take a company seriously if it had no one at all sitting at the front desk. Any publisher who defied convention that blatantly would cause potential authors or merchants or contractors to ask themselves, "If they don't feel they have to have a receptionist, what other things that publishers are normally expected to do might they just decide doesn't apply to them? Pay me, for example?"[10]

Receptionists are required as a Badge of Seriousness even if there's nothing else for them to do. Other flunkies are Badges of Importance. The following account is from Jack, who was hired as a cold caller in a low-level securities trading firm. Such firms, he explains, "operate by stolen corporate directories: internal company phonebooks that some enterprising individual has stolen a physical copy of and then sold to various firms." Brokers then call upper-level employees of the companies and try to pitch them stocks.

Jack: My job, as a cold caller, was to call these people. Not to try to sell them stocks, but rather, to offer "free research material on a promising company that is about to go public," emphasizing that I was calling on behalf of a broker. That last point was especially stressed to me during my training. The reasoning behind this was that the brokers themselves would seem, to the potential client, to be more capable and professional if they were so damn busy making money that they needed an assistant to make this call for them. There was literally no other purpose to this job than to make my neighbor the broker appear to be more successful than he actually was.

I was paid two hundred dollars per week, cash, literally from the broker's wallet, for making him look like a high roller. But this didn't just make for social capital for the broker with regards to his clients; in the office itself, being a broker with your own cold caller was a status symbol, and an important one in such a hypermasculine, hypercompetitive office environment. I was some kind of totem figure for him. Owning me could mean the difference between his getting a meeting with a visiting regional head or not; but for the most part, it just put him on a slightly higher rung on the social ladder of the workplace.

The ultimate goal of such brokers being to sufficiently impress their boss that they would be moved from the lowly "trading pit" to an office of their own upstairs. Jack's conclusion: "My position at this company was wholly unnecessary and served no purpose whatsoever other than to make my immediate superior look and feel like a big shot."

This is the very definition of a flunky job.

The pettiness of the game here—even in the 1990s, $200 was not a lot of money—helps lay bare dynamics that might express themselves in more opaque ways in larger and more complex corporate environments. There we often find cases where no one is entirely sure how or why certain positions were invented and maintained. Here is Ophelia, who works for an organization that runs social marketing campaigns:

Ophelia: My current job title is Portfolio Coordinator, and everyone always asks what that means, or what it is I actually do? I have no idea. I'm still trying to figure it out. My job description says all sorts of stuff about facilitating relationships between partners, etc., which as far as I'm concerned, just means answering occasional queries.

It has occurred to me that my actual title refers to a bullshit job. However, the reality of my working life is functioning as a Personal Assistant to the Director. And in that role, I do have actual work tasks that need doing, simply because the people I assist are either too "busy" or too important to do this stuff themselves. In fact, most of the time, I seem to be the only one at my workplace who has something to do. Some days I run around frantically, whilst most of the midlevel managers sit around and stare at a wall, seemingly bored to death and just trying to kill time doing pointless things (like that one guy who rearranges his backpack for a half hour every day).

Obviously, there isn't enough work to keep most of us occupied, but—in a weird logic that probably just makes them all feel more important about their own jobs—we are now recruiting another manager. Maybe this is to keep up the illusion that there's so much to do?

Ophelia suspects her job was originally just an empty place filler, created so that someone could boast about the number of employees he had working under him. But once it was created, a perverse dynamic began to set in, whereby managers off-loaded more and more of their responsibilities onto the lowest-ranking female subordinate (her) to give the impression that they were too busy to do such things themselves, leading, of course, to their having even less to do than previously—a spiral culminating in the apparently bizarre decision to hire another manager to stare at the wall or play Pokémon all day, just because hiring him would make it look like that was not what everyone else was doing. Ophelia ends up sometimes working frenetically; in part because the few necessary tasks (handed off to her) are augmented with completely made-up responsibilities designed to keep low-level staff bustling:

Ophelia: We are divided between two organizations and two buildings. If my boss (the boss of the whole place, in fact) goes to the other building, I have to fill in a form to book a room for her. Every time. It is absolute insanity, but it certainly keeps the receptionist over there very busy and therefore, indispensable. It also makes her appear very organized, juggling and filing all this paperwork. It occurs to me that this is what they really mean in job ads when they say that they expect you to make office procedures more efficient: that you create more bureaucracy to fill the time.

Ophelia's example highlights a common ambiguity: Whose job is really bullshit, that of the flunky? Or the boss? Sometimes, as we've seen with Jack, it's clearly the former—the flunky really does only exist to make his or her immediate superior look or feel important. In cases like that, no one minds if the flunky does absolutely nothing:

> Steve: I just graduated, and my new "job" basically consists of my boss forwarding emails to me with the message "Steve refer to the below," and I reply that the email is inconsequential or straight-up spam.

In other cases, as with Ophelia, the flunkies end up effectively doing the bosses' jobs for them. This, of course, was the traditional role of female secretaries (now relabeled "administrative assistants") working for male executives during most of the twentieth century: while in theory secretaries were there just to answer the phone, take dictation, and do some light filing, in fact, they often ended up doing 80 percent to 90 percent of their bosses' jobs, and sometimes, 100 percent of its nonbullshit aspects. It would be fascinating—though probably impossible—to write a history of books, designs, plans, and documents attributed to famous men that were actually written by their secretaries.[11]

So, in such cases, who has the bullshit job?

Here again, I think we are forced to fall back on the subjective element. The middle manager in Ophelia's office reorganizing his backpack for a half hour every day may or may not have been willing to admit his job was pointless, but those hired just to make someone like him seem important almost invariably know it and resent it—even when it doesn't involve making up unnecessary busywork:

> Judy: The only full-time job I ever had—in Human Resources in a private sector engineering firm—was wholly not necessary. It was there only because the HR Specialist was lazy and didn't want to leave his desk. I was an HR Assistant. My job took, I shit you not, one hour a day—an hour and a half max. The other seven or so hours were spent playing *2048* or watching YouTube. Phone never rang, Data were en-

tered in five minutes or less. I got paid to be bored. My boss could have easily done my job yet again—fucking lazy turd.

■ ■ ■

When I was doing anthropological fieldwork in highland Madagascar, I noticed that wherever one found the tomb of a famous nobleman, one also invariably found two or three modest graves directly at its foot. When I asked what these modest graves were, I would always be told these were his "soldiers"—really a euphemism for "slaves." The meaning was clear: to be an aristocrat meant to have the power to order others around. Even in death, if you didn't have underlings, you couldn't really claim to be a noble.

An analogous logic seems to be at work in corporate environments. Why did the Dutch publishing outfit need a receptionist? Because a company has to have three levels of command in order to be considered a "real" company. At the very least, there must be a boss, and editors, and those editors have to have some sort of underlings or assistants—at the very minimum, the one receptionist who is a kind of collective underling to all of them. Otherwise you wouldn't be a corporation but just some kind of hippie collective. Once the unnecessary flunky is hired, whether or not that flunky ends up being given anything to do is an entirely secondary consideration—that depends on a whole list of extraneous factors: for instance, whether or not there is any work to do, the needs and attitudes of the superiors, gender dynamics, and institutional constraints. If the organization grows in size, higher-ups' importance will almost invariably be measured by the total number of employees working under them, which, in turn, creates an even more powerful incentive for those on top of the organizational ladder to either hire employees and only *then* decide what they are going to do with them or—even more often, perhaps—to resist any efforts to eliminate jobs that are found to be redundant. As we'll see, testimonies from consultants hired to introduce efficiencies in a large corporation (say, a bank, or a medical supply corporation) attest to the awkward silences and outright hostility that ensue when executives realize those efficiencies will have the effect of automating away a significant portion of their subordinates. By doing so, they would effectively reduce managers to nothing. Kings of the air. For without flunkies, to whom, exactly, would they be "superior"?

2. what goons do

The use of this term is, of course, metaphorical: I'm not using it to mean actual gangsters or other forms of hired muscle. Rather, I'm referring to people whose jobs have an aggressive element, but, crucially, who exist only because other people employ them.

The most obvious example of this are national armed forces. Countries need armies only because other countries have armies.[12] If no one had an army, armies would not be needed. But the same can be said of most lobbyists, PR specialists, telemarketers, and corporate lawyers. Also, like literal goons, they have a largely negative impact on society. I think almost anyone would concur that, were all telemarketers to disappear, the world would be a better place. But I think most would also agree that if all corporate lawyers, bank lobbyists, or marketing gurus were to similarly vanish in a puff of smoke, the world would be at least a little bit more bearable.

The obvious question is: Are these really bullshit jobs at all? Would these not be more like the Mafia hit men of the last chapter? After all, in most cases, goons are clearly doing something to further the interests of those who employ them, even if the overall effect of their profession's existence might be considered detrimental to humanity as a whole.

Here again we must appeal to the subjective element. Sometimes the ultimate pointlessness of a line of work is so obvious that few involved make much effort to deny it. Most universities in the United Kingdom now have public relations offices with staffs several times larger than would be typical for, say, a bank or an auto manufacturer of roughly the same size. Does Oxford really need to employ a dozen-plus PR specialists to convince the public it's a top-notch university? I'd imagine it would take at least that many PR agents quite a number of years to convince the public

Oxford was *not* a top-notch university, and even then, I suspect the task would prove impossible. Obviously, I am being slightly facetious here: this is not the only thing a PR department does. I'm sure in the case of Oxford much of its day-to-day concerns involve more practical matters such as attracting to the university the children of oil magnates or corrupt politicians from foreign lands who might otherwise have gone to Cambridge. But still, those in charge of public relations, "strategic communications," and the like at many elite universities in the UK have sent me testimonies making it clear that they do indeed feel their jobs are largely pointless.

I have included goons as a category of bullshit job largely for this reason: because so many of those who hold them feel their jobs have no social value and ought not to exist. Recall the words of the tax litigator from the preface: "I am a corporate lawyer . . . I contribute nothing to this world and am utterly miserable all of the time." Unfortunately, it is almost impossible to ascertain how many corporate lawyers secretly share this feeling. The YouGov survey did not break down its results by profession, and while my own research confirms such feelings are by no means unique, none of those who reported such attitudes were particularly high-level. The same is true of those who work in marketing or PR.

The reason I thought the word "goon" appropriate is because in almost all cases, goons find their jobs objectionable not just because they feel they lack positive value but also because they see them as essentially manipulative and aggressive:

> Tom: I work for a very large American-owned postproduction company based in London. There are parts of my job that have always been very enjoyable and fulfilling: I get to make cars fly, buildings explode, and dinosaurs attack alien spaceships for movie studios, providing entertainment for audiences worldwide.
>
> More recently, however, a growing percentage of our customers are advertising agencies. They bring us adverts for well-known branded products: shampoos, toothpastes, moisturizing creams, washing powders, etc., and we use visual effects trickery to make it seem like these products actually work.

We also work on TV shows and music videos. We reduce bags under the eyes of women, make hair shinier, teeth whiter, make pop stars and film stars look thinner, etc. We airbrush skin to remove spots, isolate the teeth and color correct them to make them whiter (also done on the clothes in washing powder ads), paint out split ends and add shiny highlights to hair in shampoo commercials, and there are special deforming tools to make people thinner. These techniques are literally used in every commercial on TV, plus most TV drama shows, and lots of movies. Particularly on female actors but also on men. We essentially make viewers feel inadequate whilst they're watching the main programs and then exaggerate the effectiveness of the "solutions" provided in the commercial breaks.

I get paid £100,000 a year to do this.

When I asked why he considered his job to be bullshit (as opposed to merely, say, evil), Tom replied:

Tom: I consider a worthwhile job to be one that fulfills a preexisting need, or creates a product or service that people hadn't thought of, that somehow enhances and improves their lives. I believe we passed the point where most jobs were these type of jobs a long time ago. Supply has far outpaced demand in most industries, so now it is demand that is manufactured. My job is a combination of manufacturing demand and then exaggerating the usefulness of the products sold to fix it. In fact, you could argue that that is the job of every single person that works in or for the entire advertising industry. If we're at the point where in order to sell products, you have to first of all trick people into thinking they need them, then I think you'd be hard-pressed to argue that these jobs aren't bullshit.[13]

In advertising, marketing, and publicity, discontent of this sort runs so high that there is even a magazine, *Adbusters*, produced entirely by workers in the industry who resent what they are made to do for a living and wish to use the powers they've acquired in advertising for good instead of evil—for instance, by designing flashy "subvertising" that attacks consumer culture as a whole.

Tom, for his part, didn't consider his job bullshit because he objected to consumer culture in itself. He objected because he saw his "beauty work," as he called it, as inherently coercive and manipulative. He was drawing a distinction between what might be called honest illusions and dishonest ones. When you make dinosaurs attack spaceships, no one actually thinks that's real. Much as with a stage magician, half the fun is that everyone knows a trick is being played—they just don't know exactly how it's done. When you subtly enhance the appearance of celebrities, in contrast, you are trying to change viewers' unconscious assumptions about what everyday reality—in this case, of men's and women's bodies—*ought* to be like, so as to create an uncomfortable feeling that their lived reality is itself an inadequate substitute for the real thing. Where honest illusions add joy into the world, dishonest ones are intentionally aimed toward convincing people their worlds are a tawdry and miserable sort of place.

Similarly, I received a very large number of testimonies from call center employees. None considered his or her job bullshit because of conditions of employment—actually, these appear to vary enormously, from nightmarish levels of surveillance to surprisingly relaxed—but because the work involved tricking or pressuring people into doing things that weren't really in their best interest. Here's a sampling:

- "I had a bunch of bullshit call center jobs selling things that people didn't really want/need, taking insurance claims, conducting pointless market research."
- "It's a bait and switch, offering a 'free' service first, and then asking you for $1.95 for a two-week trial subscription in order for you to finish the process and get you what you went on the website to acquire, and then signing you up for an auto-renewal for a monthly service that's more than ten times that amount."
- "It's not just a lack of positive contribution, but you're making an active negative contribution to people's day. I called people up to hock them useless shit they didn't need: specifically, access to their

'credit score' that they could obtain for free elsewhere, but that we were offering (with some mindless add-ons) for £6.99 a month."

- "Most of the support covered basic computer operations the customer could easily google. They were geared toward old people or those that didn't know better, I think."
- "Our call center's resources are almost wholly devoted to coaching agents on how to talk people into things they don't need as opposed to solving the real problems they are calling about."

So once again, what really irks is (1) the aggression and (2) the deception. Here I can speak from personal experience, having done such jobs, albeit usually very, very briefly: there are few things less pleasant than being forced against your better nature to try to convince others to do things that defy their common sense. I will be discussing this issue in greater depth in the next chapter, on spiritual violence, but for now, let us merely note that this is at the very heart of what it is to be a goon.

3. what duct tapers do

Duct tapers are employees whose jobs exist only because of a glitch or fault in the organization; who are there to solve a problem that ought not to exist. I am adopting the term from the software industry, but I think it has more general applicability. One testimony from a software developer describes the industry like this:

Pablo: Basically, we have two kinds of jobs. One kind involves working on core technologies, solving hard and challenging problems, etc.

The other one is taking a bunch of core technologies and applying some duct tape to make them work together.

The former is generally seen as useful. The latter is often seen as less useful or even useless, but, in any case, much less gratifying than the first kind. The feeling is probably based on the observation that if core technologies were done properly, there would be little or no need for duct tape.

Pablo's main point is that with the growing reliance on free software (free-ware), paid employment is increasingly reduced to duct taping. Coders are often happy to perform the interesting and rewarding work on core technologies for free at night but, since that means they have less and less incentive to think about how such creations will ultimately be made compatible, that means the same coders are reduced during the day to the tedious (but paid) work of making them fit together. This is a very important insight, and I'll be discussing some of its implications at length later; but for now, let's just consider the notion of duct taping itself.

Cleaning is a necessary function: things get dusty even if they just sit there, and the ordinary conduct of life tends to leave traces that need to be tidied up. But cleaning up after someone who makes a completely gratuitous and unnecessary mess is always irritating. Having a full-time occupation cleaning up after such a person can only breed resentment. Sigmund Freud even spoke of "housewife's neurosis": a condition that he believed affected women forced to limit their life horizons to tidying up after others, and who therefore became fanatical about domestic hygiene as a form of revenge. This is often the moral agony of the duct taper: to be forced to organize one's working life around caring about a certain value (say, cleanliness) precisely *because* more important people could not care less.

The most obvious examples of duct tapers are underlings whose jobs are to undo the damage done by sloppy or incompetent superiors.

Magda: I once worked for an SME [a small or medium-size enterprise] where I was the "tester." I was required to proofread research reports written by their posh star researcher-statistician.

The man didn't know the first thing about statistics, and he struggled to produce grammatically correct sentences. He tended to avoid using verbs. He was so bad, I'd reward myself with a cake if I found a coherent paragraph. I lost twelve pounds working in that company. My job was to convince him to undertake a major reworking of every report he produced. Of course, he would never agree to correct anything, let alone undertake a rework, so I would then have to take the report to the company directors. They were statistically illiterate too, but being the directors, they could drag things out even more.

There is, it seems, a whole genre of jobs that involve correcting the damage done by a superior who holds his position for reasons unrelated to ability to do the work. (This overlaps somewhat with flunky positions where the jobholder has to do the superior's work, but it's not exactly the same thing.) Here's another example, of a programmer who got a job for a firm run by a Viennese psychologist who fancied himself an old-style scientific revolutionary, and who had invented what was, in the company, referred to simply as "the algorithm." The algorithm aimed to reproduce human speech. The company sold it to pharmacists to use on their websites. Except it didn't work:

> Nouri: The company's founding "genius" was this Viennese research psychologist, who claimed to have discovered the Algorithm. For many months, I was never allowed to see it. I just wrote stuff that used it.
>
> The psychologist's code kept failing to give sensible results. Typical cycle:
> - I demonstrate his code barfs on a ridiculously basic sentence.
> - He'd wear Confused Frown: *"Oh . . . how strange . . ."* like I just discovered the Death Star's one tiny weakness.
> - He'd disappear into his cave for two hours . . .
> - Triumphantly emerges with bug fix—now it's perfect!
> - Go to step one.

In the end, the programmer was reduced to writing very primitive Eliza scripts[14] to mimic speech for the Web pages just to cover up the fact that the Algorithm was basically gibberish, and the company, it turned out, was a pure vanity project run by a rented CEO who used to manage a gym.

Many duct-taper jobs are the result of a glitch in the system that no one has bothered to correct—tasks that could easily be automated, for instance, but haven't been either because no one has gotten around to it, or because the manager wants to maintain as many subordinates as possible, or because of some structural confusion, or because of some combination of the three. I have any number of testimonies of this sort. Here's a sampling:

- "I worked as a programmer for a travel company. Some poor person's job was to receive updated plane timetables via email several times a week and copy them by hand into Excel."
- "My job was to transfer information about the state's oil wells into a different set of notebooks than they were currently in."
- "My day consisted of photocopying veterans' health records for seven and a half hours a day . . . Workers were told time and again that it was too costly to buy the machines for digitizing."
- "I was given one responsibility: watching an in-box that received emails in a certain form from employees in the company asking for tech help, and copy and paste it into a different form. Not only was this a textbook example of an automatable job, it actually used to be automated! There was some kind of disagreement between various managers that led to higher-ups issuing a standardization that nullified the automation."

On the social level, duct taping has traditionally been women's work. Throughout history, prominent men have wandered about oblivious to half of what's going on around them, treading on a thousand toes; it was typically their wives, sisters, mothers, or daughters who were left with the responsibility of performing the emotional labor of soothing egos, calming nerves, and negotiating solutions to the problems they created. In a more material sense, duct taping might be considered a classic working-class function. The architect may come up with a plan that looks stunning on paper, but it's the builder who has to figure out how to *actually* install electrical sockets in a circular room or to use real duct tape to hold things together that in reality simply don't fit together the way the blueprints say they should.

In this latter case, we're not really talking about a bullshit job at all, any more than we're talking about a bullshit job when an orchestra conductor interprets the score of a Beethoven symphony or an actress plays Lady Macbeth. There will always be a certain gap between blueprints, schemas, and plans and their real-world implementation; therefore, there will always be people charged with making the necessary adjustments. What makes such a role bullshit is when the plan obviously can't work and any competent architect should have known it; when the system is so stupidly designed that it will fail in completely predictable ways, but rather than fix the problem, the organization prefers to hire full-time employees whose main or entire job is to deal with the damage. It's as if a homeowner, upon discovering a leak in the roof, decided it was too much bother to hire a roofer to reshingle it, and instead stuck a bucket underneath and hired someone whose full-time job was to periodically dump the water.

It goes without saying that duct tapers are almost always aware they have a bullshit job and are usually quite angry about it.

I encountered a classic example of a duct taper while working as a lecturer at a prominent British university. One day the wall shelves in my office collapsed. This left books scattered all over the floor, and a jagged half-dislocated metal frame that once held the shelves in place dangling cheerfully over my desk. A carpenter appeared an hour later to inspect the damage but announced gravely that, since there were books all over the floor, safety rules prevented him from entering the room or taking further action. I would have to stack the books and then not touch anything else, whereupon he would return at the earliest available opportunity to remove the dangling frame.

I duly stacked the books, but the carpenter never reappeared. There ensued a series of daily calls from Anthropology to Buildings and Grounds. Each day someone in the Anthropology Department would call, often multiple times, to ask about the fate of the carpenter, who always turned out to have something extremely pressing to do. By the time a week was out, I had taken to doing my work on the floor in a kind of little nest assembled from fallen books, and it had become apparent that there was one man employed by Buildings and Grounds whose entire job it was to apologize for the fact that the carpenter hadn't come. He seemed like a nice man. He was exceedingly polite and even-tempered, and always had just a slight trace of wistful melancholy about him, which made him quite well suited for the job. Still, it's hard to imagine he was particularly happy with his choice of career. Most of all: there didn't seem any obvious reason the school couldn't simply get rid of the position and use the money to *hire another carpenter*, in which case his job would not be needed anyway.

4. what box tickers do

I am using the term "box tickers" to refer to employees who exist only or primarily to allow an organization to be able to claim it is doing something that, in fact, it is not doing. The following testimony is from a woman hired to coordinate leisure activities in a care home:

> Betsy: Most of my job was to interview residents and fill out a recreation form that listed their preferences. That form was then logged on a computer and promptly forgotten about forever. The paper form was also kept in a binder, for some reason. Completion of the forms was by far the most important part of my job in the eyes of my boss, and I would catch hell if I got behind on them. A lot of the time, I would complete a form for a short-term resident, and they would check out the next day. I threw away mountains of paper. The interviews mostly just annoyed the residents, as they knew it was just bullshit paperwork, and no one was going to care about their individual preferences.

The most miserable thing about box-ticking jobs is that the employee is usually aware that not only does the box-ticking exercise do nothing toward accomplishing its ostensible purpose, it actually undermines it, since it diverts time and resources away from the purpose itself. So here Betsy was aware that the time she spent processing forms about how residents might wish to be entertained was time *not* spent entertaining them. She did manage to engage in some leisure activities with the residents ("Fortunately, I was able to play the piano for the residents every day before dinner, and that was a beautiful time, with singing, smiling, and tears"), but as so often in such situations, there was a sense that these moments were indulgences granted her as a reward for carrying out her primary duties, which consisted of the filling out and proper disposition of forms.[15]

We're all familiar with box ticking as a form of government. If a government's employees are caught doing something very bad—taking bribes, for instance, or regularly shooting citizens at traffic stops—the first reaction is invariably to create a "fact-finding commission" to get to the bottom of things. This serves two functions. First of all, it's a way of insisting that, aside from a small group of miscreants, no one had any idea that any of this was happening (this, of course, is rarely true); second of all, it's a way of implying that once all the facts are in, someone will definitely do something about it. (This is usually not true, either.) A fact-finding commission is a way of telling the public that the government is doing something it is not. But large corporations will behave in exactly the same way if, say, they are revealed to be employing slaves or child laborers in their garment factories or dumping toxic waste. All of this is bullshit, but the true bullshit *job* category applies to those who are not just there to stave off the public (this at least could be said to serve some kind of useful purpose for the company) but to those who do so within the organization itself.[16]

The corporate compliance industry might be considered an intermediary form. It is explicitly created by (US) government regulation:

> Layla: I work in a growing industry born out of the federal regulation the Foreign Corrupt Practices Act.
>
> Basically US companies have to do due diligence to make sure they aren't doing business with corrupt overseas firms. Clients are big companies—tech, auto companies, etc.—who might have myriad smallish businesses they supply or work with in places like China (my region).
>
> Our company creates due diligence reports for our clients: basically one to two hours of internet research that is then edited into a report. There is a lot of jargon and training that goes into making sure every report is consistent.

Sometimes the internet reveals something that's an easy red flag—like a company's boss had a criminal case—but I would say the realness/bullshit factor is 20/80. Unless someone has been criminally charged, I have no way of knowing from my apartment in Brooklyn if they've been handed an envelope full of cash in Guangzhou.[17]

Of course, on some level, all bureaucracies work on this principle: once you introduce formal measures of success, "reality"—for the organization—becomes that which exists on paper, and the human reality that lies behind it is a secondary consideration at best. I vividly remember the endless discussions that ensued, when I was a junior professor at Yale University, about a first-year archaeology graduate student whose husband had died in a car crash on the first day of the term. For some reason, the shock caused her to develop a mental block on doing paperwork. She still attended lectures and was an avid participant in class discussions; and she turned in papers and got excellent grades. But eventually the professor would always discover she hadn't formally signed up for the class. As the *éminence grise* of the department would point out during faculty meetings, that was all that really mattered.

"As far as the guys in Registration are concerned, if you don't get the forms in on time, you didn't take the course. So your performance is completely irrelevant." Other professors would mumble and fuss, and there would be occasional careful allusions to her "personal tragedy"—the exact nature of which was never specified. (I had to learn about it from other students later on.) But no one raised any fundamental objections to Registration's attitude. That was just reality—from an administrative point of view.

Eventually, after last-minute attempts to have her fill out a sheaf of late-application appeal documents also met with no response, and after numerous long soliloquies from the Director of Graduate Studies about just how inconsiderate it was of her to make things so difficult for those who were only trying to help her,[18] the student was expelled from the program on the grounds that anyone so incapable of handling paperwork was obviously not suited for an academic career.

This mentality seems to increase, not decrease, when government functions are reorganized to be more like a business, and citizens, for example, are redefined as "customers." Mark is Senior Quality and Performance Officer in a local council in the United Kingdom:

Mark: Most of what I do—especially since moving away from frontline customer-facing roles—involves ticking boxes, pretending things are great to senior managers, and generally "feeding the beast" with meaningless numbers that give the illusion of control. None of which helps the citizens of that council in the slightest.

I've heard an apocryphal story about a Chief Executive who turned on the fire alarm, so all the staff gathered in the car park. He then told all the employees who were with a customer when the alarm went off to return to the building immediately. The other employees could return when one of the people dealing with a customer needed them for something, and so on and so forth. If this had happened when I was at that council, I would have been in the car park for a very long time!

Mark goes on to describe local government as little more than an endless sequence of box-ticking rituals revolving around monthly "target figures." These were put up on posters in the office and coded green for "improving," amber for "stable," and red for "decline." Supervisors appeared innocent even of the basic concept of random statistical variation—or at least, pretended to be—as each month, those with green-coded figures were rewarded, while those with red urged to do a better job. Almost none of this had any real bearing on providing services:

Mark: One project I worked on was to come up with some housing "service standards." The project involved playing lip service to customers, and having long discussions with managers at meetings, before finally writing up a report that got praised (mainly because it was presented and laid out attractively) by managers in the meeting. The report then got filed away—making absolutely no difference to the residents but still somehow requiring many hours of staff time, not to mention all the hours the residents themselves spent filling in surveys or attending focus groups. In my experience, this is how most policy works in local government.[19]

Note here the importance of the physical attractiveness of the report. This is a theme that comes up frequently in testimonies about box-ticking operations and even more so in the corporate sector than in government. If the ongoing importance of a manager is measured by how many people he has working under him, the immediate material manifestation of that manager's power and prestige is the visual quality of his presentations and reports. The meetings in which such emblems are displayed might be considered the high rituals of the corporate world. And just as the retinues of a feudal lord might include servants whose only role[20] was to polish his horses' armor or tweeze his mustache before tournaments or pageants, so may present-day executives keep employees whose sole purpose is to prepare their PowerPoint presentations or craft the maps, cartoons, photographs, or illustrations that accompany their reports. Many of these reports are nothing more than props in a Kabuki-like corporate theater—no one actually reads them all the way through.[21] But this doesn't stop ambitious executives from cheerfully shelling out half a workman's yearly wages of company money just to be able to say, "Ooh yes, we commissioned a report on that."

Hannibal: I do digital consultancy for global pharmaceutical companies' marketing departments. I often work with global PR agencies on this, and write reports with titles like *How to Improve Engagement Among Key Digital Health Care Stakeholders*. It is pure, unadulterated bullshit, and serves no purpose beyond ticking boxes for marketing departments. But it is very easy to charge a very large amount of money to write bullshit reports. I was recently able to charge around twelve thousand pounds to write a two-page report for a pharmaceutical client to present during a global strategy meeting. The report wasn't used in the end because they didn't manage to get to that agenda point during their allotted meeting time, but the team I wrote it for was very happy with it nonetheless.

There are whole minor industries that exist just to facilitate such box-ticking gestures. I worked for some years for the Interlibrary Loan Office in the University of Chicago Science Library, and at least 90 percent of what people did there was photocopy and mail out articles from medical journals with titles such as the *Journal of Cell Biology*, *Clinical Endocrinology*, and the *American Journal of Internal Medicine*. (I was lucky. I did something else.) For the first few months, I was under the naïve impression that these articles were being sent to doctors. To the contrary, a bemused coworker eventually explained to me: the overwhelming majority were being sent to lawyers.[22] Apparently, if you are suing a doctor for malpractice, part of the show involves assembling an impressive pile of scientific papers to plunk down on the table at an appropriately theatrical moment and then enter into evidence. While everyone knows that no one will actually read these papers, there is always the possibility that the defense attorney or one of his expert witnesses might pick one up at random for inspection—so it is considered important to ensure your legal aides locate articles that can at least plausibly be said to bear in some way on the case.

As we will see in later chapters, there are all sorts of different ways that private companies employ people to be able to tell themselves they are doing something that they aren't really doing. Many large corporations, for instance, maintain their own in-house magazines or even television channels, the ostensible purpose of which is to keep employees up to date on interesting news and developments, but which, in fact, exist for almost no reason other than to allow executives to experience that warm and pleasant feeling that comes when you see a favorable story about you in the media, or to know what it's like to be interviewed by people who look and act exactly like reporters but never ask questions you wouldn't want them to ask. Such venues tend to reward their writers, producers, and technicians very handsomely, often at two or three times the market rate.

But I've never talked to anyone who does such work full-time who doesn't say the job is bullshit.[23]

5. what taskmasters do

Taskmasters fall into two subcategories. Type 1 contains those whose role consists entirely of assigning work to others. This job can be considered bullshit if the taskmaster herself believes that there is no need for her intervention, and that if she were not there, underlings would be perfectly capable of carrying on by themselves. Type 1 taskmasters can thus be considered the opposite of flunkies: unnecessary superiors rather than unnecessary subordinates.

Whereas the first variety of taskmaster is merely useless, the second variety does actual harm. These are taskmasters whose primary role is to create bullshit tasks for others to do, to supervise bullshit, or even to create entirely new bullshit jobs. One might also refer to them as bullshit generators. Type 2 taskmasters may also have real duties in addition to their role as taskmaster, but if all or most of what they do is create bullshit tasks for others, then their own jobs can be classified as bullshit too.

As one might imagine, it is especially difficult to gather testimonies from taskmasters. Even if they do secretly think their jobs are useless, they are much less likely to admit it.[24] But I found a small number willing to come clean.

Ben represents a classic example of type 1. He is a middle manager:

Ben: I have a bullshit job, and it happens to be in middle management. Ten people work for me, but from what I can tell, they can all do the work without my oversight. My only function is to hand them work, which I suppose the people that actually generate the work could do themselves. (I will say that in a lot of cases, the work that is assigned is a product of other managers with bullshit jobs, which makes my job two levels of bullshit.)

I just got promoted to this job, and I spend a lot of my time looking around and wondering what I'm supposed to be doing. As best I can tell, I'm supposed to be motivating the workers. I sort of doubt that I'm earning my salary doing that, even if I'm really trying!

Ben calculates that he spends at least 75 percent of his time allocating tasks and then monitoring if the underling is doing them, even though, he insists, he has absolutely no reason to believe the underlings in question would behave any differently if he weren't there. He also says he keeps trying to allocate himself real work on the sly, but when he does so, his own superiors eventually notice and tell him to cut it out. But then, when he sent in his testimony, Ben had only been at the job for two and a half months—which might explain his candor. If he does succumb eventually and accepts his new role in life, he will come to understand that, as another testimony put it, "The entire job of middle management is to ensure the lower-level people hit their 'productivity numbers' "—and will therefore start coming up with formal statistical metrics that his underlings can try to falsify.

Being forced to supervise people who don't need supervision is actually a fairly common complaint. Here, for instance, is the testimony of an Assistant Localization Manager named Alphonso:

Alphonso: My job is to oversee and coordinate a team of five translators. The problem with that is that the team is perfectly capable of managing itself: they are trained in all the tools they need to use and they can, of course, manage their time and tasks. So I normally act as a "task gatekeeper." Requests come to me through Jira (a bureaucratic online tool for managing tasks), and I pass them on to the relevant person or persons. Other than that, I'm in charge of sending periodic reports to my manager, who, in turn, will incorporate them into "more important" reports to be sent to the CEO.

This kind of combination of taskmastering and box ticking would appear to be the very essence of middle management.

In Alphonso's case, he did actually serve one useful function—but only because his team of translators, based in Ireland, was assigned so little work by the central office in Japan that he had to constantly figure out ways to finagle the reports to make it look like they were very busy and no one needed to be laid off.

■ ■ ■

Let us move on, then, to taskmasters of the second type: those who make up bullshit for others to do.

We may begin with Chloe, who held the post of Academic Dean at a prominent British university, with a specific responsibility to provide "strategic leadership" to a troubled campus.

Now, those of us toiling in the academic mills who still like to think of ourselves as teachers and scholars before all else have come to fear the word "strategic." "Strategic mission statements" (or even worse, "strategic vision documents") instill a particular terror, since these are the primary means by which corporate management techniques—setting up quantifiable methods for assessing performance, forcing teachers and scholars to spend more and more of their time assessing and justifying what they do and less and less time actually doing it—are insinuated into academic life. The same suspicions hold for any document that repeatedly uses the words "quality," "excellence," "leadership," or "stakeholder." So for my own part, my immediate reaction upon hearing that Chloe was in a "strategic leadership" position was to suspect that not only was her job bullshit, it actively inserted bullshit into others' lives as well.

According to Chloe's testimony, this was exactly the case—though, if at first, not precisely for the reasons I imagined.

Chloe: The reason that my Dean's role was a bullshit job is the same reason that all nonexecutive Deans, PVCs [Pro-Vice Chancellors], and other "strategic" roles in universities are bullshit jobs. The real roles of power and responsibility within a university trace the flow of money through the organization. An executive PVC or Dean (in other words, s/he who holds the budget) can cajole, coerce, encourage, bully, and negotiate with departments about what they can, ought, or might want to do, using the stick (or carrot) of money. Strategic Deans and other such roles have no carrots or sticks. They are nonexecutive. They hold no money, just (as was once described to me) "the power of persuasion and influence."

I did not sit on university leadership and so was not part of the bunfights about targets, overall strategy, performance measures, audits, etc. I had no budget. I had no authority over the buildings, the timetable, or any other operational matters. All I could do was come up with a new strategy that was in effect a re-spin of already agreed-upon university strategies.

So her primary role was to come up with yet another strategic vision statement, of the kind that are regularly deployed to justify the number crunching and box ticking that has become so central to British academic life.[25] But since Chloe had no actual power, it was all meaningless shadow play. What she *did* get was what all high-level university administrators now receive as their primary badge of honor: her own tiny empire of administrative staff.

Chloe: I was given a 75% full-time equivalent Personal Assistant, a 75% full-time equivalent "Special Project and Policy Support Officer," and a full-time postdoctoral Research Fellow, *plus* an "expenses" allowance of twenty thousand pounds. In other words, a shed-load of (public) money went into supporting a bullshit job. The Project and Policy Support Officer was there to help me with projects and policies. The PA was brilliant but ended up just being a glorified travel agent and diary secretary. The Research Fellow was a waste of time and money because I am a lone scholar and don't actually need an assistant.

So, I spent two years of my life making up work for myself and for other people.

Actually, Chloe appears to have been a very generous boss. As she spent her own hours developing strategies she knew would be ignored, her Special Projects Officer "ran around doing timetable scenarios" and gathering useful statistics, the Personal Assistant kept her diary, and the Research Fellow spent her time working on her own personal research. This in itself seems perfectly innocent. At least none of them was doing any harm. Who knows, maybe the Research Fellow even ended up making an important contribution to human knowledge of her own. The truly disturbing thing about the whole arrangement, according to Chloe, was her ultimate realization that if she had been given real power, she probably *would* have done harm. Because after two years as Dean, she was unwise enough to accept a gig as head of her old department and was thus able see things from the other side—that is, before quitting six months later in horror and disgust:

Chloe: My very brief stint as Head of Department reminded me that at the very minimum, ninety percent of the role is bullshit: Filling out the forms that the Faculty Dean sends so that she can write her strategy documents that get sent up the chain of command. Producing a confetti of paperwork as part of the auditing and monitoring of research activities and teaching activities. Producing plan after plan after five-year plan justifying why departments need to have the money and staff they already have. Doing bloody annual appraisals that go into a drawer never to be looked at again. And, in order to get these tasks done, as HoD, you ask your staff to help out. Bullshit proliferation.

So, what do I think? It is not capitalism per se that produces the bullshit.[26] It is managerialist ideologies put into practice in complex organizations. As managerialism embeds itself, you get entire cadres of academic staff whose job it is just to keep the managerialist plates spinning—strategies, performance targets, audits, reviews, appraisals, renewed strategies, etc., etc.—which happen in an almost wholly and entirely disconnected fashion from the real lifeblood of universities: teaching and education.

On this, I will leave Chloe the last word.

Chloe at least was allocated her staff first and only then had to figure out how to keep them occupied. Tania, who had a series of taskmaster jobs in both the public and private sectors, provides us with an explanation of how entirely new bullshit positions can come about. This last testimony is unique because it explicitly incorporates the typology developed in this chapter. Toward the end of my research, I laid out my then nascent five-part division on Twitter, to encourage comments, amendments, or reactions. Tania felt the terms fit her experience well:

> Tania: I might be a taskmaster in your taxonomy of BS jobs. I was one of two deputy directors of an administrative services office that handled HR, budget, grants, contracts, and travel for two bureaus with total resources of about $600 million and a thousand souls.
>
> At some point as a manager (or as a duct taper helping to fill functional gaps), you realize that you need to hire a new person to meet an organizational need. Most of the time, the needs I am trying to fill are either my own need for a box ticker or a duct taper, or the needs of other managers, sometimes to hire people for non-BS work or to hire their ration of goons and flunkies.
>
> The reason I need duct tapers is usually because I have to compensate for poorly functioning program-management systems (both automated and human workflows) and, in some cases, a poorly functioning box ticker and even a non-BS-job subordinate who has job tenure and twenty-five years of outstanding performance ratings from a succession of previous bosses.

This last is important. Even in corporate environments, it is very difficult to remove an underling for incompetence if that underling has seniority and a long history of good performance reviews. As in government bureaucracies, the easiest way to deal with such people is often to "kick them upstairs": promote them to a higher post, where they become somebody else's problem. But Tania was already at the top of this particular hierarchy, so an incompetent would continue to be her problem even if kicked upstairs. She was left with two options. Either she could move the incompetent into a bullshit position where he had no meaningful responsibilities, or, if no such position was currently available, she could leave him in place and hire someone else to really do his job. But if you take the latter course, another problem arises: you can't recruit someone for the incompetent's job, since the incompetent already has that job. Instead, you have to make up a new job with an elaborate job description that you know to be bullshit, because, really, you're hiring that person to do something else. Then you have to go through the motions of pretending the new person is ideally qualified to do the made-up job you don't really want him or her to do. All this involves a great deal of work.

Tania: In organizations with structured job classifications and position descriptions, there has to be an established and classified job to which you can recruit someone. (This is a whole professional universe of BS jobs and boondogglery unto itself. It's similar to the world of people who write grant proposals or contract bids.)

So the creation of a BS job often involves creating a whole universe of BS narrative that documents the purpose and functions of the position as well as the qualifications required to successfully perform the job, while corresponding to the format and special bureaucratese prescribed by the Office of Personnel Management and my agency's HR staff.

Once that's done, there has to be a narrative job announcement of the same ilk. To be eligible for hire, the applicant must present a resume incorporating all the themes and phraseology of the announcement so that the hiring software our agency uses will recognize their qualifications. After the person is hired, their duties must be spelled out in yet another document that will form the basis for annual performance appraisals.

I have rewritten candidates' resumes myself to ensure that they defeat the hiring software so I can be allowed to interview and select them. If they don't make it past the computer, I can't consider them.

To present a parable version: imagine you are a feudal lord again. You acquire a gardener. After twenty years of faithful service, the gardener develops a serious drinking problem. You keep finding him curled up in flowerbeds, while dandelions sprout everywhere and the sedge begins to die. But the gardener is well connected, and getting rid of him would offend people you don't feel it would be wise to offend. So you acquire a new servant, ostensibly to polish the doorknobs or perform some other meaningless task. In fact, you make sure the person you get as doorknob polisher is actually an experienced gardener. So far, so good. The problem is, in a corporate environment, you can't just summon a new servant, make up an impressive-sounding title for him ("High Seneschal of the Entryways"), and tell him his real job is to take over when the gardener is drunk. You have to come up with an elaborate fake description of what a doorknob polisher would, in fact, do; coach your new gardener in how to pretend he's the best doorknob polisher in the kingdom; and then use the description of his duties as the basis of periodic box-ticking performance reviews.

And if the gardener sobers up and doesn't want some young punk messing with his business—now you have a full-time doorknob polisher on your hands.

This, according to Tania, is just one of the many ways that taskmasters end up creating bullshit jobs.

on complex multiform bullshit jobs

These five categories are not exhaustive, and new types could certainly be proposed. One compelling suggestion I heard was for a category of "imaginary friends"—that is, people hired ostensibly to humanize an inhuman corporate environment but who, in fact, mainly force people to go through elaborate games of make-believe. We will be hearing about forced "creativity" and "mindfulness" seminars and obligatory charity events later on; there are workers whose entire careers are based on dressing up in costumes or otherwise designing silly games to create rapport in office environments where everyone would probably be happier just being left alone. These could be seen as box tickers of a sort, but they could equally be seen as a phenomenon unto themselves.

As the previous examples suggest, it can also sometimes be clear that a job is bullshit but still be difficult to determine precisely which of the five categories it belongs to. Often it may seem to contain elements of several. A box ticker might also be a flunky, or might end up becoming a mere flunky if the organization's internal rules change; a flunky might also be a part-time duct taper or become a full-time duct taper if a problem arises and, instead of fixing it, the boss decides it would be easier to just reassign one of his idle minions to deal with the effects.

Consider Chloe the nonexecutive Dean. In a way, she, too, was a flunky, since her post was created by higher-ups for largely symbolic reasons. But she was also a taskmaster to her own subordinates. Since she and her subordinates didn't have much to do, she spent some of her time looking for problems they could duct-tape until she finally came to the realization that even if she were given some kind of power, most of what she'd be doing would just be box-ticking exercises anyway.

I received one testimony from a man who worked for a telemarketing company with a contract with a major IT firm. (Let's say Apple. I don't know if it was Apple. He didn't tell me which one it was.) His job was to call up corporations and try to convince them to book a meeting with an Apple sales representative. The problem was that all of the firms they would call already had an Apple sales rep permanently attached to them, often working out of the same office. What's more, they were perfectly aware of this.

Jim: I often asked my managers how they would convince prospects of the value of taking a meeting with a sales rep from our technology giant customer when they already had a sales rep from that same technology giant on their premises. Some were as hapless as I was, but the more effective managers patiently explained to me that I was missing the point: an appointment-setting call is a game of social niceties.

Prospects don't take a meeting because they think it might help solve a business problem; they take it because they fear it would be impolite not to.

This is as pointless as pointless can be, but how, exactly, would one classify it? Certainly Jim, being a telemarketer, would qualify as a goon. But he was a goon whose entire purpose was to maneuver people into box ticking.

Another ambiguous multiform category are flak catchers, who might be considered a combination of flunky and duct taper but who have certain unique characteristics of their own. Flak catchers are subordinates hired to be at the receiving end of often legitimate complaints but who are given that role precisely because they have absolutely no authority to do anything about them.

The flak catcher is, of course, a familiar role in any bureaucracy. The man-whose-job-it-was-to-apologize-for-the-fact-that-the-carpenter-didn't-come might be considered a flak catcher of sorts, but if so, his position was an unusually cushy one, since he only really had to talk to university professors and administrators who were unlikely to scream, pound the table, or become visibly upset. In other contexts, flak catching can be genuinely dangerous. When I first came to the United Kingdom in 2008, one of the first things that struck me was the ubiquity of the notices in public places reminding citizens not to physically attack minor government officials. (It struck me this should rather go without saying. But apparently it doesn't.)

Sometimes flak catchers are well aware of what they're there for, as with Nathaniel, who signed up for a work-study program at a college in Canada, and was assigned to sit in the registrar's office and call people to tell them that some form was filled out incorrectly and they'd have to do it all over again. ("Since all frontline workers were students, it kept the cap on how pissed off anyone could reasonably get. The first line you used when someone became agitated was, 'Sorry, man, I know it's BS. I am a student, too.'") Other flak catchers seem touchingly innocent:

Tim: I work in a college dormitory during the summer. I have worked at this job for three years, and at this point, it is still completely unclear to me what my actual duties are.

Primarily, it seems that my job consists of physically occupying space at the front desk. This is what I spend approximately seventy percent of my time doing. While engaged in this, I am free to "pursue my own projects," which I take to mean mainly screwing around and creating rubber band balls out of rubber bands I find in the cabinets. When I am not busy with this, I might be checking the office email account (I have basically no training or administrative power, of course, so all I can do is forward these emails to my boss), moving packages from the door where they get dropped off to the package room, answering phone calls (again, I know nothing and rarely answer a question to the caller's satisfaction), finding ketchup packets from 2005 in the desk drawers, or calling maintenance to report that a resident has dropped three forks down the garbage disposal, and now the sink is spewing decayed food.

In addition, often people will yell at me for things that are clearly not my fault, such as the fact that they dropped three forks down the garbage disposal, or the fact that there is construction happening nearby, or the fact that they have not paid their outstanding rent balance, and I am forbidden from accepting $1,400 in cash, and my boss does not work on weekends; or the fact that there is no convenient TV available on which they can watch *The Bachelor*. I assume it's a kind of catharsis for them to do this yelling, since I am nineteen years old and clearly abjectly powerless.

For these duties, I am paid fourteen dollars an hour.

On the surface, it may seem as if Tim is just a flunky, like the unnecessary receptionist in the Dutch publishing house: it just wouldn't look good to have no one sitting there at all. But, in fact, it seems likely that insofar as Tim provides a real service to his employers, it's precisely by giving angry students someone they can vent at. Why else, after three years, would they still be keeping him so completely in the dark? The main reason I hesitate to make flak catcher a category of bullshit job is because this *is* a real service. Tim is not making up for a structural flaw like the man whose job it was to apologize for the fact that the carpenter didn't come.

He's there because if you gather together a large number of teenagers, a few will invariably throw temper tantrums about stupid things, and Tim's employer would prefer they direct their outrage at someone other than himself. In other words, Tim's is a shit job, but it's not entirely clear that it's a bullshit one.

a word on second-order bullshit jobs

A final ambiguous category consists of jobs which are in no sense point-less in and of themselves, but which are ultimately pointless because they are performed in support of a pointless enterprise. An obvious example would be the cleaners, security, maintenance, and other support staff for a bullshit company. Take Kurt's office that provides the paperwork required to move German soldiers' computers down the hall. Or Nouri's firm that promoted an algorithm that didn't work. Or any of a hundred fake tele-marketing or compliance firms. In every one of those offices, someone has to water the plants. Someone has to clean the toilets. Someone has to handle pest control. And while it's true that most of the companies in question operate in large office buildings hosting any number of different sorts of enterprise—which usually makes it unlikely that any one cleaner or electrician or bug sprayer is providing services exclusively for those who believe themselves to be engaged in useless occupations—if one were to measure the total proportion of cleaning or electrical work that is ulti-mately performed in support of bullshit, that number would be very high. (One would have to assume 37 percent, in fact, if the YouGov survey is accurate.[27])

If 37 percent of jobs are bullshit, and 37 percent of the remaining 63 percent are in support of bullshit, then slightly over 50 percent of all labor falls into the bullshit sector in the broadest sense of the term.[28] If you com-bine this with the bullshitization of useful occupations (at least 50 percent in office work; presumably less in other sorts), and the various professions that basically exist only because everyone is working too hard (dog wash-ers, all-night pizza deliverymen, to name a few), we could probably get the *real* workweek down to fifteen hours—or even twelve—without anyone noticing much.

a final note, with a brief return to the question: is it possible to have a bullshit job and not know it?

The idea of second-order bullshit jobs once again raises the issue of the degree to which bullshit jobs are just a matter of subjective judgment and the degree to which they have objective reality. I believe bullshit jobs to be very real—when I say we can only rely on the judgment of the worker, I'm simply talking about what we can, as observers, know about them. I would also remind the reader that I while I believe it is right to defer to the particular worker about the factual question of whether their work actually does anything at all, when it comes to the rather more subtle issue of whether the work in question does anything *of value*, I will think it's the best thing to defer to the overall opinion of those who work in the industry. Otherwise we could end up in the rather silly position of saying that of thirty legal aides working in the same office and performing the same tasks, twenty-nine have bullshit jobs because they think they do, but the one true believer who disagrees does not.

Unless one takes the position that there is absolutely no reality at all except for individual perception, which is philosophically problematic, it is hard to deny the possibility that people *can* be wrong about what they do. For the purposes of this book, this is not that much of a problem, because what I am mainly interested in is, as I say, the subjective element; my primary aim is not so much to lay out a theory of social utility or social value as to understand the psychological, social, and political effects of the fact that so many of us labor under the secret belief that our jobs lack social utility or social value.

I am also assuming that people are not *usually* wrong, so if one really did want to map out, say, which sectors of the economy are real and which are bullshit, the best way to do so would be to examine in which sectors the preponderance of workers feel their jobs are pointless and in which sectors the preponderance do not. Even more, one would try to tease out the tacit theory of social value that led them to this conclusion: if someone says, "My job is completely pointless," what are the unspoken criteria being applied? Some, like Tom the special effects artist, have thought these things through and can simply tell you. In other cases, workers are not able to articulate a theory, but you can tell that one must be there, if only on a not completely conscious level—so you have to tease out the theory by examining the language people use and observing their gut reactions to the work they do.

For me, this isn't really a problem. I'm an anthropologist: teasing out the implicit theory that lies behind people's everyday actions and reactions is what anthropologists are trained to do. But then there's the problem that people's theories are not all the same. For instance, it has come to my attention, while conducting this research, that many of those employed in the banking industry are privately convinced that 99 percent of what banks do is bullshit that does not benefit humanity in any way. I can only assume that others working in the industry disagree with this assessment. Is there any pattern here? Does it vary with seniority? Are higher-ups more likely to believe in the social benefits of banking? Or do many of them secretly agree that their work has no social value but just don't care? Maybe they even take delight in the knowledge that their work does not benefit the public, thinking of themselves as pirates, or scam artists, in some romantic sense? It's impossible to say (though Jeffrey Sachs's testimony in the last chapter at least suggests that many at the very top simply feel they have a right to whatever they can get).

The real problem for my approach comes when one has to deal with those in professions that everyone *else* regularly invokes as prime examples of bullshit jobs who don't seem to think of their jobs that way themselves. Again, no one has done detailed comparative survey work in this regard, but I did notice certain interesting patterns in my own data. I heard from only a smattering of lawyers (though from a large number of legal aides), only two PR flacks, and not a single lobbyist. Does this mean we have to conclude these are largely nonbullshit occupations? Not necessarily. There are any number of other possible explanations for their silence. For instance, perhaps fewer of them hang around on Twitter, or maybe the ones that do are more inclined to lie.

I should add as a final note there was really only one class of people that not only denied their jobs were pointless but expressed outright hostility to the very idea that our economy is rife with bullshit jobs. These were—predictably enough—business owners, and anyone else in charge of hiring and firing. (Tania appears to be something of an exception in this regard.) In fact, for many years, I have been receiving periodic unsolicited communications from indignant entrepreneurs and executives telling me my entire premise is wrong. No one, they insist, would ever spend company money on an employee who wasn't needed. Such communications rarely offer particularly sophisticated arguments. Most just employ the usual circular argument that since, in a market economy, none of the things described in this chapter could have actually occurred, that therefore they didn't, so all the people who are convinced their jobs are worthless must be deluded, or self-important, or simply don't understand their real function, which is fully visible only to those above.

One might be tempted to conclude from these responses that there is at least one class of people who genuinely don't realize their jobs are bullshit. Except, of course, what CEOs do isn't really bullshit. For better or for worse, their actions do make a difference in the world. They're just blind to all the bullshit they create.

Chapter 3

Why Do Those in Bullshit Jobs

Regularly Report Themselves Unhappy?

(On Spiritual Violence, Part 1)

Workplaces are fascist. They're cults designed to eat your life; bosses hoard your minutes jealously like dragons hoard gold.

—Nouri

In this chapter, I'd like to start exploring some of the moral and psychological effects of being trapped inside a bullshit job.

In particular, I want to ask the obvious question: Why is this even a problem? Or to phrase it more precisely: Why does having a pointless job so regularly cause people to be miserable? On the face of it, it's not obvious that it should. After all, we're talking about people who are effectively being paid—often very good money—to do nothing. One might imagine that those being paid to do nothing would consider themselves fortunate, especially when they are more or less left to themselves. But while every now and then I did hear testimonies from those who said they couldn't believe their luck in landing such a position, the remarkable thing is how very few of them there were.[1] Many, in fact, seemed perplexed by their own reaction, unable to understand why their situation left them feeling so worthless or depressed. Indeed, the fact that there was no clear explanation for their feelings—no story they could tell themselves about the nature of their situation and what was wrong about it—often contributed to their misery. At least a galley slave knows that he's oppressed. An office worker forced to sit for seven and a half hours a day pretending to type into a screen for $18 an hour, or a junior member of a consultancy team forced to give the exact same seminar on innovation and creativity week in and week out for $50,000 a year, is just confused.

In an earlier book about debt, I wrote about the phenomenon of "moral confusion." I took as my example the fact that throughout human history, most people seem to have agreed both that paying back one's debts was the essence of morality and that moneylenders were evil. While the rise of bullshit jobs is a comparatively recent phenomenon, I think it creates a similar moral embarrassment. On the one hand, everyone is encouraged to assume that human beings will always tend to seek their best advantage, that is, to find themselves a situation where they can get the most benefit for the least expenditure of time and effort, and for the most part, we do assume this—especially if we are talking about such matters in the abstract. ("We can't just give poor people handouts! Then they won't have any incentive to look for work!") On the other hand, our own experience, and those of the people we are closest to, tends to contradict these assumptions at many points. People almost never act and react to situations in quite the way our theories of human nature would predict. The only reasonable conclusion is that, at least in certain key essentials, these theories about human nature are wrong.

In this chapter, I don't just want to ask why people are so unhappy doing what seems to them meaningless make-work, but to think more deeply about what that unhappiness can tell us about what people are and what they are basically about.

about one young man apparently handed a sinecure who nonetheless found himself unable to handle the situation

I will begin with a story. The following is the tale of a young man named Eric, whose first experience of the world of work was of a job that proved absolutely, even comically, pointless.

Eric: I've had many, many awful jobs, but the one that was undoubtedly pure, liquid bullshit was my first "professional job" postgraduation, a dozen years ago. I was the first in my family to attend university, and due to a profound naïveté about the purpose of higher education, I somehow expected that it would open up vistas of hitherto-unforeseen opportunity.

Instead, it offered graduate training schemes at Pricewaterhouse-Coopers, KPMG, etc. I preferred to sit on the dole for six months using my graduate library privileges to read French and Russian novels before the dole forced me to attend an interview which, sadly, led to a job.

That job involved working for a large design firm as its "Interface Administrator." The Interface was a content management system—an intranet with a graphical user interface, basically—designed to enable this company's work to be shared across its seven offices around the UK.

Eric soon discovered that he was hired only because of a communication problem in the organization. In other words, he was a duct taper: the entire computer system was necessary only because the partners were unable to pick up the phone and coordinate with one another:

Eric: The firm was a partnership, with each office managed by one partner. All of them seem to have attended one of three private schools and the same design school (the Royal College of Art). Being unbelievably competitive fortysomething public schoolboys, they often tried to outcompete one another to win bids, and on more than one occasion, two different offices had found themselves arriving at the same client's office to pitch work and having to hastily combine their bids in the parking lot of some dismal business park. The Interface was designed to make the company supercollaborative, across all of its offices, to ensure that this (and other myriad fuckups) didn't happen again, and my job was to help develop it, run it, and sell it to the staff.

The problem was, it soon became apparent that Eric wasn't even really a duct taper. He was a box ticker: one partner had insisted on the project, and, rather than argue with him, the others pretended to agree. Then they did everything in their power to make sure it didn't work.

> Eric: I should have realized that this was one partner's idea that no one else actually wanted to implement. Why else would they be paying a twenty-one-year-old history graduate with no IT experience to do this? They'd bought the cheapest software they could find, from a bunch of absolute crooks, so it was buggy, prone to crashing, and looked like a Windows 3.1 screen saver. The entire workforce was paranoid that it was designed to monitor their productivity, record their keystrokes, or flag that they were torrenting porn on the company internet, and so they wanted nothing to do with it. As I had absolutely no background in coding or software development, there was very little I could do to improve the thing, so I was basically tasked with selling and managing a badly functioning, unwanted turd. After a few months, I realized that there was very little for me to do at all most days, aside from answer a few queries from confused designers wanting to know how to upload a file, or search for someone's email on the address book.

The utter pointlessness of his situation soon led to subtle—and then, increasingly unsubtle—acts of rebellion:

> Eric: I started arriving late and leaving early. I extended the company policy of "a pint on Friday lunchtime" into "pints every lunchtime." I read novels at my desk. I went out for lunchtime walks that lasted three hours. I almost perfected my French reading ability, sitting with my shoes off with a copy of Le Monde and a Petit Robert. I tried to quit, and my boss offered me a £2,600 raise, which I reluctantly accepted. They needed me precisely because I didn't have the skills to implement something that they didn't want to implement, and they were willing to pay to keep me. (Perhaps one could paraphrase Marx's

Economic and Philosophical Manuscripts of 1844 here: to forestall their fears of alienation from their own labor, they had to sacrifice me up to a greater alienation from potential human growth.)

As time went on, Eric became more and more flagrant in his defiance, hoping he could find something he could do that might actually cause him to be fired. He started showing up to work drunk and taking paid "business trips" for nonexistent meetings:

Eric: A colleague from the Edinburgh office, to whom I had poured out my woes when drunk at the annual general meeting, started to arrange phony meetings with me, once on a golf course near Gleneagles, me hacking at the turf in borrowed golf shoes two sizes too large. After getting away with that, I started arranging fictional meetings with people in the London office. The firm would put me up in a nicotine-coated room in the St. Athans in Bloomsbury, and I would meet old London friends for some good old-fashioned all-day drinking in Soho pubs, which often turned into all-night drinking in Shoreditch. More than once, I returned to my office the following Monday in last Wednesday's work shirt. I'd long since stopped shaving, and by this point, my hair looked like it was robbed from a Zeppelin roadie. I tried on two more occasions to quit, but both times my boss offered me more cash. By the end, I was being paid a stupid sum for a job that, at most, involved me answering the phone twice a day. I eventually broke down on the platform of Bristol Temple Meads train station one late summer's afternoon. I'd always fancied seeing Bristol, and so I decided to "visit" the Bristol office to look at "user take-up." I actually spent three days taking MDMA at an anarcho-syndicalist house party in St. Pauls, and the dissociative comedown made me realize how profoundly upsetting it was to live in a state of utter purposelessness.

After heroic efforts, Eric did finally manage to get himself replaced:

Eric: Eventually, responding to pressure, my boss hired a junior fresh out of a computer science degree to see if some improvements could be made to our graphical user interface. On this kid's first day at work, I wrote him a list of what needed to be done—and then immediately wrote my resignation letter, which I posted under my boss's door when he took his next vacation, surrendering my last paycheck over the telephone in lieu of the statutory notice period. I flew that same week to Morocco to do very little in the coastal town of Essaouira. When I came back, I spent the next six months living in a squat, growing my own vegetables on three acres of land. I read your *Strike!* piece when it first came out. It might have been a revelation for some that capitalism creates unnecessary jobs in order for the wheels to merely keep on turning, but it wasn't to me.

The remarkable thing about this story is that many would consider Eric's a dream job. He was being paid good money to do nothing. He was also almost completely unsupervised. He was given respect and every opportunity to game the system. Yet despite all that, it gradually destroyed him. Why?

To a large degree, I think, this is really a story about social class. Eric was a young man from a working-class background—a child of factory workers, no less—fresh out of college and full of expectations, suddenly confronted with a jolting introduction to the "real world." Reality, in this instance, consisted of the fact that (a) while middle-aged executives can be counted on to simply assume that any twentysomething white male will be at least something of a computer whiz (even if, as in this case, he had no computer training of any kind), and (b) might even grant someone like Eric a cushy situation if it suited their momentary purposes, (c) they basically saw him as something of a joke. Which his job almost literally was. His presence in the company was very close to a practical joke some designers were playing on one another.

Even more, what drove Eric crazy was the fact there was simply no way he could construe his job as serving any sort of purpose. He couldn't even tell himself he was doing it to feed his family; he didn't have one yet. Coming from a background where most people took pride in making, main-taining, and fixing things, or anyway felt that was the sort of thing people *should* take pride in, he had assumed that going to university and moving into the professional world would mean doing the same sorts of thing on a grander, even more meaningful, scale. Instead, he ended up getting hired precisely for what he *wasn't* able to do. He tried to just resign. They kept offering him more money. He tried to get himself fired. They wouldn't fire him. He tried to rub their faces in it, to make himself a parody of what they seemed to think he was. It didn't make the slightest bit of difference.

To get a sense of what was really happening here, let us imagine a second history major—we can refer to him as anti-Eric—a young man of a professional background but placed in exactly the same situation. How might anti-Eric have behaved differently? Well, likely as not, he would have played along with the charade. Instead of using phony business trips to practice forms of self-annihilation, anti-Eric would have used them to accumulate social capital, connections that would eventually allow him to move on to better things. He would have treated the job as a stepping-stone, and this very project of professional advancement would have given him a sense of purpose. But such attitudes and dispositions don't come naturally. Children from professional backgrounds are taught to think like that from an early age. Eric, who had not been trained to act and think this way, couldn't bring himself to do it. As a result, he ended up, for a time, at least, in a squat growing tomatoes.[2]

concerning the experience of falseness and purposelessness at the core of bullshit jobs, and the importance now felt of conveying the experience of falseness and purposelessness to youth

In a deeper way, Eric's story brings together almost everything that those with bullshit jobs say is distressing about their situation. It's not just the purposelessness—though certainly, it's that. It's also the falseness. I've al-ready mentioned the indignation telemarketers feel when they are forced to try to trick or pressure people into doing something they think is against their best interests. This is a complicated feeling. We don't even really have a name for it. When we think of scams, after all, we think of grifters, confidence artists; they are easy to see as romantic figures, rebels living by their wits, as well as admirable because they have achieved a certain form of mastery. This is why they make acceptable heroes in Hollywood movies. A confidence artist could easily take delight in what she's doing. But being *forced* to scam someone is altogether different. In such circumstances, it's hard not to feel you're ultimately in the same situation as the person you're scamming: you're both being pressured and manipulated by your employer, only in your case, with the added indignity that you're also betraying the trust of someone whose side you should be on.

One might imagine the feelings sparked by most bullshit jobs would be very different. After all, if the employee is scamming anyone, it's his employer, and he's doing it with his employer's full consent. But somehow, this is precisely what many report to be so disturbing about the situation. You don't even have the satisfaction of knowing you're putting something over on someone. You're not even living your own lie. Most of the time, you're not even quite living somebody else's lie, either. Your job is more like a boss's unzipped fly that everyone can see but also knows better than to mention.

If anything, this appears to compound the sense of purposelessness.

Perhaps anti-Eric would, indeed, have found a way to turn around that purposelessness and seen himself as in on the joke; perhaps if he were a real go-getter, he'd have used his administrative skills to effectively take over the office; but even children of the rich and powerful often find this difficult to pull off. The following testimony gives a sense of the moral confusion they can often feel:

Rufus: I got the job because my dad was a Vice President at the company. I was charged with handling complaints. Given that it was (in name) a biomedical company, all returned product was considered a biohazard. So I was able to spend a lot of time in a room all by myself, with no supervision and essentially no work to do. The bulk of my memory of the job involves either playing Minesweeper or listening to podcasts.

I did spend hours poring over spreadsheets, tracking changes on Word documents, etc., but I guarantee you that I contributed *nothing* to this company. I spent every minute at the office wearing headphones. I paid only the smallest attention possible to the people around me and the "work" I was assigned.

I hated every minute working there. In fact, more days than not, I went home early from work, took two- or three-hour lunch breaks, spent hours "in the bathroom" (wandering around), and nobody ever said a word. I was compensated for every minute.

Thinking back on it, it was kind of a dream job.

Retrospectively, Rufus understands that he got a ridiculously sweet deal—he seems rather baffled, actually, why he hated the job so much at the time. But surely he couldn't have been entirely unaware of how his coworkers must have seen him: boss's kid getting paid to goof off; feels he's too good to talk to them; supervisors clearly informed "hands off." It could hardly have evoked warm feelings.

Still, this story raises another question: If Rufus's father didn't actually expect his son to do the job, why did he insist he take it in the first place? He could presumably just as easily have given his son an allowance, or, alternately, assigned him a job that needed doing, coached him on his duties, and taken some minimal effort to make sure those tasks were actually carried out. Instead, he seems to have felt it was more important for Rufus to be able to say he had a job than to actually acquire work experience.[3]

That's puzzling. It's all the more puzzling because the father's attitude appears to be extremely common. It wasn't always so. There was once a time when most students in college whose parents could afford it, or who qualified for scholarships or assistance, received a stipend. It was considered a good thing that there might be a few years in a young man's or woman's life where money was not the primary motivation; where he or she could thus be free to pursue other forms of value: say, philosophy, poetry, athletics, sexual experimentation, altered states of consciousness, politics, or the history of Western art. Nowadays it is considered important they should work. However, it is not considered important they should work at anything useful. In fact, like Rufus they're barely expected to work at all, just to show up and pretend to do so. A number of students wrote just to complain to me about this phenomenon. Here Patrick reflects on his job as a casual retail assistant in a student union convenience store:

Patrick: I didn't actually need the job (I was getting by financially without it), but after some pressure from my family, I applied for it out of some warped sense of obligation to get experience in work to prepare me for whatever lay ahead beyond university. In reality, the job just took away time and energy from other activities I had been doing, like campaigning and activism, or reading for pleasure, which I think made me resent it even more.

The job was pretty standard for a student union convenience store and involved serving people on the till (could have easily been done by a machine) with the explicitly stated requirement, in my performance review after my trial period, that I "should be more positive and happy when serving customers." So not only did they want me to do work that could have been performed by a machine just as effectively, they wanted me to pretend that I was enjoying that state of affairs.

It was just about bearable if my shift was during lunchtime, when it got really busy, so time went by relatively quickly. Being on shift on a Sunday afternoon when nobody frequented the SU was just appalling. They had this thing about us not being able to just do nothing, even if the shop was empty. So we couldn't just sit at the till and read a magazine. Instead, the manager made up utterly meaningless work for us to do, like going round the whole shop and checking that things were in date (even though we knew for a fact they were because of the turnover rate) or rearranging products on shelves in even more pristine order than they already were.

The very, very worst thing about the job was that it gave you so much time to think, because the work was so lacking in any intellectual demand. So I just thought so much about how bullshit my job was, how it could be done by a machine, how much I couldn't wait for full communism, and just endlessly theorized the alternatives to a system where millions of human beings *have* to do that kind of work for their whole lives in order to survive. I couldn't stop thinking about how miserable it made me.

This is what happens, of course, when you first open the entire world of social and political possibility to a young mind by sending it to college and then tell it to stop thinking and tidy up already tidy shelves. Parents now feel it is important that young minds should have this experience. But what, precisely, was Patrick supposed to be learning through this exercise?

Here's another example:

Brendan: I'm at a small college in Massachusetts training to be a high school history teacher. Recently I started work at the dining commons.

A coworker told me on my first day: "Half of this job is making things *look* clean, and the other half is looking busy."

For the first couple of months, they had me "monitor" the back room. I would clean the buffet slider, restock the desserts, and wipe down tables when people left. It's not a big room, so usually I could do all my tasks in five minutes out of every thirty. I ended up being able to get a lot of reading for my coursework done.

However, sometimes one of the less understanding supervisors would be working. In that case, I would have to keep the corner of my eye open at all times in order to make sure they would always see me acting busy. I have no idea why the job description couldn't just acknowledge that I wouldn't have much to do—if I didn't have to spend so much time and energy looking busy, I could get my reading *and* the table cleaning done quicker and more efficiently.

But of course, efficiency is not the point. In fact, if we are simply talking about teaching students about efficient work habits, the best thing would be to leave them to their studies. Schoolwork is, after all, real work in every sense except that you don't get paid for it (though if you're receiving a scholarship or an allowance, you actually are getting paid for it). In fact, like almost all the other activities Patrick or Brendan might have been engaged in had they not been obliged to take on "real world" jobs, their classwork is actually more real than the largely make-work projects they ended up being forced to do. Schoolwork has real content. One must attend classes, do the readings, write exercises or papers, and be judged on the results. But in practical terms, this appears to be exactly what makes schoolwork appear inadequate to those authorities—parents, teachers, governments. administrators—who have all come to feel that they must also teach students about the real world. It's *too* results-oriented. You can study any way you want to so long as you pass the test. A successful student has to learn self-discipline, but this is not the same as learning how to operate under orders. Of course, the same is true of most of the other projects and activities students might otherwise be engaged in: whether rehearsing for plays, playing in a band, political activism, or baking cookies or growing pot to sell to fellow students. All of which might be appropriate training for a society of self-employed adults, or even one made up primarily of the largely autonomous professionals (doctors, lawyers, architects, and so forth) that universities were once designed to produce. It might even be appropriate to train young people for the democratically organized collectives that were the subject of Patrick's reveries about full communism. But as Brendan points out, it is very much *not* preparation for work in today's increasingly bullshitized workplace:

> Brendan: A lot of these student work jobs have us doing some sort of bullshit task like scanning IDs, or monitoring empty rooms, or cleaning already-clean tables. Everyone is cool with it, because we get money while we study, but otherwise there's absolutely no reason not to just give students the money and automate or eliminate the work.
>
> I'm not altogether familiar with how the whole thing works, but a lot of this work is funded by the Feds and tied to our student loans. It's part of a whole federal system designed to assign students a lot of debt—thereby promising to coerce them into labor in the future,

as student debts are so hard to get rid of—accompanied by a bullshit education program designed to train and prepare us for our future bullshit jobs.

Brendan has a point, and I'll be returning to his analysis in a later chapter. Here, though, I want to focus on what students forced into these make-work jobs actually learn from them—lessons that they do not learn from more traditional student occupations and pursuits such as studying for tests, planning parties, and so on. Even judging by Brendan's and Patrick's accounts (and I could easily reference many others), I think we can conclude that from these jobs, students learn at least five things:

1. how to operate under others' direct supervision;
2. how to pretend to work even when nothing needs to done;
3. that one is not paid money to do things, however useful or important, that one actually enjoys;
4. that one *is* paid money to do things that are in no way useful or important and that one does not enjoy; and
5. that at least in jobs requiring interaction with the public, even when one is being paid to carry out tasks one does not enjoy, one also has to pretend to be enjoying it.

This is what Brendan meant by how make-work student employment was a way of "preparing and training" students for their future bullshit jobs. He was studying to be a high school history teacher—a meaningful job, certainly, but, as with almost all teaching positions in the United States, one where the proportion of hours spent teaching in class or preparing lessons has declined, while the total number of hours dedicated to administrative tasks has increased dramatically. This is what Brendan is suggesting: that it's no coincidence that the more jobs requiring college degrees become suffused in bullshit, the more pressure is put on college students to learn about the real world by dedicating less of their time to self-organized goal-directed activity and more of it to tasks that will prepare them for the more mindless aspects of their future careers.

why many of our fundamental assumptions on human motivation appear to be incorrect

> I do not think there is any thrill that can go through the human heart like that felt by the inventor as he sees some creation of the brain unfolding to success . . . such emotions make a man forget food, sleep, friends, love, everything.
>
> —Nikola Tesla

If the argument of the previous section is correct, one could perhaps conclude that Eric's problem was just that he hadn't been sufficiently prepared for the pointlessness of the modern workplace. He had passed through the old education system—some traces of it are left—designed to prepare students to actually *do* things. This led to false expectations and an initial shock of disillusionment that he could not overcome.

Perhaps. But I don't think that's the full story. There is something much deeper going on here. Eric might have been unusually ill-prepared to endure the meaninglessness of his first job, but just about everyone does see such meaninglessness as something to be endured—despite the fact that we are all trained, in one way or another, to assume that human beings should be perfectly delighted to find themselves in his situation of being paid good money not to work.

Let us return to our initial problem. We may begin by asking why we assume that someone being paid to do nothing *should* consider himself fortunate. What is the basis of that theory of human nature from which this follows? The obvious place to look is at economic theory, which has turned this kind of thought into a science. According to classical economic theory, *homo oeconomicus*, or "economic man"—that is, the model human being that lies behind every prediction made by the discipline—is assumed to be motivated above all by a calculus of costs and benefits. All the mathematical equations by which economists bedazzle their clients, or the public, are founded on one simple assumption: that everyone, left to his own devices, will choose the course of action that provides the most of what he wants for the least expenditure of resources and effort. It is the simplicity of the formula that makes the equations possible: if one were to admit that humans have complicated motivations, there would be too many factors to take into account, it would be impossible to properly weight them, and predictions could not be made. Therefore, while an economist will say that while of course everyone is aware that human beings are not really selfish, calculating machines, assuming that they are makes it possible to explain a very large proportion of what humans do, and this proportion—and only this—is the subject matter of economic science.

This is a reasonable statement as far as it goes. The problem is there are many domains of human life where the assumption clearly doesn't hold— and some of them are precisely in the domain of what we like to call the economy. If "minimax" (minimize cost, maximize benefit) assumptions were correct, people like Eric would be delighted with their situation. He was receiving a lot of money for virtually zero expenditure of resources and energy—basically bus fare, plus the amount of calories it took to walk around the office and answer a couple of calls. Yet all the other factors (class, expectations, personality, and so on) don't determine whether someone in that situation would be unhappy—since it would appear that just about anyone in that situation would be unhappy. They only really affect *how* unhappy they will be.

Much of our public discourse about work starts from the assumption that the economists' model is correct. People have to be compelled to work; if the poor are to be given relief so they don't actually starve, it has to be delivered in the most humiliating and onerous ways possible, because otherwise they would become dependent and have no incentive to find proper jobs.[4] The underlying assumption is that if humans are offered the option to be parasites, of course they'll take it.

In fact, almost every bit of available evidence indicates that this is not the case. Human beings certainly tend to rankle over what they consider excessive or degrading work; few may be inclined to work at the pace or intensity that "scientific managers" have, since the 1920s, decided they should; people also have a particular aversion to being humiliated. But leave them to their own devices, and they almost invariably rankle even more at the prospect of having nothing useful to do.

There is endless empirical evidence to back this up. To choose a couple of particularly colorful examples: working-class people who win the lottery and find themselves multimillionaires rarely quit their jobs (and if they do, usually they soon say they regret it).[5] Even in those prisons where inmates are provided free food and shelter and are not actually required to work, denying them the right to press shirts in the prison laundry, clean latrines in the prison gym, or package computers for Microsoft in the prison workshop is used as a form of punishment—and this is true even where the work doesn't pay or where prisoners have access to other income.[6] Here we are dealing with people who can be assumed to be among the least altruistic society has produced, yet they find sitting around all day watching television a far worse fate than even the harshest and least rewarding forms of labor.

The redeeming aspect of prison work is, as Dostoyevsky noted, that at least it was seen to be useful—even if it is not useful to the prisoner himself.

Actually, one of the few positive side effects of a prison system is that, simply by providing us with information of what happens, and how humans behave under extreme situations of deprivation, we can learn basic truths about what it means to be human. To take another example: we now know that placing prisoners in solitary confinement for more than six months at a stretch inevitably results in physically observable forms of brain damage. Human beings are not just social animals; they are so intrinsically social that if they are cut off from relations with other humans, they begin to decay physically.

I suspect the work experiment can be seen in similar terms. Humans may or may not be cut out for regular nine-to-five labor discipline—it seems to me that there is considerable evidence that they aren't—but even hardened criminals generally find the prospect of just sitting around doing nothing even worse.

Why should this be the case? And just how deeply rooted are such dispositions in human psychology? There is reason to believe the answer is: very deep indeed.

■ ■ ■

As early as 1901, the German psychologist Karl Groos discovered that infants express extraordinary happiness when they first figure out they can cause predictable effects in the world, pretty much regardless of what that effect is or whether it could be construed as having any benefit to them. Let's say they discover that they can move a pencil by randomly moving their arms. Then they realize they can achieve the same effect by moving in the same pattern again. Expressions of utter joy ensue. Groos coined the phrase "the pleasure at being the cause," suggesting that it is the basis for play, which he saw as the exercise of powers simply for the sake of exercising them.

This discovery has powerful implications for understanding human motivation more generally. Before Groos, most Western political philosophers—and after them, economists and social scientists—had been inclined either to assume that humans seek power simply because of an inherent desire for conquest and domination, or else for a purely practical desire to guarantee access to the sources of physical gratification, safety, or reproductive success. Groos's findings—which have since been confirmed by a century of experimental evidence—suggested maybe there was something much simpler behind what Nietzsche called the "will to power." Children come to understand that they exist, that they are discrete entities separate from the world around them, largely by coming to understand that "they" are the thing which just caused something to happen—the proof of which is the fact that they can make it happen again.[7] Crucially, too, this realization is, from the very beginning, marked with a species of delight that remains the fundamental background of all subsequent human experience.[8] It is hard perhaps to think of our sense of self as grounded in action because when we are truly engrossed in doing something—especially something we know how to do very well, from running a race to solving a complicated logical problem—we tend to forget that we exist. But even as we dissolve into what we do, the foundational "pleasure at being the cause" remains, as it were, the unstated ground of our being.

Groos himself was primarily interested in asking why humans play games, and why they become so passionate and excited over the outcome even when they know it makes no difference who wins or loses outside the confines of the game itself. He saw the creation of imaginary worlds as simply an extension of his core principle. This might be so. But what we're concerned with here, unfortunately, is less with the implications for healthy development and more with what happens when something goes terribly wrong. In fact, experiments have also shown that if one first allows a child to discover and experience the delight in being able to cause a certain effect, and then suddenly denies it to them, the results are dramatic: first rage, refusal to engage, and then a kind of catatonic folding in on oneself and withdrawing from the world entirely. Psychiatrist and psychoanalyst Francis Broucek called this the "trauma of failed influence" and suspected that such traumatic experiences might lie behind many mental health issues later in life.[9]

If this is so, then it begins to give us a sense of why being trapped in a job where one is treated as if one were usefully employed, and has to play along with the pretense that one is usefully employed, but at the same time, is keenly aware one is *not* usefully employed, would have devastating effects. It's not just an assault on the person's sense of self-importance but also a direct attack on the very foundations of the sense that one even *is* a self. A human being unable to have a meaningful impact on the world ceases to exist.

a brief excursus on the history of make-work and particularly of the concept of buying other people's time

Boss: How come you're not working?
Worker: There's nothing to do.
Boss: Well, you're supposed to pretend like you're working.

Worker: Hey, I got a better idea. Why don't *you* pretend like I'm working? You get paid more than me.

—Bill Hicks comedy routine

Groos's theory of "the pleasure at being the cause" led him to devise a theory of play as make-believe: humans invent games and diversions, he proposed, for the exact same reason the infant takes delight in his ability to move a pencil. We wish to exercise our powers as an end in themselves. The fact that the situation is made up doesn't detract from this; in fact, it adds another level of contrivance. This, Groos suggested—and here he was falling back on the ideas of Romantic German philosopher Friedrich Schiller—is really all that freedom is. (Schiller argued that the desire to create art is simply a manifestation of the urge to play as the exercise of freedom for its own sake as well.[10]) Freedom is our ability to make things up just for the sake of being able to do so.

Yet at the same time, it is precisely the make-believe aspect of their work that student workers like Patrick and Brendan find the most infuriating—indeed, that just about anyone who's ever had a wage-labor job that was closely supervised invariably finds the most maddening aspect of her job. Working serves a purpose, or is meant to do so. Being forced to pretend to work just for the sake of working is an indignity, since the demand is perceived—rightly—as the pure exercise of power for its own sake. If make-believe play is the purest expression of human freedom, make-believe work imposed by others is the purest expression of lack of freedom. It's not entirely surprising, then, that the first historical evidence we have for the notion that certain categories of people really ought to be working at all times, even if there's nothing to do, and that work needs to be made up to fill their time, even if there's nothing that really needs doing, refers to people who are not free: prisoners and slaves, two categories that historically have largely overlapped.[11]

■ ■ ■

It would be fascinating, though probably impossible, to write a history of make-work—to explore when and in what circumstances "idleness" first came to be seen as a problem, or even a sin. I'm not aware that anyone has actually tried to do this.[12] But all evidence we have indicates that the modern form of make-work that Patrick and Brendan are complaining about is historically new. This is in part because most people who have ever existed have assumed that normal human work patterns take the form of periodic intense bursts of energy, followed by relaxation, followed by slowly picking up again toward another intense bout. This is what farming is like, for instance: all-hands-on-deck mobilization around planting and harvest, but otherwise, whole seasons taken up largely by minding and mending things, minor projects, and puttering around. But even daily tasks, or projects such as building a house or preparing for a feast, tend to take roughly this form. In other words, the traditional student's pattern of lackadaisical study leading up to intense cramming before exams and then slacking off again—I like to refer to it as "punctuated hysteria"—is typical of how human beings have always tended to go about necessary tasks if no one forces them to act otherwise.[13] Some students may engage in cartoonishly exaggerated versions of this pattern.[14] But good students figure out how to get the pace roughly right. Not only is it what humans will do if left to their own devices, but there is no reason to believe that forcing them to act otherwise is likely to cause greater efficiency or productivity. Often it will have precisely the opposite effect.

Obviously, some tasks are more dramatic and therefore lend themselves better to alternating intense, frenetic bursts of activity and relative torpor. This has always been true. Hunting animals is more demanding than gathering vegetables, even if the latter is done in sporadic bursts; building houses better lends itself to heroic efforts than cleaning them. As these examples imply, in most human societies, men tend to try, and usually succeed, to monopolize the most exciting, dramatic kinds of work—they'll set the fires that burn down the forest on which they plant their fields, for example, and, if they can, relegate to women the more monotonous and time-consuming tasks, such as weeding. One might say that men will always take for themselves the kind of jobs one can tell stories about afterward, and try to assign women the kind you tell stories during.[15] The more patriarchal the society, the more power men have over women, the more this will tend to be the case. The same pattern tends to reproduce itself whenever one group clearly is in a position of power over another, with very few exceptions. Feudal lords, insofar as they worked at all, were fighters[16]—their lives tended to alternate between dramatic feats of arms and near-total idleness and torpor. Peasants and servants obviously were expected to work more steadily. But even so, their work schedule was nothing remotely as regular or disciplined as the current nine-to-five—the typical medieval serf, male or female, probably worked from dawn to dusk for twenty to thirty days out of any year, but just a few hours a day otherwise, and on feast days, not at all. And feast days were not infrequent.

The main reason why work could remain so irregular was because it was largely unsupervised. This is true not only of medieval feudalism but also of most labor arrangements anywhere until relatively recent times. It was true even if those labor arrangements were strikingly unequal. If those on the bottom produced what was required of them, those on top didn't really feel they should have to be bothered knowing what that entailed. We see this again quite clearly in gender relations. The more patriarchal a society, the more segregated men's and women's quarters will also tend to be; as a result, the less men tend to know about women's work, and certainly, the less able men would be able to perform women's work if the women were to disappear. (Women, in contrast, usually are well aware of what men's work entails and are often able to get on quite well were the men for some reason to vanish—this is why in so many past societies, large percentages of the male population could take off for long periods for war or trade without causing any significant disruption.) Insofar as women in patriarchal societies were supervised, they were supervised by other women. Now, this did often involve a notion that women, unlike men, should keep themselves busy all the time. "Idle fingers knit sweaters for the devil," my great-grandmother used to warn her daughter back in Poland. But this kind of traditional moralizing is actually quite different from the modern "If you have time to lean, you have time to clean," because its underlying message is not that you *should* be working but that you *shouldn't* be doing anything else. Essentially, my great-grandmother was saying that anything a teenage girl in a Polish shtetl might be getting up to when she wasn't knitting was likely to cause trouble. Similarly, one can find occasional warnings by nineteenth-century plantation owners in the American South or the Caribbean that it's better to keep slaves busy even at made-up tasks than to allow them to idle about in the off-season; the reason given always being that if slaves were left with time on their hands, they were likely to start plotting to flee or revolt.

The modern morality of "You're on my time; I'm not paying you to lounge around" is very different. It is the indignity of a man who feels he's being robbed. A worker's time is not his own; it belongs to the person who bought it. Insofar as an employee is not working, she is stealing something for which the employer paid good money (or, anyway, has promised to pay good money for at the end of the week). By this moral logic, it's not that idleness is dangerous. Idleness is theft.

This is important to underline because the idea that one person's time can belong to someone else is actually quite peculiar. Most human societies that have ever existed would never have conceived of such a thing. As the great classicist Moses Finley pointed out: if an ancient Greek or Roman saw a potter, he could imagine buying his pots. He could also imagine buying the potter—slavery was a familiar institution in the ancient world. But he would have simply been baffled by the notion that he might buy the potter's *time*. As Finley observes, any such notion would have to involve two conceptual leaps which even the most sophisticated Roman legal theorists found difficult: first, to think of the potter's capacity to work, his "labor-power," as a thing that was distinct from the potter himself, and second, to devise some way to pour that capacity out, as it were, into uniform temporal containers—hours, days, work shifts—that could then be purchased, using cash.[17] To the average Athenian or Roman, such ideas would have likely seemed weird, exotic, even mystical.

How could you *buy* time? Time is an abstraction![18] The closest he would have likely been able to come would be the idea of renting the potter as a slave for a certain limited time period—a day, for instance—during which time the potter would, like any slave, be obliged to do whatever his master ordered. But for this very reason, he would probably find it impossible to locate a potter willing to enter into such an arrangement. To be a slave, to be forced to surrender one's free will and become the mere instrument of another, even temporarily, was considered the most degrading thing that could possibly befall a human being.[19]

As a result, the overwhelming majority of examples of wage labor that we do encounter in the ancient world are of people who are already slaves: a slave potter might indeed arrange with his master to work in a ceramics factory, sending half the wages to his master and keeping the rest for himself.[20] Slaves might occasionally do free contract work as well—say, working as porters at the docks. Free men and women would not. And this remained true until fairly recently: wage labor, when it did occur in the Middle Ages, was typical of commercial port cities such as Venice, or Malacca, or Zanzibar, where it was carried out almost entirely by unfree labor.[21]

So how did we get to the situation we see today, where it's considered perfectly natural for free citizens of democratic countries to rent themselves out in this way, or for a boss to become indignant if employees are not working every moment of "his" time?

First of all, it had to involve a change in the common conception of what time actually was. Human beings have long been acquainted with the notion of absolute, or sidereal, time by observing the heavens, where celestial events happen with exact and predictable regularity. But the skies are typically treated as the domain of perfection. Priests or monks might organize their lives around celestial time, but life on earth was typically assumed to be messier. Below the heavens, there is no absolute yardstick to apply. To give an obvious example: if there are twelve hours from dawn to dusk, there's little point saying a place is three hours' walk away when you don't know the season when someone is traveling, since winter hours will be half the length of summer ones. When I lived in Madagascar, I found that rural people—who had little use for clocks—still often described distance the old-fashioned way and said that to walk to another village would take two cookings of a pot of rice. In medieval Europe, people spoke similarly of something as taking "three paternosters," or two boilings of an egg. This sort of thing is extremely common. In places without clocks, time is measured by actions rather than action being measured by time. There is a classic statement on the subject by the anthropologist Edward Evan Evans-Pritchard on the subject; he's speaking of the Nuer, a pastoral people of East Africa:

> [T]he Nuer have no expression equivalent to "time" in our language, and they cannot, therefore, as we can, speak of time as though it were something actual, which passes, can be wasted, can be saved, and so forth. I do not think that they ever experience the same feeling of fighting against time or having to coordinate activities with an abstract passage of time, because their points of reference are mainly the activities themselves, which are generally of a leisurely character. Events follow a logical order, but they are not controlled by an abstract system, there being no autonomous points of reference to which activities have to conform with precision. Nuer are fortunate.[22]

Time is not a grid against which work can be measured, because the work is the measure itself.

The English historian E. P. Thompson, who wrote a magnificent 1967 essay on the origins of the modern time sense called "Time, Work Discipline, and Industrial Capitalism,"[23] pointed out that what happened were simultaneous moral and technological changes, each propelling the other. By the fourteenth century, most European towns had created clock towers—usually funded and encouraged by the local merchant guild. It was these same merchants who developed the habit of placing human skulls on their desks as memento mori, to remind themselves that they should make good use of their time because each chime of the clock brought them one hour closer to death.[24] The dissemination of domestic clocks and then pocket watches took much longer, coinciding largely with the advent of the industrial revolution beginning in the late 1700s, but once it did happen, it allowed for similar attitudes to diffuse among the middle classes more generally. Sidereal time, the absolute time of the heavens, had to come to earth and began to regulate even the most intimate daily affairs. But time was simultaneously a fixed grid, and a possession. Everyone was encouraged to see time as did the medieval merchant: as a finite property to be carefully budgeted and disposed of, much like money. What's more, the new technologies also allowed any person's fixed time on earth to be chopped up into uniform units that could be bought and sold *for* money.

Once time was money, it became possible to speak of "spending time," rather than just "passing" it—also of wasting time, killing time, saving time, losing time, racing against time, and so forth. Puritan, Methodist, and evangelical preachers soon began instructing their flocks about the "husbandry of time," proposing that the careful budgeting of time was the essence of morality. Factories began employing time clocks; workers came to be expected to punch the clock upon entering and leaving; charity schools designed to teach the poor discipline and punctuality gave way to public school systems where students of all social classes were made to get up and march from room to room each hour at the sound of a bell, an arrangement self-consciously designed to train children for future lives of paid factory labor.[25]

Modern work discipline and capitalist techniques of supervision have their own peculiar histories, too, as forms of total control first developed on merchant ships and slave plantations in the colonies were imposed on the working poor back home.[26] But the new conception of time was what made it possible. What I want to underline here is that this was both a technological and a moral change. It is usually laid at the feet of Puritanism, and Puritanism certainly had something to do with it; but one could argue equally compellingly that the more dramatic forms of Calvinist asceticism were just overblown versions of a new time sense that was, in one way or another, reshaping the sensibilities of the middle classes across the Christian world. As a result, over the course of the eighteenth and nineteenth centuries, starting in England, the old episodic style of working came increasingly to be viewed as a social problem. The middle classes came to see the poor as poor largely because they lacked time discipline; they spent their time recklessly, just as they gambled away their money.

Meanwhile, workers rebelling against oppressive conditions began adopting the same language. Many early factories didn't allow workers to bring their own timepieces, since the owner regularly played fast and loose with the factory clock. Before long, however, workers were arguing with employers about hourly rates, demanding fixed-hour contracts, overtime, time and a half, the twelve-hour day, and then the eight-hour day. But the very act of demanding "free time," however understandable under the circumstances, had the effect of subtly reinforcing the idea that when a worker was "on the clock," his time truly did belong to the person who had bought it—a concept that would have seemed perverse and outrageous to their great-grandparents, as, indeed, to most people who have ever lived.

concerning the clash between the morality of time and natural work rhythms, and the resentment it creates

It's impossible to understand the spiritual violence of modern work without understanding this history, which leads regularly to a direct clash between the morality of the employer and the common sense of the employee. No matter how much workers may have been conditioned in time discipline by primary schooling, they will see the demand to work continually at a steady pace for eight hours a day regardless of what there is to do as defying all common sense—and the pretend make-work they are instructed to perform as absolutely infuriating.[27]

I well remember my very first job, as a dishwasher in a seaside Italian restaurant. I was one of three teenage boys hired at the start of the summer season, and the first time there was a mad rush, we naturally made a game of it, determined to prove that we were the very best and most heroic dishwashers of all time, pulling together into a machine of lightning efficiency, producing a vast and sparkling pile of dishes in record time.

We then kicked back, proud of what we'd accomplished, pausing per-haps to smoke a cigarette or scarf ourselves a scampi—until, of course, the boss showed up to ask us what the hell we were doing just lounging around.

"I don't care if there are no more dishes coming in right now, you're on my time! You can goof around on your own time. Get back to work!"

"So what are we supposed to do?"

"Get some steel wool. You can scour the baseboards."

"But we already scoured the baseboards."

"Then get busy scouring the baseboards again!"

Of course, we learned our lesson: if you're on the clock, do not be *too* efficient. You will not be rewarded, not even by a gruff nod of acknowl-edgment (which is all we were really expecting). Instead, you'll be pun-ished with meaningless busywork. And being forced to pretend to work, we discovered, was the most absolute indignity—because it was impossi-ble to pretend it was anything but what it was: pure degradation, a sheer exercise of the boss's power for its own sake. It didn't matter that we were only pretending to scrub the baseboard. Every moment spent pretending to scour the baseboard felt like some schoolyard bully gloating at us over our shoulders—except, of course, this time, the bully had the full force of law and custom on his side.

So the next time a big rush came, we made sure to take our sweet time.

■ ■ ■

It's easy to see why employees might characterize such make-work tasks as bullshit, and many of the testimonies I received enlarged on the resent-ment this produced. Here is an example of what might be called "tradi-tional make-work," from Mitch, a former ranch hand in Wyoming. Ranch work, he wrote, is hard but rewarding, and if you are lucky enough to work for an easygoing employer, it tends to alternate cheerfully between intense bursts of effort and just sort of hanging around. Mitch was not so lucky. His boss, "a very old and well-respected member of the community, of some regional standing in the Mormon church," insisted as a matter of principle that whenever there was nothing to do, free hands had to spend their time "picking rocks."

> Mitch: He would drop us off in some random field, where we were told to pick up all the rocks and put them in a pile. The idea, we were told, was to clear the land so that tractor implements wouldn't catch on them.
>
> I called BS on that right off. Those fields had been plowed many times before I ever saw them, plus the frost heaves of the severe winters there would just raise more rocks to the surface over time. But it kept the paid hands "busy" and taught us proper work ethic (meaning obedience, a very high principle as taught in Mormonism), blah, blah.
>
> Riiiight. A hundred-square-foot area of dirt would have hundreds of rocks the size of a fist or bigger.
>
> I remember once spending several hours in a field, by myself, picking rocks, and I honestly tried to do my best at it (God knows why), though I could see how futile it was. It was backbreaking. When the old boss came back to pick me up to do something else, he looked disapprovingly at my pile and declared that I hadn't really done very much work. As if being told to do menial labor for menial labor's sake wasn't degrading enough, it was made more so by my being told that my hours of hard work, performed entirely by hand with no wheelbarrow or any other tool whatsoever, simply wasn't good enough. Gee, thanks. What's more, no one ever came to haul off the rocks I had collected. From that day, they sat in that field exactly where I had piled them, and I wouldn't be surprised if they were still there to this day.
>
> I hated that old man every day until the day he died.

Mitch's story highlights the religious element: the idea that dutiful submission even to meaningless work under another's authority is a form of moral self-discipline that makes you a better person. This, of course, is a modern variant of Puritanism. For now, though, I mainly want to emphasize how this element just adds an even more exasperating layer to the perverse morality whereby idleness is a theft of someone else's time.

Despite the humiliation, Mitch could not help but try to treat even the most pointless task as a challenge to be overcome, at the same time feeling a visceral rage at having no choice but to play a game of make-believe he had not invented, and which was arranged in such a way that he could never possibly win.

Almost as soul destroying as being forced to work for no purpose is being forced to do nothing at all. In a way it's even worse, for the same reason that any prison inmate would prefer spending a year working on a chain gang breaking rocks to a year staring at the wall in solitary.

Occasionally the very rich hire their fellow human beings to pose as statues on their lawns during parties.[28] Some "real" jobs seem very close to this: although one does not need to stand quite as still, one must also do it for much longer periods of time:

> Clarence: I worked as a museum guard for a major global security company in a museum where one exhibition room was left unused more or less permanently. My job was to guard that empty room, ensuring no museum guests touched the . . . well, *nothing* in the room, and ensure nobody set any fires. To keep my mind sharp and attention undivided, I was forbidden any form of mental stimulation, like books, phones, etc.
>
> Since nobody was ever there, in practice I sat still and twiddled my thumbs for seven and a half hours, waiting for the fire alarm to sound. If it did, I was to calmly stand up and walk out. That was it.

In a situation like that—I can attest to this because I have been in roughly analogous situations—it's very hard not to stand there calculating "Just how much longer would it likely take me to notice a fire if I were sitting here reading a novel or playing solitaire? Two seconds? Three seconds? That is assuming I wouldn't actually notice it quicker because my mind would not, as it is now, be so pulped and liquified by boredom that it had effectively ceased to operate. But even assuming that it *was* three seconds, just how many seconds of my life have been effectively taken from me to eliminate that hypothetical three-second gap? Let's work it out (I have a lot of time on my hands anyway): 27,000 seconds a work shift; 135,000 seconds a week; 3,375,000 seconds a month." Hardly surprising that those assigned such utterly empty labor rarely last a year unless someone upstairs takes pity and gives them something else to do.

Clarence lasted six months (roughly twenty million seconds) and then took a job at half the pay that afforded at least a modicum of mental stimulation.

■ ■ ■

These are obviously extreme examples. But the morality of "You're on my time" has become so naturalized that most of us have learned to see the world from the point of view of the restaurant owner—to the extent that even members of the public are encouraged to see themselves as bosses and to feel indignant if public servants (say, transit workers) seem to be working in a casual or dilatory fashion, let alone just lounging around. Wendy, who sent me a long history of her most pointless jobs, reflected that many of them seem to come about because employers can't accept the idea that they're really paying someone to be on call in case they're needed:

> Wendy: Example one: as a receptionist for a small trade magazine, I was often given tasks to perform while I was waiting for the phone to ring. Fair enough—but the tasks were almost uniformly BS. One I will remember for the rest of my life: one of the ad sales people came to my desk and dumped thousands of paper clips on my desk and asked me to sort them by color. I thought she was joking, but she wasn't. I did it, only to observe that she then used them interchangeably without the slightest attention to the color of the clip.
>
> Example two: my grandmother, who lived independently in an apartment in New York City into her early nineties. She did need help, though, so we hired a very nice woman to live with her and keep an eye out. Basically, she was there in case my grandmother fell or needed help, and to help her do shopping and laundry, but if all went well,

there was basically nothing for her to do. This drove my grandmother crazy. "She's just sitting there!" she would complain. We would explain that was the point.

To help my grandmother save face, we asked the woman if she would mind straightening out cabinets when she wasn't otherwise occupied. She said no problem. But the apartment was small, the closets and cabinets were quickly put in order, and there was nothing to do again. Again, my grandmother was going crazy that she was just sitting there. Ultimately, the woman quit. When she did, my mother said to her, "Why? My mother looks great!" To which the woman responded famously, "Sure, *she* looks great. *I've* lost fifteen pounds, and my hair is falling out. I can't take her anymore." The job wasn't BS, but the need to construct a cover by way of creating so much BS busywork was deeply demeaning to her. I think this is a common problem for people working for the elderly. (It comes up with babysitting, too, but in a very different way.)[29]

Not just. Once you recognize the logic, it becomes easy to see that whole jobs, careers, and even industries can come to conform to this logic—a logic that not so very long ago would have been universally considered utterly bizarre. It has also spread across the world. Ramadan Al Sokarry, for example, is a young Egyptian engineer working for a public enterprise in Cairo:

Ramadan: I graduated from the Electronics and Communications Department in one of the best engineering schools in my country, where I had studied a complicated major, and where all the students had high expectations of careers tied to research and the development of new technologies.

Well, at least that's what our studies made us think. But it wasn't the case. After graduation, the only job I could find was as a control and HVAC [heating, ventilating, and air-conditioning] engineer in a corporatized government company—only to discover immediately that I hadn't been hired as an engineer at all but really as some kind of a technical bureaucrat. All we do here is paperwork, filling out checklists and forms, and no one actually cares about anything but whether the paperwork is filed properly.

The position is described officially as follows: "heading a team of engineers and technicians to carry out all the preventive maintenance, emergency maintenance operations, and building new systems of control engineering to achieve maximum efficiency." In reality, it means I make a brief daily check on system efficiency, then file the daily paperwork and maintenance reports.

To state the matter bluntly: the company really just needed to have a team of engineers to come in every morning to check if the air conditioners were working and then hang around in case something broke. Of course, management couldn't admit that. Ramadan and the other members of his team could have just as easily been sitting around playing cards all day, or—who knows?—even working on some of those inventions they'd been dreaming about in college, so long as they were ready to leap into action if a convector malfunctioned. Instead, the firm invented an endless array of forms, drills, and box-ticking rituals calculated to keep them busy eight hours a day. Fortunately, the company didn't have anyone on staff who cared enough to check if they were actually complying. Ramadan gradually figured out which of the exercises did need to be carried out, and which ones nobody would notice if he ignored and used the time to indulge a growing interest in film and literature.

Still, the process left him feeling hollow:

Ramadan: In my experience, this was psychologically exhausting and it left me depressed, having to go every workday to a job that I considered pointless. Gradually I started losing interest in my work, and started watching films and reading novels to fill the empty shifts. I now even leave my workplace for hours almost each shift without anyone noticing.

Once again, the end result, however exasperating, doesn't seem all that impossibly bad. Especially once Ramadan had figured out how to game the system. Why couldn't he see it, then, as stealing back time that he'd sold to the corporation? Why did the pretense and lack of purpose grind him down?

It would seem we are back at the same question with which we started. But at this point, we are much better equipped to find the answer. If the most hateful aspect of any closely supervised wage-labor job is having to pretend to work to appease a jealous boss, jobs such as Ramadan's (and Eric's) are essentially organized based on the same principle. They might be infinitely more pleasant than my experience of having to spend hours (it seemed like hours) applying steel wool to clean perfectly clean baseboards. Such jobs are likely to be not waged but salaried. There may not even be an actual boss breathing down one's neck—in fact, usually there isn't. But ultimately, the need to play a game of make-believe *not of one's own making*, a game that exists only as a form of power imposed on you, is inherently demoralizing.

So the situation was not, in the final analysis, all that fundamentally different from when me and my fellow dishwashers had to pretend to clean the baseboards. It is like taking the very worst aspect of most wage-labor jobs and substituting it for the occupation that was otherwise supposed to give meaning to your existence. It's no wonder the soul cries out. It is a direct assault on everything that makes us human.

Chapter 4

What Is It Like to Have a Bullshit Job?

(On Spiritual Violence, Part 2)

The official line is that we all have rights and live in a democracy. Other unfortunates who aren't free like we are have to live in police states. These victims obey orders or else, no matter how arbitrary. The authorities keep them under regular surveillance. State bureaucrats control even the smallest details of everyday life. The officials who push them around are answerable only to higher-ups, public or private. Either way, dissent or disobedience are punished. Informers report regularly to the authorities. All this is supposed to be a very bad thing.

And so it is, although it is nothing but a description of the modern workplace.

—Bob Black, "The Abolition of Work"

In the last chapter, we asked why it was that human beings so regularly find being paid to do nothing an exasperating, insufferable, or oppressive experience—often, even when the conditions of employment are quite good. I suggested the answer reveals certain truths about human nature largely overlooked by economic science and even by the more cynical versions of popular common sense. Humans are social beings that begin

101

to atrophy—even to physically decay—if they are denied regular contact with other humans; insofar as they do have a sense of being an autonomous entity separate from the world and from others, it is largely from conceiving themselves as capable of acting on the world and others in predictable ways. Deny humans this sense of agency, and they are nothing. What's more, in bullshit jobs, the ability to perform acts of make-believe, which under ordinary circumstances might be considered the highest and most distinctly human form of action—especially to the extent that the make-believe worlds so created are in some way actually brought into reality—is turned against itself. Hence, my inquiry into the history of pretend work and the social and intellectual origins of the concept that one's time can belong to someone else. How does it come to seem morally wrong to the employer that workers are not working, even if there is nothing obvious for them to do?

If being forced to pretend to work is so infuriating because it makes clear the degree to which you are entirely under another person's power, then bullshit jobs are, as noted above, entire jobs organized on that same principle. You're working, or pretending to work—not for any good reason, at least any good reason you can find—but just for the sake of working. Hardly surprising it should rankle.

But there's one obvious difference, too, between bullshit jobs and a dishwasher being made to clean the baseboards in a restaurant. In the latter case, there is a demonstrable bully. You know exactly who is pushing you around. In the case of bullshit jobs, it's rarely so clear-cut. Who exactly is forcing you to pretend to work? The company? Society? Some strange confluence of social convention and economic forces that insist no one should be given the means of life without working, even if there is not enough real work to go around? At least in the traditional workplace, there was someone against whom you could direct your rage.

This is one of the things that comes through strongly in the testimonies I assembled: the infuriating ambiguity. There is something terrible, ridiculous, outrageous going on, but it's not clear whether you are even allowed to acknowledge it, and it's usually even less clear who or what can be blamed.

why having a bullshit job is not always necessarily that bad

Before exploring these themes, though, it's important to acknowledge that those who hold bullshit jobs are not uniformly miserable. As I mentioned in the last chapter, there were a handful of largely positive testimonials from workers who were quite satisfied with their bullshit jobs. It's hard to generalize about their common features because there really weren't all that many of them, but perhaps we can try to tease out a few:

> Warren: I work as a substitute teacher in a public school district in Connecticut. My job just involves taking attendance and making sure the students stay on task with whatever individual work they have. Teachers rarely if ever actually leave instructions for teaching. I don't mind the job, however, since it allows me lots of free time for reading and studying Chinese, and I occasionally have interesting conversations with students. Perhaps my job could be eliminated in some way, but for now I'm quite happy.

It's not entirely clear this is even a bullshit job; as public education is currently organized, someone does have to look after the children in a given class period if a teacher calls in sick.[1] The bullshit element seems to lie in pretending that instructors such as Warren are there to teach, when everyone knows they're not: presumably this is so the students will be more likely to respect their authority when they tell them to stop running around and do their assignments. The fact that the role isn't entirely useless must help somewhat. Crucially, too, it is unsupervised, nonmonotonous, involves social interaction, and allows Warren to spend a lot of time doing whatever he likes. Finally, it's clearly not something he envisions doing for the rest of his life.

This is about as good as a bullshit job is likely to get.

Some traditional bureaucratic jobs can also be quite pleasant, even if they serve little purpose. This is especially true if by taking the job one becomes part of a great and proud tradition, such as the French civil service. Take Pauline, a tax official in Grenoble:

> Pauline: I'm a technical bankruptcy advisor in a government ministry equivalent to Britain's Inland Revenue Service. About 5 percent of my job is giving technical advice. The rest of the day, I explain incomprehensible procedures to my colleagues, help them locate directives that serve no purpose, cheer up the troops, and reassign files that "the system" has misdirected.
>
> Oddly enough, I enjoy going to work. It's as if I were being paid sixty thousand dollars a year to do the equivalent of Sudoku or crossword puzzles.[2]

This sort of carefree, happy-go-lucky government office environment is not as common as it used to be. It appears to have been extremely common in the mid-twentieth century, before internal market reforms ("reinventing government," as the Clinton administration put it) massively increased the degree of box-ticking pressure on public officials; but it still exists in certain quarters.[3] What makes Pauline's job so pleasant, it seems, is that she clearly gets along with her coworkers and is running her own show. Combine that with the respect and security of government employment and then the fact that she's aware it's ultimately a rather silly show becomes not nearly so much of a problem.

Both of these examples share another factor in common: everyone knows that jobs like substitute teacher (in America) or tax official (in France) are mostly bullshit—so there's little room for disillusionment or confusion. Those who apply for such jobs are well aware of what they're getting into, and there are already clear cultural models in their heads for how a substitute teacher or tax official is supposed to behave.

There does seem to be a happy minority, then, who enjoy their bullshit jobs. It is difficult to estimate their total numbers. The YouGov poll found that while 37 percent of all British workers felt their work served no purpose, only 33 percent of workers found it unfulfilling. Logically, then, at least 4 percent of the working population feel their jobs are pointless but enjoy them anyway. Probably the real number is somewhat higher.[4] The Dutch poll reported roughly 6 percent—that is, 18 percent of the 40 percent of workers who considered their jobs pointless also said they were at least somewhat happy doing them.

No doubt there are many reasons why this might be true in any individual case. Some people hate their families or find domestic life so stressful they treasure any excuse to get away from it. Others simply like their coworkers and enjoy the gossip and camaraderie. A common problem in large cities, especially in the North Atlantic world, is that most middle-class people now spend so much time at work that they have few social ties outside it; as a result, much of the day-to-day drama of gossip and personal intrigue that makes life entertaining for inhabitants of a village or small town or close-knit urban neighborhood, insofar as it exists at all, comes to be confined largely to offices or experienced vicariously through social media (which many mostly access in the office while pretending to work). But if that's true, and people's social life really is often rooted in the office, then it's all the more striking that the overwhelming majority of those in bullshit occupations claim to be so miserable.

on the misery of ambiguity and forced pretense

Let us return to the subject of make-believe. Obviously, a lot of jobs require make-believe. Almost all service jobs do to a certain extent. In a classic study of Delta Airlines flight attendants, *The Managed Heart: Commercialization of Human Feeling*, sociologist Arlie Russell Hochschild introduced the notion of "emotional labor." Hoschschild found air hostesses typically had to spend so much effort creating and maintaining a perky, empathetic, good-natured persona as part of their conditions of employment that they often became haunted by feelings of emptiness, depression, or confusion, unsure of who or what they really were. Emotional labor of this sort is not limited to service workers, of course: many firms expect such work even in inward-facing office workers—especially women.

In the last chapter, we observed Patrick's indignation at first encountering the demand to pretend to enjoy being a cashier. Now, flight attendant is not a bullshit job—as I've observed, few service workers feel that the services they provide are entirely pointless. The kind of emotional labor required by those in most bullshit jobs, however, is usually rather different. Bullshit jobs, too, require maintaining a false front and playing a game of make-believe—but in their case, the game has to be played in a context where one is rarely quite sure what the rules are, why it is being played, who's on your team, and who isn't. At least flight attendants know exactly what's expected of them. What is expected of bullshit jobholders is usually far less onerous, but it is complicated by the fact that they are never sure exactly what it is. One question I asked regularly was "Does your supervisor know that you're not doing anything?" The overwhelming majority said they didn't know. Most added that they found it hard to imagine their supervisors could be totally oblivious, but they couldn't be sure because discussing such matters too openly appeared to be taboo. But tellingly, they weren't even entirely sure about exactly how far that taboo extended.

To every rule there must be exceptions. Some did report supervisors who were relatively open about the fact that there was nothing to do and who would tell their underlings that it was acceptable to "pursue their own projects." But even then, such tolerance was only within reasonable parameters and what sort of parameters were considered reasonable was rarely self-evident; such matters had to be worked out by trial and error. I never heard a single case of a supervisor just sitting down with an employee and spelling out the rules, simply and honestly, regarding when she had to work, when she didn't, and how she could and could not behave when she wasn't working.

Some managers communicate indirectly, by their own behavior. In the local British government office in which Beatrice worked, for example, supervisors indicated the appropriate level of pretense (just a little) during the week by livestreaming important sports events and similar acts of self-indulgence. On weekend shifts, in contrast, no pretense was required:

Beatrice: On other occasions, my role models known as "senior management" would stream World Cup football matches live into the office onto their desktops. I understood this gesture to be a form of multitasking, so I started to research my own projects whenever I had nothing to do at work.

On the other hand, my weekend role was a breeze. It was quite a sought-after position in the authority because of the high rate of overtime pay. In that office, we did nothing. We made Sunday dinners, and I even heard stories of someone bringing a sunbed-recliner into work so they could relax on it whilst we put the TV on. We surfed the internet, watched DVDs—but more often, we just went to sleep, as there was nothing to do. We would get some rest in before Monday morning started.

In other cases, the rules are set out explicitly, but in such a way that they are clearly made to be broken.[5] Robin, hired as a temp in North Carolina but not assigned any duties, managed to turn technical competence into a way to mitigate the experience—to a degree:

Robin: I was told that it was very important that I stay busy, but I wasn't to play games or surf the Web. My primary function seemed to be occupying a chair and contributing to the decorum of the office.

At first, this seemed pretty easy, but I quickly discovered that looking busy when you aren't is one of the least pleasant office activities imaginable. In fact, after two days, it was clear that this was going to be the worst job I had ever had.

I installed Lynx, a text-only Web browser that basically looks like a DOS [disk operating system] window. No images, no Flash, no Java-Script—just monospaced text on an endless black background. My absentminded browsing of the internet now appeared to be the work of a skilled technician, the Web browser a terminal into which diligently typed commands signaled my endless productivity.

This allowed Robin to spend most of his time editing Wikipedia pages.

As far as temporary jobs are concerned, the worker is often effectively being tested for his or her ability to just sit there and pretend to work. In most cases, one is not, like Robin, told explicitly whether they are allowed to play computer games; but if there are a lot of temporary hires, it's usually possible to make discreet inquiries of one's fellows and get some sense of what the ground rules are and just how flagrantly one has to violate them to actually get fired.

Sometimes in longer-term positions, there is enough camaraderie among employees that they can discuss the situation openly and find common strategies to use against supervisors. Solidarity in such circumstances can bring a sense of common purpose. Robert speaks of the legal aides at a crooked law firm:

> Robert: The weirdest thing about this job is how, in a twisted way, it was kind of enjoyable. The legal assistants were all smart and interesting people, and working a job that was so clearly meaningless led to a great deal of bonding and gallows humor among the team. I managed to maneuver my way into a desk with its back to the wall, so I could spend as much time as possible surfing the internet or teaching myself computer programming. Much of what we did was obviously inefficient, like manually relabeling thousands of files, so I'd automate it and then use the time it would have taken me to complete it manually to do whatever I wanted. I also always made sure to have at least two projects run by different bosses, so that I could tell both of them that I was spending a lot of time on the other project.

At the very least, there can be a conspiracy of silence on such shirking strategies; sometimes, active cooperation. In other cases, one can be lucky enough to find a supervisor who is both willing to be fairly honest and agreeable enough to set almost explicit parameters for loafing. The emphasis here is on "almost." One can never simply ask. Here's someone who has an on-call job at a travel insurance company. He's basically a duct taper, there to straighten out things once every month or two when something goes predictably awry in their relation to their partner company. Otherwise:

Calvin: Any given week, there will be a few situations where [our partner company] is supposed to reach out to my team for advisory. So for up to twenty minutes a week, we have actual work to do. Ordinarily, though, I send five or eight fifteen-word emails a day, and every few days, there's a ten-minute team meeting. The rest of the workweek is functionally mine, though not in any way I can flaunt. So I flit through social media, RSS aggregation, and coursework in a wide but short browser window I keep discreetly on the second of my two monitors. And every few hours, I'll remember I'm at a workplace and respond to my one waiting email with something like: "We agree with the thing you said. Please proceed with the thing." Then I only have to pretend to be visibly overworked for seven more hours each day.

David: So if you didn't look busy, who would notice? Does that person know there's nothing really to do and just wants you to look busy, do you think, or do they actually believe it's a real full-time job?

Calvin: Our team manager seems to know what's up, but she's never let on to having problems with it. Occasionally, I will have days with zero work at all, so I'll let her know that and volunteer to help out another department if they're bogged down in some way. That help is never needed, it seems, so my letting her know is my way of declaring, "I'm going to be on Twitter a full eight hours, but I told you in advance, so it's actually extremely noble of me." She schedules hourlong weekly meetings that haven't once had ten minutes of content—we spend the rest of them chatting casually. And since her bosses, up however high, are aware of the genuine problems the other company can cause, I think it's presumed we're wrangling their nonsense, or at least might have to at any given second.

Not all supervisors, then, subscribe to the ideology of "You're on my time." Particularly in large organizations where managers don't have much of a proprietary feeling anyway and don't have reason to believe they'll get in much trouble with their own superiors if they notice one of their subordinates slacking off, they might well let matters take their own course.[6] This kind of polite, coded, mutual consideration is perhaps about as close to honesty in such situations as one is likely to get. But even in such maximally benevolent circumstances, there is a taboo on being too explicit. The one thing that could never, apparently, happen, is for anyone to actually say, "Basically, you're just here in case of emergencies. Otherwise, do what you like and try not to get in anybody's way." And even Calvin feels obliged to pretend to be overworked, just as a reciprocal gesture of appreciation and respect.

More typically supervisors simply find subtle ways to say "Just shut up and play along."

> Maria: My first meeting on arriving to start this job was with my line manager, who was very quick to explain that she had absolutely no idea what the person who used to do my job actually did. But luckily for me, that predecessor was still around. She had just moved up inside the team and would be able to show me everything that she had done in her former role. She did. It took about an hour and a half.

"Everything she had done" also turned out to be virtually nothing. Maria couldn't handle the idleness. She begged her coworkers to let her do a share of their work; something to make herself feel she had some reason to be around. Driven to distraction, she finally made the mistake of openly complaining to her manager:

> Maria: I spoke to my manager, who very clearly told me not to "advertise the fact" that I wasn't mega busy. I asked her to at least send any unclaimed work my way, and she told me she would show me a few of the things she does, but never did.

This is as close to being told directly to pretend to work as one is likely to get. Even more dramatic, but in no way unusual, is the experience of

Lilian, hired as Digital Product Project Manager in the IT department of a major publishing house. Despite the somewhat pretentious-sounding title, Lilian insists that such positions are not necessarily bullshit—she'd had a similar gig before, and while it was relatively undemanding, she did get to work with a small, friendly team solving genuine problems. "This new place, however . . ."

As best she could reconstruct what happened (much of it had occurred just before she arrived), her immediate supervisor, an arrogant blowhard obsessed with the latest business fads and buzzwords, had sent out a series of bizarre and contradictory directives that had the unintended consequence of leaving Lilian with no responsibilities at all. When she gently pointed out there was a problem, her concerns were brushed aside with eye rolls and similar gestures of impatient dismissal.

> Lilian: One would think that, as a Project Manager, I would somehow be "running" the process. Except there is no room in the process for that to happen. No one is running this process. Everyone is confused.
>
> Other people expect me to help them and organize things and give them the confidence that people usually look to a Project Manager for because I've been given that title. But I have no authority and no control over anything.
>
> So I read a lot. I watch TV. I have no idea what my boss thinks I do all day.

As a result of her situation, Lilian has to come up with two quite difficult false fronts: one for her superior and another for her underlings. In the first case, because she can only speculate what, if anything, her supervisor actually wants her to do; in the second, in the fact that about the only positive contribution she is allowed to make is to adopt an air of cheerful confidence that might inspire her subordinates to do a better job. ("Cheer up the troops," as Pauline might put it.) Or at least not infect them with her own desperation and confusion. Underneath, Lilian was riddled with anxiety. It's worth quoting her comments at length because they give a sense of the spiritual toll such a situation can take:

Lilian: What's it like to have a job like this? Demoralizing. Depressing. I get most of the meaning in my life from my job, and now my job has no meaning or purpose.

It gives me anxiety because I think that at any moment someone is actually going to realize that nothing would change if I were not here and they could save themselves the money.

It also trashes my confidence. If I'm not constantly being met by challenges that I am overcoming, how do I know that I'm capable? Maybe all my ability to do good work has atrophied. Maybe I *don't* know anything useful. I wanted to be able to handle bigger and more complex projects, but now I handle nothing. If I don't exercise those skills, I'll lose them.

It also makes me afraid that other people in the office think the problem is me; that I'm choosing to slack off or I'm choosing to be useless, when nothing about this is my choice, and all my attempts to make myself more useful or give myself more work are met with rejection and not a small amount of derision for attempting to rock the boat and challenge my boss's authority.

I have never been paid so much to do so little, and I know I'm not earning it. I know my coworkers with other job titles do significantly more work. I might even get paid more than them! How bullshit would *that* be? I'd be lucky if they didn't hate me on that basis alone.

Lilian testifies eloquently to the misery that can ensue when the only challenge you can overcome in your own work is the challenge of coming to terms with the fact that you are not, in fact, presented with any challenges; when the only way you can exercise your powers is in coming up with creative ways to cover up the fact that you cannot exercise your powers; of managing the fact that you have, completely against your choosing, been turned into a parasite and fraud. An employee would have to be confident indeed not to begin to doubt herself in such a situation. (And such confidence can be pernicious in itself: it was her boss's idiotic cocksureness, after all, that created the situation to begin with.)

Psychologists sometimes refer to the kind of dilemmas described in this section as "scriptlessness." Psychological studies, for instance, find that men or women who had experienced unrequited love during adolescence were in most cases eventually able to come to terms with the experience and showed few permanent emotional scars. But for those who had been the *objects* of unrequited love, it was quite another matter. Many still struggled with guilt and confusion. One major reason, researchers concluded, was precisely the lack of cultural models. Anyone who falls in love with someone who does not return their affections has thousands of years' worth of romantic literature to tell them exactly how they are supposed to feel; however, while this literature provides detailed insight on the experience of being Cyrano, it generally tells you very little about how you are supposed to feel—let alone what you're supposed to do—if you're Roxane.[7]

Many, probably most, bullshit jobs involve a similar agonizing scriptlessness. Not only are the codes of behavior ambiguous, no one is even sure what they are supposed to say or how they are supposed to feel about their situation.

on the misery of not being a cause

Whatever the ambiguities, almost all sources concur that the worst thing about a bullshit job is simply the knowledge that it's bullshit. As noted in chapter 3, much of our sense of being a self, a being discrete from its surrounding environment, comes from the joyful realization that we can have predictable effects on that environment. This is true for infants and remains true throughout life. To take away that joy entirely is to squash a human like a bug. Obviously, the ability to affect one's environment cannot be taken away completely—rearranging objects in one's backpack or playing Fruit Mahjong is still acting on the world in *some* way—but most people in the world today, certainly in wealthy countries, are now taught to see their work as their principal way of having an impact on the world, and the fact that they are paid to do it as proof that their efforts do indeed have some kind of meaningful effect. Ask someone "What do you do?" and he or she will assume you mean "for a living."

Many speak of the intense frustration of learning gradually that they are instead paid to do nothing. Charles, for instance, started out of college working in the video game industry. In his first job, at Sega, he began as a tester but was soon promoted to "localization," only to discover it was a typical on-call job where he was expected to sit around pretending to work in between dealing with problems that came up only once a week, on average. Like Lilian, the situation made him doubt his own value: "Working for a company that essentially was paying me to sit around doing nothing made me feel completely worthless." He quit after superiors bawled him out for being late to work and threw himself instead into a whirlwind romance. A month later, he tried again.

At first, he thought the new job, also for a gaming company, was going to be different:

Charles: In 2002 I was hired by [BigGameCo], in LA, as an associate producer. I was excited about this job because I was told I would be in charge of writing the design document that bridged the desires of the artists with the realities of what the programmers could do. For the first few months, though, there was nothing to do. My big duty every day was ordering dinner from a delivery place for the rest of the staff.

Again, just sitting around, doing emails. Most days, I would go home early, because, why the fuck not?

With so much time on my hands, I started dreaming of having my own business and began using all the free time to start making the website for it. Eventually the producer above me threatened to report me to the owner for doing this though. So I had to stop.

Finally, I was allowed to start work on the sound design document. I threw myself into this work. I was so happy to be doing it. When it was done, the producer told me to upload it to the shared server for everyone working on the game.

Immediately there was uproar. The producer who hired me hadn't realized there was a sound design department a floor below us that makes these documents for each game. I had done someone else's job. This producer had already made some other big mistake, so he asked me to take the blame for this so he wouldn't get fired. Every ounce of my soul rebelled against doing this. My friends in programming, though, who were actually enjoying having an incompetent producer because it meant they had the freedom to do whatever they wanted, asked me to take the bullet for them. They didn't want the producer replaced by someone that would rein them in. So I accepted responsibility, quit the next day, and haven't worked for someone else since then.

Thus did Charles say farewell to the world of formal paid employment and began playing guitar for a living and sleeping in his van.

Things are rarely quite as obvious as this: cases where the worker is basically doing nothing at all (though as we've seen, this certainly can happen). It's more common for there to be at least a modicum of work, and for the worker to either immediately, or gradually, come to understand that work is pointless. Most employees do think about the social value of what they do, and whatever tacit yardstick they apply, once they judge their work to be pointless, this judgment cannot fail but affect the experience of doing that work—whatever the nature of the work or conditions of employment. Of course, when those conditions are also bad, matters often become intolerable.

Let's look at a worst-case scenario: unpleasant work, bad conditions, obvious uselessness. Nigel was a temp worker hired by a company that had won a contract to scan the application forms for hundreds of thousands of company loyalty cards. Since the scanning equipment the company used was imperfect, and since its contract stated that each form would be checked for errors no fewer than three times before being approved, the company was obliged to bus in a small army of temps every day to act as "Data Perfecters." This is how he describes his work:

Nigel: It is hard to explain what this level of entranced boredom was like. I found myself conversing with God, pleading for the next record to contain an error, or the next one, or the next. But the time seemed to pass quickly, like some kind of near-death experience.

There was something about the sheer purity of the social uselessness of this job, combined with the crippling austerity of the process, that united the Data Perfecters. We all knew that this was bullshit. I really think that if we had been processing applications for something that had a more obvious social value—organ transplant registration, say, or tickets to [the] Glastonbury [rock festival]—then it would have felt different. I don't mean that the process would have been any less tedious—an application form is an application form—but the knowledge that no one cared about this work, that there was really nothing of any value riding on how we did the job, made it feel like some sort of personal test of stamina, like Olympic endurance boredom for its own sake.

It was really weird.

Finally, there came a point where a few of us decided we just couldn't take it anymore. We complained one day about one of the supervisors being rude, and the very next morning, we got a call from the agency saying we were no longer needed.

Fortunately for Nigel, his fellow workers were all temps with no loyalty to the organization and no reason to keep quiet about what was going on—at least with one another. Often in more long-term assignments, it's hard to know exactly who one can and can't confide in.

Where for some, pointlessness exacerbates boredom, for others it exacerbates anxiety. Greg spent two years working as a designer of digital display advertising for a marketing agency, "creating those annoying banner ads you see on most websites." The entire enterprise of making and selling banner ads, he was convinced, is basically a scam. The agencies that sell the ads are in possession of studies that made clear that Web surfers largely didn't even notice and almost never clicked on them. This didn't stop them, however, from basically cooking the books and holding junkets with their clients where they presented them with elaborate "proof" of the ads' effectiveness.

Since the ads didn't really work, client satisfaction was everything. Designers were told to indulge their clients' every whim, no matter how technically difficult, self-indulgent, or absurd.

Greg: High-paying clients generally want to reproduce their TV commercials within the banner ads and demand complex storyboards with multiple "scenes" and mandatory elements. Automotive clients would come in and demand that we use Photoshop to switch the steering wheel position or fuel tank cap on an image the size of a thumbnail.

Such exacting demands were made, and had to be accommodated, as designers stewed in the knowledge that no Web surfer would possibly be able to make out such tiny details in a rapidly moving image from the corner of her eye. All this was barely tolerable, but once Greg actually saw the abovementioned studies, which also revealed that even if the surfer did see them, she wouldn't click on the banner anyway, he began to experience symptoms of clinical anxiety.

Greg: That job taught me that pointlessness compounds stress. When I started working on those banners, I had patience for the process. Once I realized that the task was more or less meaningless, all that patience evaporated. It takes effort to overcome cognitive dissonance—to actually care about the process while pretending to care about the result.

Eventually the stress became too much for him, and he quit to take another job.

■ ■ ■

Stress was another theme that popped up regularly. When, as with Greg, one's bullshit job involves not just sitting around pretending to work but actually working on something everyone knows—but can't say—is pointless, the level of ambient tension increases and often causes people to lash out in arbitrary ways. We've already met Hannibal, who makes extraordinary amounts of money writing reports designed to be waved around in pharmaceutical marketing meetings and later thrown away. In fact, he confines the bullshit aspects of his employment to a day or two a week—just enough to pay the bills—and spends the rest of his time engaged in medical research aimed at eradicating tuberculosis in the Global South—which no one seems to want to pay for. This gives him the opportunity to compare behavior in both his workplaces:

> Hannibal: That's the other thing I've noticed: the amount of workplace aggression and stress I see in people is inversely correlated with the importance of the work they're doing: "The client's going fucking apeshit because they're under pressure from their boss to get this presentation ready for the Q3 planning meeting on Monday! They're threatening to cancel the entire fucking contract unless we get it delivered by *tomorrow morning*! We're all going to need to stay late to finish it! (Don't worry, we'll order some shitty junk food pizzas and pissy lager in so we can work through the night...)." This is typical for the bullshit reports. Whereas working on meaningful stuff always has more of a collaborative atmosphere, everyone working together toward a greater goal.

Similarly, while few offices are entirely free of cruelty and psychological warfare, many respondents seemed to feel they were particularly prevalent in offices where everyone knew, but did not wish to admit, that they weren't really doing much of anything.[8]

> Annie: I worked for a medical care cost management firm. I was hired to be part of a special tasks team that performed multiple functions within the company.
> They never provided me with this training, and instead my job was to:
>
> • pull forms from the pool into the working software;
> • highlight specific fields on those forms;
> • return the forms to the pool for someone else to do something with them.
>
> This job also had a very rigid culture (no talking to others), and it was one of the most abusive environments I ever worked in.

In particular, I made one highlighting error consistently during my first two weeks of employment. I learned this was wrong and immediately corrected it. However, for the entire remainder of my time at this company, every time someone found one of these mis-highlighted forms, I would be pulled aside to talk about it. Every time, like it was a new issue. Every time, like the manager didn't know these were all done during the same period, and it wasn't happening anymore—even though I *told her* every time.

Such minor acts of sadism should be familiar to most of us who have worked in office environments. You have to ask yourself: What was the supervisor who called in Annie time and time again to "talk to her" about a mistake that she knew perfectly well had long since been corrected, actually thinking? Did she somehow forget, each time, that the problem had been resolved? That seems unlikely. Her behavior appears to be a pure exercise of power for its own sake. The pointlessness of the exercise—both Annie and her boss knew nothing would really be achieved by telling someone to fix a problem that's already been fixed—made it nothing more than a way for the boss to rub that fact—that this *was* a relation of pure arbitrary power—in Annie's face. It was a ritual of humiliation that allows the supervisor to show who's boss in the most literal sense, and it puts the underling in her place, justified no doubt by the sense that underlings are generically guilty at the very least of spiritual insubordination, of resenting the boss's tyranny, in the same way that police who beat suspects they know to be innocent will tell themselves the victim is undoubtedly guilty of something else.

> Annie: I did this for six months before deciding I'd rather die than continue. This was also, however, the first time I made a living wage doing anything. Before that, I was a preschool teacher, and while what I was doing was very important, I made $8.25 an hour (in the Boston area).

This leads us to another issue: the effects of such situations on employees' physical health. While I lack statistical evidence, if the testimonials are anything to go by, stress-related ailments seem a frequent consequence of bullshit jobs. I've read multiple reports of depression, anxiety overlapping with physical symptoms of every sort, from carpal tunnel syndrome that mysteriously vanishes when the job ends, to what appears, while it's happening, like autoimmune breakdown. Annie, too, became increasingly ill. Part of the reason, she felt in retrospect, was the extreme contrast between the work environments of her previous job and this one:

> **David:** I'm trying to imagine what it must have been like to move from a real job, teaching and taking care of children, to something so entirely pointless and humiliating, just to pay the rent. Do you think there are a lot of people in that situation?

> **Annie:** I imagine it has to be pretty common! Low-paying child-care jobs have really high turnover. Some people get additional training and can move on to something more sustaining, but a lot of the ones I've watched leave (mostly women) end up in some office or retail management.
>
> One part of the experience I think about a lot is that I went from an environment where I was touched and touching all day long—picking kids up, getting hugs, giving piggybacks, rocking to sleep—into an environment where nobody talked to each other, let alone touched each other. I didn't recognize the effect this had on my body while it was happening, but now in retrospect I see what a *huge* impact it had on my physical and mental health.

I suspect that not only is Annie right, but she is describing an unusually dramatic example of what is, in fact, a very common dynamic. Annie was convinced that not only was her particular job pointless but also that the entire enterprise shouldn't really exist: at best, it was a giant exercise in duct taping, making up for some bits of the damage caused by the notoriously dysfunctional American health care system, of which it was an intrinsic part. But of course, no one was allowed to discuss such matters in the office. No one was allowed to discuss anything in the office. The physical isolation was continuous with the social isolation. Everyone there was forced to become a little bubble unto himself or herself.

In such minimal, but clearly unequal, social environments, strange things can start to happen. Back in the 1960s, the radical psychoanalyst Erich Fromm first suggested that "nonsexual" forms of sadism and necrophilia tend to pervade everyday affairs in highly puritanical and hierarchical environments.[9] In the 1990s, the sociologist Lynn Chancer synthesized some of these ideas with those of feminist psychoanalyst Jessica Benjamin to devise a theory of Sado-Masochism in Everyday Life.[10] What Chancer found was that unlike members of actual BDSM subcultures, who are entirely aware of the fact that they are playing games of make-believe, purportedly "normal" people in hierarchical environments typically ended up locked in a kind of pathological variation of the same sadomasochistic dynamic: the (person on the) bottom struggles desperately for approval that can never, by definition, be forthcoming; the (person on the) top going to greater and greater lengths to assert a dominance that both know is ultimately a lie—for if the top were really the all-powerful, confident, masterly being he pretends to be, he wouldn't need to go to such outrageous lengths to ensure the bottom's recognition of his power. And, of course, there is also the most important difference between make-believe S&M play—and those engaged in it actually do refer to it as "play"—and its real-life, nonsexual enactments. In the play version, all the parameters are carefully worked out in advance by mutual consent, with both parties knowing the game can be called off at any moment simply by invoking an agreed-on safe-word. For example, just say the word "orange," and your partner will immediately stop dripping hot wax on you and transform from the wicked marquis to a caring human being who wants to make sure you aren't really hurt. (Indeed, one might argue that much of the bottom's pleasure comes from knowing she has the power to affect this transformation at will.[11]) This is precisely what's lacking in real-life sadomasochistic situations. You can't say "orange" to your boss. Supervisors never work out in advance in what ways employees can and cannot be chewed out for different sorts of infractions, and if an employee is, like Annie, being reprimanded or otherwise humiliated, she knows there is nothing she can say to make it stop; no safe-word, except, perhaps, "I quit." To pronounce these words, however, does more than simply break off the scenario of humiliation; it breaks off the work relationship entirely—and might well lead to one's ending up playing a very different game, one where you're desperately scrounging around to find something to eat or how to prevent one's heat from being shut off.

on the misery of not feeling entitled to one's misery

I am suggesting, then, that the very meaninglessness of bullshit employment tends to exacerbate the sadomasochistic dynamic already potentially present in any top-down hierarchical relationship. It's not inevitable; some supervisors are generous and kind. But the lack of any feeling of common purpose, any reason to believe one's collective actions in any way make life better for those outside the office or really have *any* significant effect on anyone outside the office, will tend to magnify all the minor indignities, distempers, resentments, and cruelties of office life, since, ultimately, office politics is all that's really going on.

Many, like, Annie, were terrified by the health effects. Just as a prisoner in solitary confinement inevitably begins to experience brain damage, the worker deprived of any sense of purpose often experiences mental and physical atrophy. Nouri, whom we met in chapter 2, repairing code for an incompetent Viennese psychologist, kept something of a diary of each of his successive bullshit jobs and their effects upon his mind and body:

Nouri:

Job 1: Programmer, (pointless) start-up.
Effect on me: I first learned self-loathing. Got a cold every month.
Imposter syndrome killed my immune system.

Job 2: Programmer, (vanity project) start-up.
Effect on me: I pushed myself so hard that I damaged my eye, forcing me to relax.

Job 3: Software Developer, (scam) small business.
Effect on me: usual depression, unable to find energy.

Job 4: Software developer, (doomed, dysfunctional) ex-start-up.
Effect on me: relentless mediocrity and fear due to my inability to focus crippled my mind; I got a cold every month; warping my consciousness to motivate myself killed my immune system. PTSD. My thoughts were thoroughly mediocre . . .

Nouri had the misfortune to stumble through a series of relentlessly absurd and/or abusive corporate environments. He managed to keep himself sane—at least to the degree of fending off complete mental and physical breakdown—by finding a different sense of purpose: he began to carry out a detailed analysis of the social and institutional dynamics that lie behind failed corporate projects. Effectively, he became an anthropologist. (This has been very useful to me. Thanks, Nouri!) Then he discovered politics, and began diverting time and resources toward plotting to destroy the very system that created such ridiculous jobs. At this point, he reports, his health began to markedly improve.

Even in relatively benign office environments, the lack of a sense of purpose eats away at people. It may not cause actual physical and mental degeneration, but at the very least, it leaves workers struggling with feelings of emptiness or worthlessness. These feelings are typically in no sense mitigated, but actually compounded by the prestige, respect, and generous compensation that such positions often confer. Like Lilian, bullshit job-holders can be secretly tortured by the suspicion that they are being paid more than their actually productive underlings ("How bullshit would *that* be?"), or that others have legitimate reason to hate them. This left many genuinely confused about how they *should* feel. No moral compass was available. One might consider this a kind of moral scriptlessness.

Here is a relatively mild case. Finn works for a company that licenses software on a subscription basis:

> Finn: From the moment I first read the "Bullshit Jobs" essay a couple of years back, it resonated with me. I continue to pull it out occasionally to read and refer friends to.
>
> I'm a manager of technical support for a software-as-a-service company. My job seems to mostly consist of sitting in meetings, emailing, communicating coming changes to my team, serving as an escalation point for client issues, and doing performance reviews.

Performance reviews, Finn admits, are bullshit, explaining, "Everyone already knows who the slackers are." Actually, he acknowledges readily that most of his responsibilities are bullshit. The useful work he performs consists mainly of duct taping: solving problems caused by various unnecessarily convoluted bureaucratic processes within the company. Plus, the company itself is fairly pointless.

> Finn: Still, sitting down to write this, there's part of my brain that wants to defend my bullshit job. Mostly because the job provides for me and my family. I think that's where the cognitive dissonance comes in. From an emotional standpoint, it's not like I'm invested in my job or the company in any way. If I showed up on Monday and the building had disappeared, not only would society not care, I wouldn't, either. If there's any satisfaction that comes from my job, it's being an expert in navigating the waters of our disorganized organization and being able to get things done. But being an expert in something that is unnecessary is, as you can imagine, not *all* that fulfilling.
>
> My preference would be to write novels and opinion essays, which I do in my spare time, but I fear the leap from my bullshit job will mean being incapable of making ends meet.

This is, of course, a commonplace dilemma. The job itself may be unnecessary, but it's hard to see it as a bad thing if it allows you to feed your children. You might ask what kind of economic system creates a world where the only way to feed one's children is to spend most of one's waking hours engaged in useless box-ticking exercises or solving problems that shouldn't exist. But, then, you can equally well turn this question on its head and ask whether all this can really be as useless as it seems if the economic system that created these jobs also enables you to feed your children. Do we really want to second-guess capitalism? Perhaps every aspect of the system, no matter how apparently pointless, is just the way it has to be.

Yet at the same time, one cannot also dismiss one's own experience that something is terribly amiss.

Many others spoke, like Lilian, of the agonizing disparity between the outward respect they received from society and the knowledge of what they actually did. Dan, an administrative contractor for a British corporation's offices in Toronto, was convinced he did only about an hour or two of real work a week—work he could have easily done from home. The rest was entirely pointless. Putting on the suit and coming to the office was, he felt, just an elaborate sacrificial ritual; a series of meaningless gestures he had to perform in order to prove himself worthy of a respect he did not deserve. At work, he wondered constantly if his coworkers felt the same way:

> Dan: It felt like some Kafkaesque dream sequence that only I had the misfortune of realizing how stupid so much of what we were doing was, but deep down inside, I felt as if this experience had to be a silently shared one. We must have all known! We were an office of six people, and we were all "managers" . . . There were easily more managers in the building than actual employees. The situation was completely absurd.

In Dan's case, everyone played along with the charade. The environment was in no way abusive. The six managers and their supervising managers-of-managers were polite, friendly, mutually supportive. They all told one another what a terrific job they were doing and what a disaster it would be for everyone else if they weren't there as part of the team—but only, Dan felt, as a way of consoling one another in the secret knowledge they were hardly doing anything, that their work was of no social value, and that if they weren't there, it would make no difference. It was even worse outside the office, where he began to be treated as the member of his family who had really made something of his life. "It's honestly hard to describe how mad and useless I felt. I was being taken seriously as a 'young professional'—but did any of them know what it was I really did?"

Eventually Dan quit to become a science teacher in a Cree Indian community in northern Quebec.

■ ■ ■

It doesn't help that higher-ups in such situations will regularly insist that perceptions of futility are self-evidently absurd. It doesn't always happen. Some managers, as we've seen, will basically wink and smile; a precious few might honestly discuss at least part of what's going on. But since middle managers generally see their role as one of maintaining morale and work discipline, they will often feel they have little choice but to rationalize the situation. (In effect, doing so is the only part of their jobs that *isn't* bullshit.) Plus, the higher you climb in the hierarchy, the more oblivious the managers are likely to be—but at the same time, the more formal authority they tend to have.

Vasily works as a research analyst for a European foreign affairs office: his office, he reports, has just as many supervisors as researchers, and every sentence of any document produced by a researcher invariably ends up being passed up two levels of hierarchy to be read, edited, and passed down again, repeatedly, until it makes no sense. Granted, this would be more of a problem if there were a chance that anyone outside the office would ever read them, or, for that matter, be aware they existed. Vasily does occasionally try to point all this out to his superiors:

Vasily: If I question the utility or sense of our work, my bosses look at me as if I'm from another planet. Of course they do: for them, it is crucial that the work we're doing is not seen as total nonsense. If that would be the case, the positions would be canceled, and the result would be having no job.

In this case, it's not the capitalist economic system but the modern international state system that between the various consular services, United Nations, and Bretton Woods instututions, creates untold thousands of (usually high-paid, respectable, comfortable) jobs across the planet. One can argue, as in all things, about which of these positions are truly useful and for what. Presumably some do important work—preventing wars, for instance. Others arrange and rearrange furniture. What's more, there are pockets inside the apparatus that appear, to their low-ranking denizens, at least, as entirely superfluous. This perception, says Vasily, creates feelings of guilt and shame:

> Vasily: When I am in public and people ask me about my job, I don't want to. There is nothing to say, nothing to be proud of. Working for the foreign ministry has a high reputation, so when I am saying, "I am working for the foreign ministry," people usually react with a mix of respect and not really knowing what I am doing. I think the respect makes it even worse.

There are a million ways to make a human feel unworthy. The United States, so often a pioneer in such areas, has, among other things, perfected a quintessentially American mode of political discourse that consists in lecturing others about what jerks they are to think they have a right to something. Call it "rights-scolding." Rights-scolding has many forms and manifestations. There is a right-wing version, which centers on excoriating others for thinking the world owes them a living, or owes them medical treatment when they are gravely ill, or maternity leave, or workplace safety, or equal protection under the law. But there is also a left-wing version, which consists of telling people to "check their privilege" when they feel they are entitled to pretty much anything that some poorer or more oppressed person does not have.

According to these standards, even if one is beaten over the head by a truncheon and dragged off to jail for no reason, one can only complain about the injustice if one first specifies all the categories of people to which this is more likely to occur. Rights-scolding may have seen its most baroque development in North America, but it has spread all over the world with the rise of neoliberal market ideologies. Under such conditions, it's understandable that demanding an entirely new, unfamiliar, right—such as the right to meaningful employment[12]—might seem a hopeless project. It's hard enough nowadays being taken seriously when asking for things you're already supposed to have.

The burden of rights-scolding falls above all on the younger generations. In most wealthy countries, the current crop of people in their twenties represents the first generation in more than a century that can, on the whole, expect opportunities and living standards substantially worse than those enjoyed by their parents. Yet at the same time, they are lectured relentlessly from both left and right on their sense of entitlement for feeling they might deserve anything else. This makes it especially difficult for younger people to complain about meaningless employment.

Let us end, then, with Rachel, to express the horror of a generation.

Rachel was a math whiz with an undergrad degree in physics, but from a poor family. She aspired to pursue a graduate degree, but with British university tuition fees having tripled, and financial assistance cut to the bone, she was forced to take a job as Catastrophe Risk Analyst for a big insurance company to raise the requisite funds. A year out of her life, she told herself, but hardly the end of the world:

Rachel: "It's not the worst thing in the world: learn some new skills, earn some money, and do a bit of networking while you're at it." Such was my thinking. "Realistically, how bad is it going to be?" And obviously, in the back of your head, the resounding, "Loads of people spend their whole lives doing boring, backbreaking work for barely any money. What on earth makes *you* too special for one year in a boring office job?"

That last one is an overarching fear for self-aware millennials. I can barely scroll through Facebook without hitting some preachy think piece about my generation's entitlement and reluctance to just do a bloody day's work, for Christ's sake! It is sort of hard to gauge whether my standards for an "acceptable" job are reasonable or just the result of ridiculous, Generation Snowflakey "entitled bollocks" (as my grandma likes to say).

This is, incidentally, a particularly British variation of rights-scolding (though it increasingly infects the rest of Europe): older people who grew up with cradle-to-grave welfare state protections mocking young people for thinking they might be entitled to the same thing. There was also another factor, much though Rachel was slightly embarrassed to admit it: the position paid extremely well; more than either of her parents was making. For someone who'd spent her entire adult existence as a penniless student supporting herself through temping, call center, and catering jobs, it would be refreshing to finally get a taste of bourgeois life.

> Rachel: I'd done the "office thing" and the "crap job thing," so how bad could a crap office job be, really? I had no concept of the bottom-of-the-ocean black depths of boredom I would sink to under a bulk of bureaucracy, terrible management, and myriad bullshit tasks.

Rachel's job was necessitated by various capital holding requirement regulations which, like all corporations in a similar situation, her employer had no intention of respecting. Thus, a typical day consisted of taking in emails each morning with data on how much money different branches of the firm would expect to lose in some hypothetical catastrophe scenario, "cleaning" the data, copying the data into a spreadsheet (whereupon the spreadsheet program invariably crashed and had to be rebooted), and coming up with a figure for overall losses. Then, if there was a potential legal problem, Rachel was expected to massage the numbers until the problem went away. That's when things were going well. On a bad day, or bad month, when there was nothing else to do, her supervisors would make up elaborate and obviously pointless exercises to keep her busy, such as constructing "mind maps"[13]. Or just leave her with nothing—but always with the proviso that while doing nothing, she had to actively pretend not to be:

Rachel: The weirdest and (apart from the title) maybe most bullshitty thing about my job was that while it was generally acknowledged that there wasn't really enough work to do, you weren't allowed to conspicuously not work. In a hark back to the days of the early internet, even Twitter and Facebook were banned.

My academic degree was pretty interesting and involved a lot of work, so, again, I had no concept of the horrible dread I would feel getting up in the morning to spend all day sitting in an office trying to inconspicuously waste time.

The final straw came after months of complaining, when I met my friend Mindy for a drink after a week of peak bullshit. I had just been asked to color coordinate a mind map to show "the nice-to-haves, must-haves, and would-like-to-have-in-futures." (No, I have no idea what that means, either.) Mindy was working on a similarly bullshit project, writing branded content for the pages of a company newspaper nobody reads.

She ranted at me, and I ranted at her. I made a long, impassioned speech that ended with me shouting, "I cannot wait for the sea levels to rise and the apocalypse to come because I would rather be out hunting fish and cannibals with a spear I'd fashioned out of a fucking pole than doing this fucking bollocks!" We both laughed for a long time, and then I started crying. I quit the next day. That is one massive benefit of having done all manner of weird menial jobs through university: you can almost always find work quickly.

So, yes, I am the queen crystal of Generation Snowflake, melting in the heat of a pleasantly air-conditioned office, but, good Lord, the working world is crap.

From thinking a "crap office job" was hardly the end of the world, Rachel was finally forced to the conclusion that the end of the world would, in fact, be preferable.[14]

on the misery of knowing that one is doing harm

There is one other, slightly different form of social suffering that ought to be acknowledged: the misery of having to pretend you're providing some kind of benefit to humanity, when you know the exact opposite is in fact the case. For obvious reasons, this is most common among social service providers who work for government or nongovernmental organizations (NGOs). Most are engaged in box-ticking rituals, at least to a certain degree, but many are aware that what they're doing is worse than useless: they are harming the people they are supposedly there to help. Shihi is now an artist, but she was once a community therapist in New York City:

> Shíhi: I used to work as a therapist in a community mental health center in the Bronx in the 1990s and 2000s. I have a social work degree.
>
> My clients ended up either being mandated to "treatment" after being incarcerated for minor stuff (Clinton's crime bill), lost their jobs and apartments after being jailed, or just needed to prove to welfare-to-work or Social Security offices that they need SSI [Supplemental Security Income] or other food/rent subsidies because they were mentally ill.
>
> Some were indeed severely mentally ill, but many others were just extremely poor people who were constantly being harassed by the police. Their living conditions would make anyone "mentally ill."
>
> My job was to do therapy to essentially tell them it was their own fault and their responsibility to make their lives better. And if they attended the program daily, so the company could bill their Medicaid, staff would copy their medical records to send to the Social Security office so they could be reviewed for disability payments. The more paperwork in their charts, the better their chances.
>
> I had groups to run like "anger management," "coping skills" . . . They were so insulting and irrelevant! How do you cope with lack of decent food or control your rage toward the police when they abuse you?

My job was useless and harmful. So many NGOs profit from the misery created by inequality. I made a very poor living doing what I did, but it still pains me deeply that I was a poverty pimp.

It is interesting and important to note that many of the petty officials who do absurd and terrible things in the name of paperwork are keenly aware of what they are doing and of the human damage that is likely to result—even if they usually feel they must remain stone-faced when dealing with the public. Some rationalize it. A few take sadistic pleasure. But any victim of the system who has ever asked herself, "How can such people live with themselves?" might take some comfort in the fact that, in many cases, they can't. Meena's job for a local government council in an English town sometimes referred to as "Little Skidrow-by-the-Sea" was represented to her, when she took it, as working with the homeless. She found this was true in a sense:

> Meena: My job was not to place, to advise, or help homeless people in any way. Instead, I had to try to collect their paperwork (proof of ID, National Insurance number, proof of income, etc.) so that the temporary homeless unit could claim back housing benefit. They had three days to provide it. If they couldn't or wouldn't provide the necessary paperwork, I had to ask their caseworkers to kick them out of their temporary accommodations. Obviously, homeless people with drug addictions tend to have difficulties providing two proofs of income, among many other things. But so do fifteen-year-olds whose parents have abandoned them, and veterans with PTSD, and women fleeing domestic violence.

So ultimately, Meena explains, her role was to threaten to make formerly homeless people homeless again, "all so that one department could claim a cash transfer from another." What was it like? "Soul destroying." After six months, she couldn't take it and gave up on government service entirely.

Meena quit. Beatrice, who worked for a different local authority, also couldn't take it after witnessing colleagues laughing over letters sent to pensioners that contained intentional errors designed to confuse the recipients so as to allow the council to falsely bill them for late payment. Only a handful of her coworkers, she said, took an active pleasure in defrauding the public they were hired to serve, but it cast a terrible pall upon an otherwise easygoing and friendly office environment. She tried to complain to higher-ups ("Surely this isn't right!"), but they looked at her as if she were crazy. So Beatrice took her first opportunity to find another job.

George, who worked for Atos, a French firm hired by the British government to knock as many citizens as possible from the disability rolls (in the years following, more than two thousand were discovered to have died not long after having been found "fit to work"),[15] soldiers on. He reports that everyone who works for the company does understand what's going on and "hates Atos with a quiet desperation." In other cases, government workers are convinced that they are the only ones in their office who've figured out how useless or destructive the work they're doing is—though when asked if they have ever presented their views to colleagues directly, most invariably say they haven't, leaving open the possibility that their coworkers are equally convinced they are the only ones who know what's really going on.[16]

In all this, we are moving into somewhat different territory. Much of what happens in such offices is simply pointless, but there is an added dimension of guilt and terror when it comes to knowing you are involved in actively hurting others. Guilt, for obvious reasons. Terror, because in such environments, dark rumors will always tend to circulate about what is likely to happen to whistle-blowers. But on a day-to-day basis, all this simply deepens the texture and quality of the misery attendant on such jobs.

coda: on the effects of bullshit jobs on human creativity, and on why attempts to assert oneself creatively or politically against pointless employment might be considered a form of spiritual warfare

Let me conclude by returning to the theme of spiritual violence.

It's hard to imagine anything more soul destroying than, as Meena put it, being forced to commit acts of arbitrary bureaucratic cruelty against one's will. To become the face of the machine that one despises. To become a monster. It has not escaped my notice, for example, that the most frightening monsters in popular fiction do not simply threaten to rend or torture or kill you but to turn you into a monster yourself: think here of vampires, zombies, werewolves. They terrify because they menace not just your body but also your soul. This is presumably why adolescents in particular are drawn to them: adolescence is precisely when most of us are first confronted with the challenge of how not to become the monsters we despise.

Useless or insidious jobs that involve pretenses to public service are perhaps the worst, but almost all of the jobs mentioned in this chapter can be considered soul destroying in different ways. Bullshit jobs regularly induce feelings of hopelessness, depression, and self-loathing. They are forms of spiritual violence directed at the essence of what it means to be a human being.

If what I have argued in the last chapter—that the integrity of the human psyche, even human physical integrity (insofar as these two can ever be entirely distinguished), is caught up in relations with others, and the sense of one's capacity to affect the world—then such jobs could hardly be anything other than spiritual violence.

This is not to say, however, that the soul has no means for resistance. It might be well to conclude this chapter by taking note of the resulting spiritual warfare, and document some of the ways workers keep themselves sane by involving themselves in other projects. Call it, if you like, guerrilla purpose. Robin, the temp who fixed his screen to look like he was programming when, in fact, he was surfing the Web, used that time to perform free editorial work for a number of Wikipedia pages he monitored (including, apparently, mine), and to help maintain an alternative-currency initiative. Others start businesses, write film scripts and novels, or secretly run sexy maid services.

Yet others escape into Walter Mitty–style reverie, a traditional coping mechanism for those condemned to spend their lives in sterile office environments. It's probably no coincidence that nowadays many of these involve fantasies not of being a World War I flying ace, marrying a prince, or becoming a teenage heartthrob, but of having a better—just utterly, ridiculously better—job. Boris, for instance, works for "a major international institution" writing bullshit reports. Here is his (obviously somewhat self-mocking) report:

> Boris: It is clearly a bullshit job because I have tried everything, self-help books, sneaky onanistic breaks, calling my mother and crying, realizing all my life choices have been pure shite—but I keep carrying on because I have a rent to pay.
>
> What's more, this situation, which causes me a mild to severe depression, also obliges me to postpone my true life's calling: being J.Lo's or Beyoncé's Personal Assistant (either separately or concomitantly). I am a hardworking, results-driven person so I believe I could handle it well. I would be willing to work for one of the Kardashians, too, particularly Kim.

Still, most testimonies focus on creativity as a form of defiance—the dogged fortitude with which many attempt to pursue art, or music, or writing, or poetry, serves as an antidote to the pointlessness of their "real" paid work. Obviously, sample bias may be a factor here. The testimonies sent to me were largely drawn from my followers on Twitter, a population likely to be both more artsy and more politically engaged than the public at large. So I will not speculate on how common this is. But certain interesting patterns emerge.

For instance, workers hired for a certain skill, but who are then not really allowed to exercise it, rarely end up exercising that skill in a covert way when they discover they have free time on their hands. They almost invariably end up doing something else. We've already observed in chapter 3 how Ramadan, the engineer who dreamed of working at the cutting edge of science and technology, simply gave up when he discovered he was really expected to sit around doing paperwork all day. Rather than pursuing scientific projects on the sly, he threw himself into film, novels, and the history of Egyptian social movements. This is typical. Faye, who has been contemplating writing a pamphlet on "how to keep your soul intact in corporate environments," falls back on music:

> Faye: The frustrated musician in me has come up with ways of silently learning music while stuck at my corporate desk. I studied Indian classical music for a while and have internalized two of their rhythmic systems. Indian approaches are abstract, numerical, and nonwritten, and so open up ways for me to silently and invisibly practice in my head.
>
> This means I can improvise music while stuck in the office, and even incorporate inputs from the world around me. You can groove off the ticking clock as dull meetings drag on or turn a phone number into a rhythmic poem. You can translate the syllables of corporate jargon into quasi hip-hop, or interpret the proportions of the filing cabinet as a polyrhythm. Doing this has been a shield to more aggregate boredom in the workplace than I can possibly explain. I even gave a talk to friends a few months ago about using rhythm games to alleviate workplace boredom, demonstrating how you can turn aspects of a dull meeting into a funk composition.

Lewis, who describes himself as a "fake investment banker" for a financial consulting firm in Boston, is working on a play. When he realized his role in the company was basically pointless, he began to lose motivation and with it the ability to concentrate on the one or two hours per day he actually did need to work. His supervisor, a stickler for time and "optics" who seemed remarkably indifferent to productivity, didn't seem to mind what Lewis did so long as he didn't leave the office before she did, but what he describes as his Midwestern American guilt complex drove him to come up with a means to carry on:

> Lewis: Happily, I have an automatic standing desk and lots of mildly guilt-ridden BS-free time. So, over the last three months, I've used that time to write my first play. Strangely, the creative output began out of necessity rather than desire. I found that I'm way more productive and efficient once I've chewed on a scene or dialogue. In order to do the

seventy minutes or so of actual work I need to get done in a given day, I'll need another three to four hours of creative writing.

Faye and Lewis are unusual. The most common complaint among those trapped in offices doing nothing all day is just how difficult it is to re-purpose the time for anything worthwhile. One might imagine that leav-ing millions of well-educated young men and women without any real work responsibilities but with access to the internet—which is, poten-tially, at least, a repository of almost all human knowledge and cultural achievement—might spark some sort of Renaissance. Nothing remotely along these lines has taken place. Instead, the situation has sparked an efflorescence of social media (Facebook, YouTube, Instagram, Twitter): basically, of forms of electronic media that lend themselves to being pro-duced and consumed while pretending to do something else. I am con-vinced this is the primary reason for the rise of social media, especially when one considers it in the light not just of the rise of bullshit jobs but also of the increasing bullshitization of real jobs. As we've seen, the spe-cific conditions vary considerably from one bullshit job to another. Some workers are supervised relentlessly; others are expected to do some token task but are otherwise left more or less alone. Most are somewhere in be-tween. Yet even in the best of cases, the need to be on call, to spend at least a certain amount of energy looking over one's shoulder, maintaining a false front, never looking too obviously engrossed, the inability to fully collaborate with others—all this lends itself much more to a culture of computer games, YouTube rants, memes, and Twitter controversies than to, say, the rock 'n' roll bands, drug poetry, and experimental theater cre-ated under the midcentury welfare state. What we are witnessing is the rise of those forms of popular culture that office workers can produce and consume during the scattered, furtive shards of time they have at their disposal in workplaces where even when there's nothing for them to do, they still can't admit it openly.

Some testimonies similarly bemoaned the fact that traditional forms of artistic expression simply cannot be pursued under bullshit conditions. Padraigh, an Irish art school graduate shepherded into a pointless job at a foreign tech multinational owing to the complexities of the Irish welfare and tax system—which, he says, makes it almost impossible to be self-employed unless you're already rich—has been forced to abandon his life's calling:

> Padraigh: But what kills me most is the fact that outside of work, I have been unable to paint, to follow my creative impulses to draw or scrape out ideas on canvas. I was quite focused on it whilst I was unemployed. But that didn't pay. So now I have the money and not the time, energy, or headspace to be creative.[17]

He still manages to keep up a political life as an anarchist determined to destroy the economic system that does not allow him to pursue his life's true calling. Meanwhile, a New York legal aide, James, is reduced to acts of subtle protest: "Spending all day in a sterile office environment, I'm too mentally numb to do anything but consume meaningless media," he says. "And on occasion, yeah, I do feel quite depressed about it all: the isolation, the futility, the tiredness. My one small act of rebellion is wearing a black-and-red-star pin into work every day—they have no fucking idea!"

Finally, a British psychologist who, owing to Prime Minister Tony Blair's higher education reforms of the 1990s, was laid off as a teacher and rehired as a "Project Assessor" to determine the effects of laying off teachers:

> Harry: What surprises me is that it's astonishingly difficult to re-purpose time for which one is being paid. I'd have felt guilty if I'd dodged the BS work and, say, used the time to have a go at writing a novel. I felt obliged to do my best to carry out the activities I was contracted to carry out—even if I knew those activities were entirely futile.

> David: You know, that's one theme that keeps cropping up in the testimonies I've been reading: jobs that should be wonderful, since they pay you lots of money to do little or nothing and often don't even insist you pretend to work, somehow drive people

crazy anyway because they can't figure out a way to channel the time and energy into anything else.

Harry: Well here's one thing that bears out your assertion. These days, I work as Training Manager in a bus depot. Not all that glamorous, of course, but much more purposeful work. And I actually do more freelance work for pleasure now (short stories, articles) than I did in that completely unchallenging BS job.

David: Maybe we're onto something here!

Harry: Yes, it's really interesting.

So utilizing a bullshit job to pursue other projects isn't easy. It requires ingenuity and determination to take time that's been first flattened and homogenized—as all work time tends to be in what James calls "sterile office environment[s]"—then broken randomly into often unpredictably large fragments, and use that time for projects requiring thought and creativity. Those who manage to do so have already sunk a great deal of their—presumably finite—creative energies just into putting themselves in a position where they can use their time for anything more ambitious than cat memes. Not that there's anything wrong with cat memes. I've seen some very good ones. But one would like to think our youth are meant for greater things.

About the only accounts I received from workers who felt they had largely overcome the mental destruction caused by bullshit jobs were from those that had found a way to keep those jobs down to one or two days a week. Needless to say, this is logistically extremely difficult, and usually impossible, for either financial or career reasons. Hannibal might serve as a success story in this regard. The reader may recall him as the man who writes bullshit reports for marketing agencies for as much as £12,000 a go and tries to limit this work if possible to one day a week. During the rest of the week, he pursues projects that he considers utterly worthwhile but knows that he couldn't possibly self-finance:

Hannibal: One of the projects I'm working on is to create an image-processing algorithm to read low-cost diagnostic strips for TB patients in the developing world. Tuberculosis is one of the world's biggest killers, causing one and a half million deaths a year with up to eight million infected at any one time. Diagnosis is still a significant problem, so if you can improve the treatment of just one percent of those eight million infected patients, then you can count lives improved in the tens of thousands per year. We're already making a difference. This work is rewarding for all those involved. It's technically challenging, involves problem solving and working collaboratively to achieve a greater goal that we all believe in. It is the antithesis of a bullshit job. However, it is proving virtually impossible to raise more than a very small amount of money to do this.

Even after spending much time and energy trying to convince various health executives there might be potentially lucrative spin-offs of one sort or another, he only raised enough to pay the expenses of the project itself, certainly not enough to provide any sort of compensation for those working on it, including himself. So Hannibal ends up writing meaningless word spaghetti for marketing forums in order to fund a project that will actually save lives.

Hannibal: If I get the opportunity, I ask people who work in PR or for global pharmaceutical companies what they think of this state of affairs, and their reactions are interesting. If I ask people more junior than me, they tend to think I am setting them some kind of test or trying to catch them out. Perhaps I'm just trying to get them to admit that what they do is worthless so I can persuade their boss to make them redundant? If I ask people more senior than me what they think about this, they will usually start by saying something along the lines of "Welcome to the real world," like I'm some teenage dropout yet to "get it," and accept that I can't stay at home playing video games and smoking weed all day. I must admit that I spent quite a lot of time doing that as a teenager, but I'm no longer a teenager. In fact, I'm usually charging them a huge amount of money to write bullshit reports, so I often then detect that there's a moment of reflection as they internally question who it is that really doesn't "get it."

Hannibal is at the top of his game: an accomplished researcher who can walk with confidence in the corridors of corporate power. He's aware, too, that in the professional world, playing the part is everything: form is always valued over content, and from all indications, he can perform the role with consummate skill.[18] Thus, he can see his bullshit activities as basically a kind of scam; something he's putting over on the corporate world. He can even see himself as a kind of modern-day Robin Hood in a world where, as he put it, merely "doing something worthwhile is subversive."

Hannibal's is a best-case scenario. Others turn to political activism. This can be extremely beneficial to a worker's emotional and physical health,[19] and is usually easier to integrate with the fragmented nature of office time—this is true of digital activism, at least—than more conventional creative pursuits. Still, the psychological and emotional labor required to balance meaningful interests and bullshit work is often daunting. I've already mentioned Nouri's work-related health problems, which began to improve markedly when he began working to unionize his workplace. It required definite mental discipline, yes, but not nearly so great as the mental discipline required to operate effectively in a high-pressure corporate environment where one knew one's work had no effect at all:

Nouri: I used to have to go literally "insane" to get into work. Scrub away "me" and become the thing that can do this work. Afterward, I'd often need a day to recover; to remember who I am. (If I didn't, I'd become an acerbic, nitpicky person to people in my private life, enraged over tiny things.)

So I'd have to find all sorts of mental technologies to make my work bearable. The most effective motivations were deadlines and rage. (For example, pretending I was slighted, so I'd "show them" with my excellent productivity.) But as a result, it was hard to organize the different parts of me, the ancient things which cohere into "me"; they quickly went off-kilter.

In contrast, I could stay up late for hours working on workplace organizer stuff, like teaching coworkers how to negotiate, programming, project management . . . I was most fully myself then. My imagination and logic worked in concert. Until I saw dreams and had to sleep.

Nouri, too, experienced working on something meaningful as entirely different. True, unlike Hannibal, he wasn't working with a collaborative team. But even working toward a larger meaningful purpose, he felt, allowed him to reintegrate a shattered self. And eventually he did begin to find the seeds of a community, at least in the minimal form of a fellow isolated workplace organizer:

Nouri: I began to introduce myself to people by saying that programming is my day job, and workplace organizer is my real job. My workplace subsidizes my activism.

Recently I found someone very much like me online; we've become deep, deep friends, and as of last week, I find it so much easier to get into "the zone" for work. I think it's because someone understands me. For all my other "close" friends, I'm an active listener, a sounding board—because they simply don't understand the things I care about. Their eyes glaze over when I even mention my activism.

But even now, I still must empty my mind for work. I listen to Sigur Rós—"Varðeldur," which my new friend sent me. Then I go into a sort of meditative trance. When the song's done, my mind's empty, and I can run fairly nimbly through work.

It's always a good idea to end a bleak chapter on a note of redemption, and these stories demonstrate that it is possible to find purpose and meaning despite even the worst of bullshit jobs. It also makes clear that this takes a great deal of doing. The "art of skiving," as it's sometimes called in England, may be highly developed and even honored in certain working-class traditions, but proper shirking does seem to require something real to shirk.

In a truly bullshit job, it's often entirely unclear what one is really supposed to be doing, what one can say about what one is and isn't doing, who one can ask and what one can ask them, how much and within what parameters one is expected to pretend to be working, and what sorts of things it is or is not permissible to do instead. This is a miserable situation. The effects on health and self-esteem are often devastating. Creativity and imagination crumble.

Sadomasochistic power dynamics frequently emerge. (In fact, I would argue they will almost invariably emerge within top-down situations devoid of purpose unless explicit efforts are made to ensure that they do not—and sometimes even despite such efforts.) It is not for nothing that I've referred to the results as spiritual violence. This violence has affected our culture. Our sensibilities. Above all, it has affected our youth. Young people in Europe and North America in particular, but increasingly throughout the world, are being psychologically prepared for useless jobs, trained in how to pretend to work, and then by various means shepherded into jobs that almost nobody really believes serve any meaningful purpose.[20]

How this has come to happen, and how the current situation has become normalized or even encouraged, is a topic we will explore in chapter 5. It needs to be addressed, because this is a genuine scar across our collective soul.

Chapter 5

Why Are Bullshit Jobs Proliferating?

In the Scilly Islands . . . the natives of that group are popularly said to have eked out a precarious livelihood by taking in each other's washing.

—obscure nineteenth-century joke

A bourgeois paradise will supervene, in which everyone will be free to exploit—but there will be no one to exploit. On the whole, one must suppose that the type of it would be that town that I have heard of, whose inhabitants lived by taking in each other's washing.

—William Morris, 1887

If the preceding chapters merely described forms of pointless employ-ment that have always been with us in one way or another—or even that have always been with us since the dawn of capitalism—then matters would be distressing enough. But the situation is more dire still. There is every reason to believe that the overall number of bullshit jobs, and, even more, the overall percentage of jobs considered bullshit by those who hold them, has been increasing rapidly in recent years—alongside the ever-increasing bullshitization of useful forms of employment. In other words, this is not just a book about a hitherto neglected aspect of the world of work. It's a book about a real social problem. Economies around the world have, increasingly, become vast engines for producing nonsense.

How did this happen? And why has it received so little public attention? One reason it has been so little acknowledged, I think, is that under our current economic system, this is precisely what is not supposed to happen: in the same way as the fact that so many people feel so unhappy being paid to do nothing defies our common assumptions about human nature, the fact that so many people are being paid to do nothing in the first place defies all our assumptions about how market economies are supposed to work. For much of the twentieth century, state Socialist regimes dedicated to full employment created bogus jobs

Figure 2   Distribution of the labor force by sector, 1840–2010

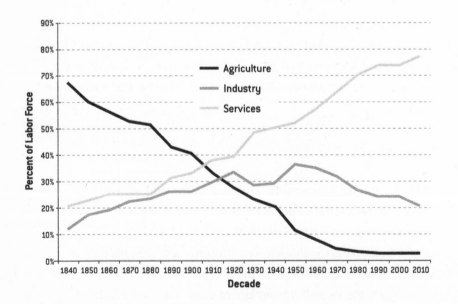

as a matter of public policy, and their social democratic rivals in Europe and elsewhere at least colluded in featherbedding and overstaffing in the public sector or with government contractors, when they weren't establishing self-conscious make-work programs like the Works Progress Administration (WPA), as the United States did at the height of the Great Depression. All of this was supposed to have ended with the collapse of the Soviet bloc and worldwide market reforms in the nineties. If the joke under the Soviet Union was "We pretend to work; they pretend to pay us," the new neoliberal age was supposed to be all about efficiency. But if patterns of employment are anything to go by, this seems to be exactly the opposite of what actually happened after the Berlin Wall came down in 1989.

So part of the reason no one has noticed is that people simply refused to believe that capitalism *could* produce such results—even if that meant writing off their own experiences or those of their friends and family as somehow anomalous.

Another reason the phenomenon has been able to sail past people's heads is that we have developed a way of talking about changes in the nature of employment that seems to explain a lot of what we see and hear happening around us in this regard, but is, in fact, profoundly deceptive. I'm referring to the rise of what's called the "service economy." Since the 1980s, all conversations on changes in the structure of employment have had to begin with an acknowledgment that the overall global trend, especially in rich countries, has been for a steady decline in farming and manufacturing, and a steady increase in something called "services." Here, for instance, is a typical long-term analysis of the US labor force by sector (see figure 2, page 146).[1]

Often it's assumed that the decline of manufacturing—which, incidentally, hasn't declined *that* much in terms of employment in the United States, by 2010 only returning to about what it was at the outbreak of the Civil War—simply meant that factories were relocated to poorer countries. This is obviously true to an extent, but it's interesting to observe that the same overall trends in the composition of employment can be observed even in the countries to which the factory jobs were exported. Here, for instance, is India (see figure 3, below).

The number of industrial jobs has remained constant or increased slightly, but otherwise the picture is not so very different.

The real problem here is with the concept of a "service economy" itself. There is a reason I just put the term in quotation marks. Describing a country's economy as dominated by the service sector leaves one with the impression that people in that country are supporting themselves principally by serving each other iced lattes or pressing one another's shorts. Obviously, this isn't really true. So what else might they be doing? When economists speak of a fourth, or quaternary, sector (coming after farming, manufacturing, and service provision), they usually define it as the FIRE sector (finance, insurance, real estate). But back in 1992, Robert Taylor, a library scientist, suggested it would be more useful to define it as information work. The results were telling (see figure 4).

As we can see, even in 1990, the proportion of the workforce made up of actual waiters, barbers, salesclerks, and the like was really quite small. It also remained remarkably steady over time, holding for more

Figure 3 Sector contribution to GDP (%), India

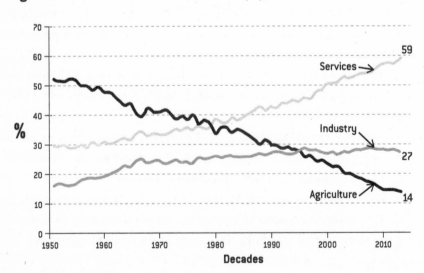

Figure 4   Information as a Component of the Economy

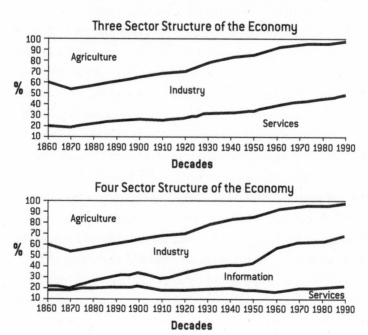

Three Sector Structure of the Economy

Four Sector Structure of the Economy

than a century at roughly 20 percent. The vast majority of those others included in the service sector were really administrators, consultants, clerical and accounting staff, IT professionals, and the like. This was also the part of the service sector that was actually increasing—and increasing quite dramatically from the 1950s onward. And while no one, to my knowledge, has pursued this particular breakdown through to the present, the percentage of information jobs was already rapidly on the increase even in the latter half of the twentieth century. It seems reasonable to conclude this trend continued, and that the bulk of the new service jobs added to the economy were really of this same sort.

This, of course, is precisely the zone where bullshit jobs proliferate. Obviously, not all information workers feel they are engaged in bullshit (Taylor's category includes scientists, teachers, and librarians), and by no means all those who felt they are engaged in bullshit are information workers; but if our surveys are to be trusted, it seems evident that a majority of those classed as information workers do feel that if their jobs were to vanish, it would make very little difference to the world.

I think this is important to emphasize because despite the lack of statistics, there has been a great deal of discussion since the 1990s about the rise of information-oriented jobs and their larger effect on society. Some, like former US Labor Secretary Robert Reich, spoke of the rise of a new tech-savvy middle class of "symbolic analysts" who threatened to gain all the benefits of growth and leave the old-fashioned laboring classes languishing in poverty; others spoke of "knowledge workers" and "information society"; some Marxists even became convinced that new forms of what they called "immaterial labor"—founded in marketing, entertainment, and the digital economy but spilling outside as well into our increasingly brand-saturated, iPhone-happy daily lives—had become the new locus of value creation— leading to prophecies of the eventual rebellion of the digital proletariat.[2] Almost everyone assumed that the rise of such jobs had something to do with the rise of finance capital—even if there was no consensus as to how. It just seemed to make sense that, just as Wall Street profits were derived less and less from firms involved in commerce or manufacturing, and more and more from debt, speculation, and the creation of complex financial instruments, so did an ever-increasing proportion of workers come to make their living from manipulating similar abstractions.

These days, it's hard to recall the almost mystical aura with which the financial sector had surrounded itself in the years leading up to 2008. Financiers had managed to convince the public—and not just the public, but social theorists, too (I well remember this)—that with instruments such as collateralized debt obligations and high-speed trading algorithms so complex they could be understood only by astrophysicists, they had, like modern alchemists, learned ways to whisk value out of nothing by means that others dared not even try to understand. Then, of course, came the crash, and it turned out that most of the instruments were scams. Many weren't even particularly sophisticated scams.

In a way, one could argue that the whole financial sector is a scam of sorts, since it represents itself as largely about directing investments toward profitable opportunities in commerce and industry, when, in fact, it does very little of that. The overwhelming bulk of its profits comes from colluding with government to create, and then to trade and manipulate, various forms of debt. All I am really arguing in this book is that just as much of what the financial sector does is basically smoke and mirrors, so are most of the information-sector jobs that accompanied its rise as well.

But here we return to the question already raised in the last chapter: If these are scams, who, exactly, is scamming whom?

a brief excursus on causality and the nature of sociological explanation

In this chapter, then, I want to address the rise of bullshit jobs and to suggest some reasons this may be happening.

Of course, in earlier chapters, particularly chapter 2, we looked at some of the more immediate causes for the creation of useless employment: managers whose prestige is caught up in the total number of their administrative assistants or underlings; weird corporate bureaucratic dynamics; bad management; poor information flow. These are important in understanding the overall phenomenon, but they don't really explain it. We still have to ask, Why were such bad organizational dynamics more likely to occur in 2015 than they were in, say, 1915, or 1955? Has there been a change in organization culture, or is it something deeper: a change, perhaps, in our very conceptions of work?

We are faced here with a classic problem in social theory: the problem of levels of causality. In the case of any given real-world event, there are any number of different reasons why one can say it happened. These, in turn, can be sorted into different kinds of reason. If I fall into an open manhole, one might attribute this to absentmindedness. But if we discover there has been a sudden statistical increase in the number of people falling into manholes in a given city, one must seek a different sort of explanation—either one must understand why overall rates of absentmindedness are going up there, or, more likely, why more manholes are being left open. This is an intentionally whimsical example. Let's consider a more serious one.

At the end of the last chapter, Meena noted that while many people who end up homeless have a history of addiction to alcohol or other drugs, or other personal foibles, many others are teenagers abandoned by their parents, veterans with PTSD, and women fleeing domestic violence. No doubt if you were to pick a random person sleeping on the streets or in a shelter and examine his or her life history, you would find a confluence of several such factors, usually combined with a great deal of just plain bad luck.

No one individual, then, could be said to be sleeping on the streets simply because he or she was morally reprobate; but even if everyone sleeping on the streets really was morally reprobate in some way, it would be unlikely to do much to explain the rise and fall of levels of homelessness in different decades, or why rates of homelessness vary from country to country at any given time. This is a crucial point. After all, consider the matter in reverse. There have been moralists throughout the ages who have argued that the poor are poor because of their moral turpitude: after all, we are often reminded, it's easy to find examples of people born poor who became wealthy owing to sheer grit, determination, and entrepreneurial spirit. Clearly, then, the poor remain poor because they didn't make an effort they *could* have made. This sounds convincing if you look just at individuals; it becomes much less so when one examines comparative statistics and realizes that rates of upward class mobility fluctuate dramatically over time. Did poor Americans just have less get-up-and-go during the 1930s than during previous decades? Or might it have had something to do with the Great Depression? It becomes harder still to hold to a purely moral approach when one also considers the fact that rates of mobility also vary sharply from country to country. A child born to parents of modest means in Sweden is much more likely to become wealthy than a similar child is in the United States. Must one conclude that Swedes overall have more grit and entrepreneurial spirit than Americans?

I doubt most contemporary conservative moralists would wish to argue this.

One must, then, seek a different sort of explanation: access to education, for example, or the fact that the poorest Swedish children aren't nearly as poor as the poorest American ones.[3] This doesn't mean that personal qualities do not help explain why *some* poor Swedish children succeed and others do not. But these are different kinds of questions and different levels of analysis. The question of why one player won a game rather than another is different from the question of how hard the game is to play.

■ ■ ■

Or why people are playing the game to begin with. That's a third question. Similarly, in cases like these, where one is looking at a broad pattern of social change, such as the rise of bullshit jobs, I would propose we really need to look not at two but at three different levels of explanation: (1) the particular reasons any given individual ends up homeless; (2) the larger social and economic forces that lead to increased levels of homelessness (say, a rise in rents, or changes in the family structure); and, finally (3), the reasons why no one intervened. We might refer to this last as the political and cultural level. It's also the easiest to overlook, since it often deals specifically with things people are *not* doing. I well remember the first time I discussed the phenomenon of homelessness in America with friends in Madagascar. They were flabbergasted to discover that in the wealthiest and most powerful country in the world, there were people sleeping on the streets. "But aren't Americans ashamed?" one friend asked me. "They're so rich! Doesn't it bother them to know everyone else in the world will see it as a national embarrassment?"

I had to concede it was a good question. Why *didn't* Americans see people sleeping on the streets as a national embarrassment? In certain periods of US history, they certainly would have. If large numbers of people were living on the streets in major cities in the 1820s, or even the 1940s, there would have been an outcry and some kind of action would have been taken. It might not have been very nice action. At some points, it would probably have meant rounding up vagrants and placing them in workhouses; at other times, it might have involved building public housing; but whatever it might have been, they would not have been left to languish in cardboard boxes on public thoroughfares. Since the 1980s, the same American was more likely to react not with outrage at how social conditions could have come to this pass, but by appeal to explanations of the first level—and conclude that homelessness was nothing more than the inevitable result of human weakness. Humans are fickle beings. They always have been. There's nothing anyone can do to change this fact.[4]

This is why I emphasize that the third level is simultaneously political and cultural—it bears on basic assumptions about what people are, what can be expected of them, and what they can justifiably demand of one another. Those assumptions, in turn, have an enormous influence in determining what is considered to be a political issue and what is not. I don't want to suggest that popular attitudes are the only factor here. Political authorities often ignore the popular will. Polls regularly find roughly two-thirds of Americans favor a national health care system but no major political party there has ever supported this. Polls also show most Britons favor reinstating the death penalty, but no major political party has taken this up either.[5] Still, the larger cultural climate is clearly a factor.

■ ■ ■

In the case of bullshit jobs, this means we can ask three questions:

1. On the individual level, why do people agree to do and put up with their own bullshit jobs?
2. On social and economic levels, what are the larger forces that have led to the proliferation of bullshit jobs?
3. On the cultural and political levels, why is the bullshitization of the economy not seen as a social problem, and why has no one done anything about it?[6]

Much of the confusion that surrounds debate about social issues in general can be traced back to the fact that people will regularly take these different explanations as alternatives rather than seeing them as factors that all operate at the same time. For example, people sometimes tell me that any attempt to explain bullshit jobs in political terms is wrongheaded; such jobs, they insist, exist because people need the money—as if this consideration had somehow never occurred to me before. Looking at the subjective motives of those who take such jobs is then treated as an alternative to asking why so many people find themselves in a position where the only way they can get money is by taking such jobs to begin with.

It's even worse on the cultural-political level. There has come to be a tacit understanding in polite circles that you can ascribe motives to people only when speaking about the individual level. Therefore, any suggestion that powerful people ever do anything they don't say they're doing, or even do what they can be publicly observed to be doing for reasons other than what they say, is immediately denounced as a "paranoid conspiracy theory" to be rejected instantly. Thus, to suggest that some "law and order" politicians or social service providers might not feel it's in their best interest to do much about the underlying causes of homelessness, is treated as equivalent to saying homelessness itself exists only because of the machinations of a secret cabal. Or that the banking system is run by lizards.

sundry notes on the role of government in creating and maintaining bullshit jobs

This is relevant because when, in the original 2013 essay about bullshit jobs, I suggested that while our current work regime was never designed consciously, one reason it might have been allowed to remain in place was because the effects are actually quite convenient politically to those in power; this was widely denounced as crazy talk. So another thing this chapter can do is clarify a few things in that regard.

Social engineering does happen. The regime of make-work jobs that existed in the Soviet Union or Communist China, for example, was created from above by a self-conscious government policy of full employment. To say this is in no sense controversial. Pretty much everyone accepts that it is the case. Still, it's hardly as if anyone sitting in the Kremlin or the Great Hall of the People actually sent out a directive saying "I hereby order all officials to invent unnecessary jobs until unemployment is eliminated."

The reason no such orders were sent out was because they didn't have to be. The policy spoke for itself. As long as you don't say "Aim for full employment, but do not create jobs unless they conform to the following standards"—and make it clear you will be very punctilious about ensuring those standards are met—then one can be sure of the results. Local officials will do what they have to do.

While no central directives of this kind were ever sent out under capitalist regimes, at least to my knowledge, it is nonetheless true that at least since World War II, all economic policy has been premised on an ideal of full employment. Now, there is every reason to believe that most policy makers don't actually want to fully achieve this ideal, as genuine full employment would put too much "upward pressure on wages." Marx appears to have been right when he argued that a "reserve army of the unemployed" has to exist in order for capitalism to work the way it's supposed to.[7] But it remains true that "More Jobs" is the one political slogan that both Left and Right can always agree on.[8] They differ only about the most expedient means to produce the jobs. Banners held aloft at a union march calling for jobs never also specify that those jobs should serve some useful purpose. It's just assumed that they will—which, of course, means that often they won't. Similarly, when right-wing politicians call for tax cuts to put more money in the hands of "job creators," they never specify whether those jobs will be good for anything; it's simply assumed that if the market produced them, they will be. In this climate, one might say that political pressure is being placed on those managing the economy similar to the directives once coming out of the Kremlin; it's just that the source is more diffuse, and much of it falls on the private sector.

Finally, as I've emphasized, there is the level of conscious public policy. A Soviet official issuing a planning document, or an American politician calling for job creation, might not be entirely aware of the likely effects of their action. Still, once a situation is created, even as an unintended side effect, politicians can be expected to size up the larger political implications of that situation when they make up their minds what—if any-thing—to do about it.

Does this mean that members of the political class might actually col-lude in the maintenance of useless employment? If that seems a daring claim, even conspiracy talk, consider the following quote, from an inter-view with then US president Barack Obama about some of the reasons why he bucked the preferences of the electorate and insisted on maintain-ing a private, for-profit health insurance system in America:

> "I don't think in ideological terms. I never have," Obama said, continu-ing on the health care theme. "Everybody who supports single-payer health care says, 'Look at all this money we would be saving from insurance and paperwork.' That represents one million, two million, three million jobs [filled by] people who are working at Blue Cross Blue Shield or Kaiser or other places. What are we doing with them? Where are we employing them?"[9]

I would encourage the reader to reflect on this passage because it might be considered a smoking gun. What is the president saying here? He acknowledges that millions of jobs in medical insurance companies like Kaiser or Blue Cross are unnecessary. He even acknowledges that a social-ized health system would be more efficient than the current market-based system, since it would reduce unnecessary paperwork and reduplication of effort by dozens of competing private firms. But he's also saying it would be undesirable for that very reason. One motive, he insists, for maintain-ing the existing market-based system is precisely its inefficiency, since it is better to maintain those millions of basically useless office jobs than to cast about trying to find something else for the paper pushers to do.[10]

So here is the most powerful man in the world at the time publicly reflecting on his signature legislative achievement—and he is insisting that a major factor in the form that legislature took is the preservation of bullshit jobs.[11]

That a political culture where "job creation" is everything might pro-duce such results should not be shocking (though for some reason, it is, in fact, treated as shocking); but it does not in itself explain the economic and social dynamics by which those jobs first come into being. In the remainder of this chapter, we will consider these dynamics and then return briefly to the role of government.

concerning some false explanations for the rise of bullshit jobs

Before mapping out what actually happened, it will first be necessary to dispose of certain very common, if ill-conceived, explanations for the rise of apparently pointless employment frequently proposed by market enthusiasts. Since libertarians, "anarcho-capitalists," enthusiasts for Ayn Rand or Friedrich Hayek and the like are extremely common in pop economic forums, and since such market enthusiasts are committed to the assumption that a market economy could not, by definition, create jobs that serve no purpose,[12] one tends to hear these arguments quite a lot. So we might as well address them.[13]

Basically such arguments fall into two broad types. Proponents of each are happy to admit that at least some of those who believe they hold pointless jobs in the public sector are correct. However, the first group argues that those who harbor similar suspicions in the private sector are not correct. Since competing firms would never pay workers to do nothing, their jobs must be useful in some way that they simply do not understand.

The second group admits useless paper-pushing jobs do exist in the private sector, and even that they have proliferated. However, this group insists that private sector bullshit jobs must necessarily be a product of government interference.

A perfect example of the first kind of argument can be found in a piece in the *Economist*, published about a day and a half after the appearance of my original "bullshit jobs" essay in 2013.[14] It had all the trappings of a rush job,[15] but the very fact that this bastion of free market orthodoxy felt the need to respond almost instantly shows that the editors knew how to identify an ideological threat. They summed up their argument as follows:

Over the past century, the world economy has grown increasingly complex. The goods being provided are more complex; the supply chains used to build them are more complex; the systems to market, sell, and distribute them are more complex; the means to finance it all is more complex; and so on. This complexity is what makes us rich. But it is an enormous pain to manage. I'd say that one way to manage it all would be through teams of generalists—craftsman managers who mind the system from the design stage right through to the customer service calls—but there is no way such complexity would be economically workable in that world (just as cheap, ubiquitous automobiles would have been impossible in a world where teams of generalist mechanics produced cars one at a time).

No, the efficient way to do things is to break businesses up into many different kinds of tasks, allowing for a very high level of specialization. And so you end up with the clerical equivalent of repeatedly affixing Tab A to Frame B: shuffling papers, management of the minutiae of supply chains, and so on. Disaggregation may make it look meaningless, since many workers end up doing things incredibly far removed from the end points of the process; the days when the iron ore goes in one door and the car rolls out the other are over. But the idea is the same.

In other words, the author claims that when we speak of "bullshit jobs,"[16] we're really just talking about the postindustrial equivalent of factory-line workers, those with the unenviable fate of having to carry out the repetitive, mind-numbingly boring but still very necessary tasks required to manage increasingly complicated processes of production. As robots replace the factory workers, these are increasingly the only jobs left. (This position is sometimes combined with a rather condescending argument about self-importance: if so many people feel their jobs are useless, it's really because today's educated workforce is full of philosophy or Renaissance literature majors who believe they are cut out for better things. They consider being a mere cog in administrative machinery beneath their dignity.)

I don't think I really need to dwell too much on the second argument, since the reader is likely to have encountered variations of it a thousand times before. Anyone who truly believes in the magic of the marketplace will always insist that any problem, any injustice, any absurdity that might seem to be produced by the market is really caused by government interference with same. This must be true because the market is freedom, and freedom is always good. Putting it this way might sound like a caricature, but I have met libertarians willing to say exactly that, in almost exactly those words.[17] Of course, the problem with any such argument is that it's circular; it can't be disproved. Since all actually existing market systems are to some degree state regulated, it's easy enough to insist that any results one likes (say, high levels of overall wealth) are the result of the workings of the market, and that any features one doesn't like (say, high levels of overall poverty) are really due to government interference in the workings of the market—and then insist that the burden of proof is on anyone who would argue otherwise. No real evidence in favor of the position is required because it is basically a profession of faith.[18]

Now, this being said, I should hasten to point out I am not saying government regulation plays *no* role in the creation of bullshit jobs (particularly of the box-ticker variety). Clearly, it does. As we've already seen, whole industries, such as corporate compliance, would not exist at all were it not for government regulations. But the argument here is not that such regulations are one reason for the rise of bullshit jobs, it's that they are the primary or, even, the only reason.

To sum up, then, we have two arguments: first, that globalization has rendered the process of production so complicated that we need ever more office workers to administer it, so these are not bullshit jobs; second, that while many of them are indeed bullshit jobs, they only exist because increases in government regulation have not only created an ever-burgeoning number of useless bureaucrats but also forced corporations to employ armies of box tickers to keep them at bay.

Both these arguments are wrong, and I think a single example can refute both of them. Let us consider the case of private universities in the

United States. Here are two tables, both drawn from Benjamin Ginsberg's book *The Fall of the Faculty*, about the administrative take-over of American universities, which give us pretty much all we need to know. The first shows the growth in the proportion of administrators and their staff in American universities overall. During the thirty years in question, a time during which tuition skyrocketed, the overall number of teachers per student remained largely constant (in fact, the period ended with slightly fewer teachers per student than before). At the same time, the number of administrators and, above all, administrative staff ballooned to an unprecedented degree (see figure 5).

Is this because the process of "production"—in this case, this would presumably mean teaching, reading, writing, and research—had become two or three times more complicated between 1985 and 2005, so that it now requires a small army of office staff to administer it?[19] Obviously not. Here I can speak from personal experience. Certainly, things have changed a bit since I was in college in the 1980s—lecturers are now expected to provide PowerPoint displays instead of writing on blackboards; there's greater use of class blogs, Moodle pages, and the like. But all this is pretty minor stuff. It's nothing even remotely comparable to, say, the containerization of shipping, Japanese-style "just in time"

Figure 5   Changes in the Supply of and Demand for Administrative Services, 1985–2005

Staff	+240%
Administrators	+85%
Student Enrollments	+56%
Faculty	+50%
No. of Degree-Granting Institutions	+50%
No. of BA Degrees Granted	+47%

Source: Calculated from NCES, "Digest," 2006

production regimes, or the globalization of supply chains. For the most part, teachers continue to do what they have always done: give lectures, lead seminars, meet students during office hours, and grade papers and exams.[20]

What about the heavy hand of government, then? Ginsberg provides us with a refutation to that claim, too, again in one easy table (see figure 6).

In reality, the number of administrators and managers at private institutions increased at *more than twice the rate* as it did at public ones. It seems extremely unlikely that government regulation caused private sector administrative jobs to be created at twice the rate as it did within the government bureaucracy itself. In fact, the only reasonable interpretation of these numbers is precisely the opposite: public universities are ultimately answerable to the public, and hence, under constant political pressure to cut costs and not engage in wasteful expenditures. This may lead to some peculiar priorities (in most US states, the highest-paid public servant is a football or basketball coach at a state university), but it does tend to limit the degree to which a newly appointed dean can simply decide that, since he is obviously a very important person, it is only natural that he should have five or six additional administrative staff working under him—and only then begin trying to figure out what said staff are actually

Figure 6 Administrative Growth at Public and Private Institutions, 1975–2005

	1975	1995	2005	Change
Administrators and Managers at Public Colleges	60,733	82,396	101,011	+66%
Administrators and Managers at Private Colleges	40,530	65,049	95,313	+135%

Source: Calculated from NCES, "Digest," 2006

going to do. Administrators at private universities are answerable only to their board of trustees. Trustees are usually extremely rich. If they are not themselves creatures of the corporate world, they are at the very least used to moving in environments shaped by its mores and sensibilities—and as a result, they tend to view such a dean's behavior as entirely normal and unobjectionable.

Ginsberg himself sees the increase in the numbers and power of university administrators as a simple power grab—one which, he says, has resulted in a profound shift in assumptions about the very nature of universities and the reasons for their existence. Back in the 1950s or 1960s, one could still say that universities were one of the few European institutions that had survived more or less intact from the Middle Ages. Crucially, they were still run on the old medieval principle that only those involved in a certain form of production—whether this be the production of stonework or leather gloves or mathematical equations—had the right to organize their own affairs; indeed that they were also the only people qualified to do so. Universities were basically craft guilds run for and by scholars, and their most important business was considered to be producing scholarship, their second-most, training new generations of scholars. True, since the nineteenth century, universities had maintained a kind of gentleman's pact with government, that they would also train civil servants (and later, corporate bureaucrats) in exchange for otherwise being largely left alone. But since the eighties, Ginsberg argues, university administrators have effectively staged a coup. They wrested control of the university from the faculty and oriented the institution itself toward entirely different purposes. It is now commonplace for major universities to put out "strategic vision documents" that barely mention scholarship or teaching but go on at length about "the student experience," "research excellence" (getting grants), collaboration with business or government, and so forth.

All this rings very true for anyone familiar with the university scene, but the question remains: If this was a coup, how did the administrators manage to get away with it? One has to assume that even in the 1880s, there were university administrators who would have been delighted to seize power in this way and each hire themselves a retinue of minions. What happened in the intervening century that put them in a position to actually do so? And whatever it was, how is it connected to the rise of the total proportion of managers, administrators, and meaningless paper pushers outside the academy that occurred during the same period of time?

Since this is the period that also saw the rise of finance capitalism, it might be best to return to the FIRE sector (finance, insurance, real estate) to seek insight into what overall dynamic in the economy sparked such changes. If those whom the *Economist* believes to be administering complex global supply chains are not, in fact, administering complex global supply chains, then what exactly *are* they doing? And does what is happening in those offices provide any sort of window on what is happening elsewhere?

why the financial industry might be considered a paradigm for bullshit job creation

- expedited frictionless convergences
- coordinated interactive market institutions
- contracted virtual clearinghouses
- directed margin adjustments [21]

On a superficial level, of course, the immediate mechanisms that create bullshit jobs in the FIRE sector are the same ones that produce them anywhere else. I listed some of these in chapter 2, when I described the five basic types of bullshit jobs and how they came about. Flunky positions are created because those in powerful positions in an organization see underlings as badges of prestige; goons are hired due to a dynamic of one-upmanship (if our rivals employ a top law firm, then so, too, must we); duct-taper positions are created because sometimes organizations find it more difficult to fix a problem than to deal with its consequences; box-ticker positions exist because, within large organizations, paperwork attesting to the fact that certain actions have been taken often comes to be seen as more important than the actions themselves; taskmasters exist largely as side effects of various forms of impersonal authority. If large organizations are conceived as a complex play of gravitational forces, pulling in many contradictory directions, one could say there will always be a certain pull in any of these five. Even so, one must ask: Why is there not a greater pressure pulling in the opposite direction? Why is this not seen as more of a problem? Firms like to represent themselves as lean and mean.

It seems to me that those creating, playing around with, and destroying large amounts of money in the FIRE sector provide the perfect place to begin to ask this question—in part because many who work in this sector are convinced that almost everything done in it is basically a scam.[22]

> Elliot: So I did a job for a little while working for one of the "big four" accountancy firms. They had been contracted by a bank to provide compensation to customers that had been involved in the PPI scandal. The accountancy firm was paid by the case, and we were paid by the hour. As a result, they purposefully mis-trained and disorganized staff so that the jobs were repeatedly and consistently done wrong. The systems and practices were changed and modified all the time, to ensure no one could get used to the new practice and actually do the work correctly. This meant that cases had to be redone and contracts extended.

In case the reader is unaware, the PPI (payment protection insurance) scandal broke in the United Kingdom in 2006, when a large number of banks were found to have been unloading unwanted and often wildly disadvantageous account insurance policies on their clients. Courts ordered much of the money returned, and the result was an entire new industry organized around resolving PPI claims. As Elliot reported it, at least some of those hired to process these claims were intentionally dragging their feet to milk the contract for all they could.

Elliot: The senior management had to be aware of this, but it was never explicitly stated. In looser moments, some of the management said things like "We make money from dealing with a leaky pipe—do you fix the pipe, or do you let the pipe keep leaking?" (or words to that effect). There had been vast sums set aside by the bank to pay compensation for the PPI.

This is actually a fairly common story in the testimonies I received: I heard about similar things going on in law firms involved with asbestos compensation payments as well. Whenever a very large sum of money, in the hundreds of millions, is set aside to compensate an entire class of people, a bureaucracy must be set up to locate claimants, process claims, and portion out the money. This bureaucracy may often involve hundreds or even thousands of people. Since the money that pays their salaries is ultimately coming from the same pot, they have no particular incentive to distribute the spoils efficiently. That would be killing the goose that laid the golden egg! According to Elliot, this often led to "crazy, surreal stuff" like intentionally placing offices in different cities and forcing people to commute between them, or printing and destroying the same documents a half dozen times—all the while threatening legal action against anyone who revealed such practices to outsiders.[23] Clearly, the point was to siphon off as much of the money as possible before it got to the claimants; the longer the lower-level people took, the more the company would earn; but owing to the peculiar dynamic discussed in the last chapter, the very pointlessness of the exercise seemed to exacerbate levels of stress and abusive behavior.

Elliot: The cynicism involved was remarkable. I guess it works out to a form of parasitism. As it happens, the job was also extremely difficult and stressful: it appeared that part of their business model was placing impossible targets which would increase all the time so that turnover was high and more staff would regularly have to be brought in and mis-trained, so that, I imagine, the firm could plausibly ask their client that the contract be extended further.

This was demoralizing, of course. I'm now working as a cleaner, which is the least bullshit/alienated job I have ever had.

David: So this sounds like a whole new category: jobs intentionally done wrong! How common do you think that is?

Elliot: From what I've heard among other people in different companies, the PPI industry is basically built around this principle, on the basis that apparently it's only large accountancy firms that really have the capacity to take on contracts like that.

David: Well, I see how one could make the argument that in any system where you are basically dealing with the distribution of spoils, it makes sense to create as many layers of parasites in between as possible. But who were they ultimately milking? Their clients? Or who?

Elliot: I'm not sure who was ultimately paying for this. The bank? An insurance company that insured the bank against losses on fraud activities in the first place? Of course, ultimately it would be the consumer and taxpayer who pay; all these companies need to know is how to milk it.

As long ago as 1852, Charles Dickens, in *Bleak House*, was already making fun of the legal profession with the case of *Jarndyce and Jarndyce*—in which two teams of barristers keep the battle over a huge estate alive for more than a lifetime, until they've devoured the whole thing, whereupon they simply declare the matter moot and move on. The moral of the story is that when a profit-seeking enterprise is in the business of distributing a very large sum of money, the most profitable thing for it to do is to be as inefficient as possible.

Of course, this is basically what the entire FIRE sector does: it creates money (by making loans) and then moves it around in often extremely complicated ways, extracting another small cut with every transaction. The results often leave bank employees feeling that the entire enterprise is just as pointless as the accountancy company's intentionally mis-training employees to milk a cash cow. Surprising numbers of bank employees can't even figure out what the real justification for their particular species of bank is supposed to be.

> Bruce: I work as a fund accountant at a custodian bank. I've never really figured out what custodian banks do. I understand the concepts associated with custodian banks, but I always thought of them as just an unnecessary added layer of accounting. Custodian banks safeguard concepts such as stocks and bonds. How do they actually do that? Can Russian hackers steal these concepts? As far as I can see, the entire custodian bank industry is bullshit.

One reason for the confusion, perhaps, is that the level of general fear, stress, and paranoia appears to be much greater in banks than in most of the other enterprises we've been considering so far. Employees are under enormous pressure not to ask too many questions. One rebel banker, who described to me in detail the machinations by which the biggest banks would lobby the government to introduce regulations to their advantage and then expect everyone to play along with the pretense that the regulations had simply been imposed, told me he thought it's almost as bad as coming out as gay would have been in the 1950s: "There are many people who have read 'on the phenomenon of bullsh*t jobs' and know of the reality of our industry, yet they (including myself) are consumed by fear of losing our jobs, so we don't talk about or discuss these issues openly. We lie to ourselves, our colleagues, and our families."

Such sentiments were commonplace. Almost all bank workers I corresponded with insisted on elaborate secrecy, effacing any detail that might possibly connect them to their employer. At the same time, many emphasized how cathartic it was to be able to finally express things that had been percolating through their minds for so many years. Here, for instance, is the testimony of Rupert, an economic refugee from Australia now working in the City of London, on bullshitization within the financial institution where he presently works:

Rupert: So in banking, obviously the entire sector adds no value and is therefore bullshit. But let's leave that to the side for a minute and look at those within banking who literally do nothing. There actually are not all that many of these because banking is a weird mix. Overall we do nothing, yet within that nothing it's efficient, meritocratic, and in general lean.

Still, the most obvious is the cheerleader Human Resources Department. At some point, banking realized that everyone hates them, and that their staff knows this, too, so they set about trying to make the staff feel better about it all. We have an intranet that HR was told to make into a kind of internal "community," like Facebook. They set it up; nobody used it. So they then started to try and bully everyone into using it, which made us hate it even more. Then they tried to entice people in by having HR post a load of touchy-feely crap or people writing "internal blogs" that nobody cared about. Still nobody comes.

Three years they've been at this, the internal intranet Facebook page is just full of HR people saying something cheesy about the company and then other HR people saying "Great post! I really agree with this." How they can stand this, I have no idea. It's a monument to the total lack of cohesiveness in banking.

Another one is they have some big drive to do charity for a week. I refuse to participate as though I give to charity, I will not give through my bank, as for them it's just a big advertising drive in an attempt to shore up morale internally and make it look like banking isn't appropriating labor through usury. They put out a "target" of, say, ninety percent participation—all "voluntary"—and then for two months, they try to get people to sign up. If you don't sign up, they note your name, and then people come and ask you why you haven't signed up. In the last two weeks before the end of it, we get automated mails that look like they come from the CEO "encouraging" you to sign up. The last time, I was actually worried about losing my job over holding out. For me, this would have been bad, as I'm in a foreign country on a work visa with no right to remain. But hold on I did.

The number of man-hours spent chasing this "voluntary" charity work is amazing. "Voluntold" is, I believe the technical term.

The charity work itself is totally empty. Things like two hours of litter picking. Giving bad sandwiches to the homeless where someone else organizes all the sandwich packages, etc., and bank employees just turn up and hand them out then go home again in their nice cars. A lot of the charity work is driven by "best company to work for in X" awards that stipulate criteria like "charitable work." The bank then has to hit that criteria to be considered, which will then help them with recruiting. They spend god knows how many hours every year trying to do this.

Okay, next: the time sheet guy . . .

After listing a few positions that could easily be automated away and seem to exist only to provide employment, Rupert ends with the most apparently useless position of all:

Rupert: Finally, middle management. The other day, I had to get an approval from someone at middle-management level. I clicked on a system to email out approval requests. Twenty-five middle managers were listed (only one needed to approve). I had only ever heard of one of them. What are these people doing all day long? Are they not worried about being found out and having to work at McDonald's?

According to those middle managers who've contacted me, the answer to "What are these people doing all day long" would be, in many cases, at least, "Not much." So in Rupert's estimation, at least, in the lower echelons, competence and efficiency actually do seem to be the reigning values; the higher one goes up the ladder, the less true this appears to be.

Rupert's account is fascinating from any number of perspectives. Take the theme of how artificial contests operate as a mechanism of bullshitization, one that cropped up in numerous other contexts as well. Many of the follies of local government in the UK, for instance, are driven by a similar desire to be named "best council" in a given region, or in the country as a whole. In every case, such contests set off a frenzy of box-ticking rituals, climaxing, in this case, in the ridiculous simulations of charity demanded of present employees so as to be able to tell potential future employees that their company has been voted one of the best places to work. Most of the other elements in Rupert's testimony appear in other accounts from inside major financial institutions as well: the confused mix of frenetic, stressful, but almost magic efficiency in some sectors, the obvious bloat in others; all in a context where no one was quite sure what the bank really did or if it was even a legitimate enterprise; the fact that such questions could never be discussed.

Another common theme was the way many of those laboring in financial institutions—to a much larger degree than those in most large corporations—had little or no idea how their work contributed to the bank as a whole. Irene, for example, worked for several major investment banks in "Onboarding"—that is, monitoring whether the bank's clients (in this case, various hedge funds and private equity funds) were in compliance with government regulations. In theory, every transaction the bank engaged in had to be assessed. The process was self-evidently corrupt, since the real work was outsourced to shady outfits in Bermuda, Mauritius, and or the Cayman Islands ("where bribes are cheap"), and they invariably found everything to be in order. Nonetheless, since a 100% percent approval rate would hardly do, an elaborate edifice had to be erected so as to make it look as if sometimes, they did indeed find problems sometimes. So Irene would report that the outsider reviewers had okayed the transaction, and a Quality Control board would review Irene's paperwork and duly locate typos and other minor errors. Then the total number of "fails" in each department would be turned over to be tabulated by a metrics division, this allowing everyone involved to spend hours every week in meetings arguing over whether any particular "fail" was real.

Irene: There was an even higher caste of bullshit, propped atop the metrics bullshit, which were the data scientists. Their job was to collect the fail metrics and apply complex software to make pretty pictures out of the data. The bosses would then take these pretty pictures to their bosses, which helped ease the awkwardness inherent in the fact that they had no idea what they were talking about or what any of their teams actually did. At [Big Bank A], I had five bosses in two years. At [Big Bank B], I had three. The vast majority were installed, cherry-picked by higher-ups, and "gifted" these castles of shit. In many cases, sadly, it was how the companies met their minorities-in-management quota.

So once again, we have the same combination of fraud, pretense (no one was allowed to talk about the shady companies in the Cayman Islands), a system designed not to be understood, which was then pushed off on managers who had no idea what was going on below them, largely because it made no sense. It was all just a meaningless ritual. What's entirely unclear is whether anyone on top of the food chain—the data crunchers, the just-passing-through executives, even the higher-ups who chose them—actually knew how pointless it all was.

Finally, on top of the usual artificially induced stress and tension and barking about deadlines, the usual sadomasochistic interpersonal relations, and the usual fearful silences (that is, all the things that typically happen when pointless projects are organized on top-down lines), there was the intense pressure on employees to take part in a different set of rituals designed to prove the institution really cared. In Irene's case, these were not staged charity events, but New Agey seminars that often drove her to the point of tears:

Irene: On top of the metrics, there were the cruel, patronizing "flexibility" and "mindfulness" seminars. No, you can't work fewer hours. No you can't get paid more. No, you can't choose which bullshit projects to decline. But you can sit through this seminar, where the bank tells you how much it values flexibility.

The mindfulness seminars were even worse. They attempted to reduce the unfathomable beauty and stupefying sadness of the human experience into the raw physicality of breathing, eating, and shitting.

Breathe mindfully. Eat mindfully. Shit mindfully, and you can be successful in business.

All of this, presumably, to remind the employee that if one reduced life to pure physicality, the fact that some abstractions were more "real" than others, and that some office tasks seemed to serve a legal and moral or even economic purpose and others did not, was not really all that important. It's as if they first forbid you to acknowledge you are engaging in empty ritual, then force you to attend seminars where hired gurus tell you, "In the final analysis, isn't everything we do just empty ritual?"

What we've seen so far from Elliot, Rupert, and Irene are all partial, situated perspectives on very large and complicated organizations. None of them has an overall, panoptic view. But it's not entirely clear if anyone else does, either. One has to assume the higher-ups in Irene's story, who intentionally assign executives from minority backgrounds to the onboarding sector, are aware that most of what goes on in that part of the company is bullshit. Even they might not know precisely how and why. Nor would it be possible to create some kind of secret survey to determine what percentage of bank workers secretly believe their jobs to be bullshit and the divisions in which they tend to be concentrated. The closest I was able to find to general insight came from a certain Simon, who had been employed by a series of large international banks in risk management, which basically, he says, means to analyze and "find problems in their internal processes."

Simon: I spent two years analyzing the critical payment and operations processes at one bank, with the sole aim to work out how a staff member might use the computer systems to commit fraud and theft, and thereby recommend solutions to prevent this. What I discovered by chance was that most people at the bank didn't know why they were doing what they were doing. They would say that they are only supposed to log into this one system and select one menu option and type certain things in. They didn't know why.

So Simon's job was basically to be the all-seeing eye that determined how different parts of a bank's many moving parts fit together and iron out any incoherences, vulnerabilities, or redundancies he might find. In other words, he's about as qualified to answer the question as anyone could be. His conclusions?

> Simon: In my conservative estimation, eighty percent of the bank's sixty thousand staff were not needed. Their jobs could either completely be performed by a program or were not needed at all because the programs were designed to enable or replicate some bullshit process to begin with.

In other words, forty-eight thousand of the bank's sixty thousand employees did nothing useful—or nothing that couldn't easily be done by a machine. These were, Simon believed, de facto bullshit jobs, even if the bank workers themselves were deprived of the means to assess or collectively analyze the situation, and expected to keep any suspicions to themselves. But why didn't the bank's higher-ups figure this out and do something about it? Well, the easiest way to answer that question is to observe what happened when Simon did suggest reforms:

> Simon: In one instance, I created a program that solved a critical security problem. I went to present it to an executive, who included all his consultants in the meeting. There were twenty-five of them in the boardroom. The hostility I faced during and after the meeting was severe, as I slowly realized that my program automated everything they were currently being paid to do by hand. It's not as if they enjoyed it; it was tedious work, monotonous and boring. The cost of my program was five percent of what they were paying those twenty-five people. But they were adamant.
>
> I found many similar problems and came up with solutions. But in all my time, not one of my recommendations was ever actioned. Because in every case, fixing these problems would have resulted in

people losing their jobs, as those jobs served no purpose other than giving the executive they reported to a sense of power.

So even if these jobs didn't originate as flunky jobs, which presumably most didn't, they ended up being maintained as such. The threat of automation, of course, is an ongoing concern in any large enterprise—I've heard of companies where programmers will show up to work wearing T-shirts that say "Go Away or I Will Replace You with a Very Small Shell Script"—but in this case, and many like it, the concern went to the very top: to the very executives who (if, for instance, they are involved in private equity in any way) pride themselves on the ruthlessness with which they acquired other corporations and saddled them with enormous debts in the name of downsizing and efficiency. These very same executives prided themselves on their own bloated staffs. In fact, if Simon is also correct, they did so because that's what a large bank really was: it was made up of a series of feudal retinues, each answerable to some lordly executive.[24]

on some ways in which the current form of managerial feudalism resembles classical feudalism, and other ways in which it does not

The upper quintile is growing in size and income because all the value created by actual productive workers in the lower quintiles gets extracted by those at the top. When the top classes rob everybody else, they need a lot more guard labor to keep their stolen loot secure.

—Kevin Carson

If we return to the example of the feudal overlord in chapter 2, this actually makes perfect sense. I was using feudal overlords and retainers as a metaphor at that point. But in the case of banks, at least, it's not clear how much is metaphor and how much is literal truth. As I pointed out, feudalism is essentially a redistributive system. Peasants and craftsmen produce things, to a large extent autonomously; lords siphon off a share of what they produce, usually by dint of some complex set of legal rights and traditions ("direct juro-political extraction" is the technical phrase I learned in college),[25] and then go about portioning out shares of the loot to their own staff, flunkies, warriors, retainers—and to a lesser extent, by sponsoring feasts and festivals and by occasional gifts and favors, giving some of it back to the craftsmen and peasants once again. In such an arrangement, it makes little sense to speak of separate spheres of "politics" and "the economy" because the goods are extracted through political means and distributed for political purposes. In fact, it was only with the first stirrings of industrial capitalism that anyone started talking about "the economy" as an autonomous sphere of human activity in the first place.

Under capitalism, in the classic sense of the term, profits derive from the management of production: capitalists hire people to make or build or fix or maintain things, and they cannot take home a profit unless their total overhead—including the money they pay their workers and contractors—comes out less than the value of the income they receive from their clients or customers. Under classic capitalist conditions of this sort it does indeed make no sense to hire unnecessary workers. Maximizing profits means paying the least number of workers the least amount of money possible; in a very competitive market, those who hire unnecessary workers are not likely to survive. Of course, this is why doctrinaire libertarians, or, for that matter, orthodox Marxists, will always insist that our economy can't really be riddled with bullshit jobs; that all this must be some sort of illusion. But by a feudal logic, where economic and political considerations overlap, the same behavior makes perfect sense. As with the PPI distributors, the whole point is to grab a pot of loot, either by stealing it from one's enemies or extracting it from commoners by means of fees, tolls, rents, and levies, and then redistributing it. In the process, one creates an entourage of followers that is both the visible measure of one's pomp and magnificence, and at the same time, a means of distributing political favor: for instance, by buying off potential malcontents, rewarding faithful allies (goons), or creating an elaborate hierarchy of honors and titles for lower-ranking nobles to squabble over.

If all of this very much resembles the inner workings of a large corporation, I would suggest that this is no coincidence: such corporations are less and less about making, building, fixing, or maintaining things and more and more about political processes of appropriating, distributing, and allocating money and resources. This means that, once again, it's increasingly difficult to distinguish politics and economics, as we have seen with the advent of "too-big-to-fail" banks, whose lobbyists typically write the very laws by which government supposedly regulates them, but even more, by the fact that financial profits themselves are gathered largely through direct juro-political means. JPMorgan Chase & Co., for example, the largest bank in America, reported in 2006 that roughly two-thirds of its profits were derived from "fees and penalties," and "finance" in general really refers to trading in other people's debts—debts which, of course, are enforceable in courts of law.[26]

It's almost impossible to get accurate figures about exactly what proportion of a typical family's income in, say, America, or Denmark, or Japan, is extracted each month by the FIRE sector, but there is every reason to believe it is not only a very substantial chunk but also is now a distinctly greater chunk of total profits than those the corporate sector derives directly from making or selling goods and services in those same countries. Even those firms we see as the very heart of the old industrial order—General Motors and General Electric in America, for example— now derive all, or almost all, of their profits from their own financial divisions. GM, for example, makes its money not from selling cars but rather from interest collected on auto loans.

Still, there is one crucial difference between medieval feudalism and the current, financialized version. We've already mentioned it earlier in the chapter. Medieval feudalism was based on a principle of self-governance in the domain of production. Anyone whose work was based on some kind of specialized knowledge, whether lace makers, wheelwrights, merchants, legal scholars, was expected to collectively regulate their own affairs, or including who would be allowed to enter the profession and how they would be trained, with minimal supervision from anybody else. Guilds and similar organizations typically had elaborate hierarchies within (though not always so much as they do today: in many medieval universities, for instance, students elected their professors), but at the very least, a medieval sword smith or soap maker could go about his work in the confidence that he would never have anyone who was not himself a sword smith or a soap maker telling him he was not going about it correctly. Industrial capitalism obviously changed all that, and the rise of managerialism in the twentieth century drove the process even further; but rather than this in any sense reversing under financialized capitalism, the situation has actually worsened. "Efficiency" has come to mean vesting more and more power to managers, supervisors, and other presumed "efficiency experts," so that actual producers have almost zero autonomy.[27] At the same time, the ranks and orders of managers seem to reproduce themselves endlessly.

■ ■ ■

If one wants a parable for what seems to have happened to capitalism over the last forty-odd years, perhaps the best example I know is the Elephant Tea factory outside Marseille, France, currently occupied by its employees. I visited the plant a few years ago, and one of the occupiers—who took me and some friends on a tour of the grounds—told us the story of what happened. Originally, it was a local enterprise, but during the age of mergers and acquisitions, the company was bought up by Unilever, owner of Lipton, the world's largest tea producer. At first, the company left the organization of the plant more or less alone. The workers, however, were in the habit of tinkering with the machinery, and by the nineties, they had introduced a series of improvements that sped up production by more than 50 percent, thus markedly increasing profits.

Now, in the fifties, sixties, and seventies, there was a tacit understanding in much of the industrialized world that if productivity in a certain enterprise improved, a certain share of the increased profits would be redistributed to the workers in the form of improved wages and benefits. Since the eighties, this is no longer the case. So here.

"Did they give any of that money to us?" our guide asked. "No. Did they use it to hire more workers, or new machinery, to expand operations? No. They didn't do that, either. So what did they do? They started hiring more and more white-collar workers. Originally, when I started working here, there were just two of them: the boss and the HR guy. It had been like that for years. Now suddenly there were three, four, five, seven guys in suits wandering around. The company made up different fancy titles for them, but basically all of them spent their time trying to think of something to do. They'd be walking up and down the catwalks every day, staring at us, scribbling notes while we worked. Then they'd have meetings and discuss it and write reports. But they still couldn't figure out any real excuse for their existence. Then finally, one of them hit on a solution: 'Why don't we just shut down the whole plant, fire the workers, and move operations to Poland?'"

Generally speaking, extra managers are hired with the ostensible purpose of improving efficiency. But in this case, there was little to be improved; the workers themselves had boosted efficiency about as much as it was possible to do. But the managers were hired anyway. What this suggests is that what we are really dealing with here has nothing to do with efficiency but everything to do with changing understandings of the moral responsibilities of corporations. From roughly 1945 to 1975, there was what is sometimes referred to as a "Keynesian bargain" between workers, employers, and government—and part of the tacit understanding was that increases in worker productivity would indeed be matched by increases in worker compensation. A glance at the diagram on the next page confirms that this was exactly what happened. In the 1970s, the two began to part ways, with compensation remaining largely flat, and productivity taking off like a rocket (see figure 7).

These figures are for the United States, but similar trends can be observed in virtually all industrialized countries.

Where did the profits from this increased productivity go? Well, much of it, as we are often reminded, ended up swelling the fortunes of the wealthiest 1 percent: investors, executives, and the upper echelons of the professional-managerial classes. But if we take the Elephant Tea factory as a microcosm for the corporate world as a whole, it becomes obvious that wasn't all that happened. Another considerable chunk of the benefits of increased productivity went to creating entirely new and basically pointless professional-managerial positions, usually—as we've seen in the case of universities—accompanied by small armies of equally pointless administrative staff. As we have seen so often, first the staff is allocated and *then* someone has to figure out what, if anything, they will actually do.

In other words, the feudal analogy is not even really an analogy. Managerialism has become the pretext for creating a new covert form of feudalism, where wealth and position are allocated not on economic but

Figure 7

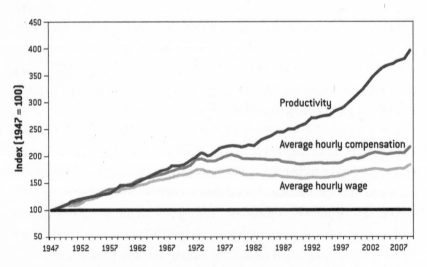

Source: EPI analysis of Bureau of Economic Analysis and Bureau of Labor Statistics data.

political grounds—or rather, where every day it's more difficult to tell the difference between what can be considered "economic" and what is "political."

Another classic feature of medieval feudalism is the creation of hierarchies of ranked nobles or officials: a European king might grant land to a baron in exchange for providing a certain number of knights to his army; the baron, in turn, would grant most of that land to some local vassal on the same basis, and so on. Such devolution would proceed, through a process of "sub-infeudation," down to local lords of the manor. This was the process by which the elaborate ranks of dukes, earls, viscounts, and so forth that still exist in places like England originally came into being. In India and China, matters were typically more indirect; the usual practice was to simply allocate the income from a certain territory or province to officials who were likely to actually live in the nearest city, but for our purposes here, the result is not so very different.[28]

As a general principle, I would propose the following: in any political-economic system based on appropriation and distribution of goods, rather than on actually making, moving, or maintaining them, and therefore, where a substantial portion of the population is engaged in funneling resources up and down the system, that portion of the population will tend to organize itself into an elaborately ranked hierarchy of multiple tiers (at least three, and sometimes ten, twelve, or even more). As a corollary, I would add that within those hierarchies, the line between retainers and subordinates will often become blurred, since obeisance to superiors is often a key part of the job description. Most of the important players are lords and vassals at the same time.

how managerial feudalism manifests itself in the creative industries through an endless multiplication of intermediary executive ranks

Every dean needs his vice-dean and sub-dean, and each of them needs a management team, secretaries, admin staff; all of them

only there to make it harder for us to teach, to research, to carry
out the most basic functions of our jobs.

—anonymous British academic[29]

The rise of managerial feudalism has produced a similar infatuation
with hierarchy for its own sake. We have already seen the phenomenon
of managers whose job it is to manage other managers, or the elaborate
mechanisms Irene described whereby banks set up a hierarchy of offices
to endlessly rarify what's ultimately an arbitrary and meaningless set of
data. Often, this kind of managerial sub-infeudation is a direct result of
the unleashing of "market forces." Recall here Kurt, with whom we began
chapter 1, who was working for a subcontractor to a subcontractor to a
subcontractor to the German military. His position was the direct outcome of market reforms supposedly designed to make government more
efficient.

The same phenomenon can be observed in a dozen different fields.
For instance, the multiplication of levels of managers whose basic job is
to sell things to one another has come to dominate almost all "creative industries"—from books, where editors at academic presses in many cases
don't even read half the books they are supposed to have edited, because
they are expected to spend most of their time marketing things to other
editors; to the visual arts, where recent decades have seen the rise of a
whole new stratum of managerial intermediaries called curators, whose
work assembling the work of artists is now often considered of equal
value and importance to the art itself; to even journalism, where the relationship between editors and reporters has been complicated by an additional level of "producers."[30] Film and television have fared particularly
badly. At least, so it seems from testimonials within the industry. Where
once the Hollywood studio system relied on a relatively simple relation
between producers, directors, and writers, recent decades have witnessed
an apparently endless process of managerial sub-infeudation, resulting in
a daunting array of producers, subproducers, executive producers, consultants, and the like, all in constant search for something, anything, to
actually do.[31]

I received several testimonies from workers in TV "development"—that is, small companies in the business of coming up with programming ideas to pitch to larger ones. Here's an example that illustrates just how much the introduction of market elements within the process has changed things:

Owen: I work in development. This part of the television industry has expanded exponentially in the last twenty years. TV used to be commissioned by one channel controller who would ask producers he liked to make whatever shows they wanted. There was no "development." There was just making the show.

Now every company in TV (and film, too) has its own development team, staffed by three to ten people, and there are more and more commissioners whose job it is to listen to their pitches. None of these people make TV shows.

I have not gotten a show sold for four years. Not because we are particularly bad but because of nepotism and politics. That's four years that have amounted to precisely nothing. I could have sat with my thumb up my arse for four years, and nothing would be any different. Or I could have been making films.

I would say the average development team gets one show commissioned every three to four months. It's bullshit through and through.

Such complaints are similar to what one regularly hears in academia: it's not just the senselessness of the process that rankles, but as with all box-ticking rituals, the fact that one ends up spending so much more time pitching, assessing, monitoring, and arguing about what one does than one spends actually doing it. In film, television, and even radio, the situation becomes even more distressing, because owing to internal marketization of the industry, a substantial chunk of those who work in it spend their time working on shows that do not and will never exist. Apollonia, for instance, did a stint for a development team pitching ideas for reality TV shows with titles such as *Snipped* (where men voted too promiscuous by the audience underwent a vasectomy live on the air), *Transsexual*

Housewives, and—this was a real title—*Too Fat to Fuck*. All were cast and promoted, even though not one was ever produced.

> Apollonia: What would happen is we would come up with ideas together and then sell them to networks. Which involves sourcing the talent, building a sizzle video (a thirty-second promo for something that doesn't exist yet), and then shopping that sizzle around to try and sell it to a network. While I was there, we didn't sell any shows, presumably because my boss was an idiot.

Apollonia did all the work, so that the Vice President and the Senior Vice President—who were the only other members of her team—could helicopter around the city meeting other vice presidents and senior vice presidents for lunch, and generally acting like high-powered media executives. During the time she worked there, the result of such efforts was precisely zero.

How did this happen? And what happens when an idea *is* accepted? One current Hollywood scriptwriter was kind enough to send me his insider's analysis of what went wrong and how things now play out:

> Oscar: In the Golden Age of Hollywood, from the 1920s to the 1950s, studios were vertical operations. They were also companies headed by one man, who took all the decisions and who banked his own money. They were not yet owned by conglomerates, and they had no board of directors. These studio "heads" were far from intellectuals, or artists, but they had gut instincts, took risks, and had an innate sense about what made a movie work. Instead of armies of executives, they would actually hire armies of writers for their story department. Those writers were on the payroll, supervised by the producers, and everything was in-house: actors, directors, set designers, actual film stages, etc.

Starting in the sixties, he continues, this system came under attack as vulgar, tyrannical, and stifling of artistic talent. For a while, the resulting ferment did allow some innovative visions to shine through, but the ultimate result was a corporatization far more stifling than anything that had come before.

Oscar: There were openings in the sixties and seventies (New Holly-wood: Beatty, Scorsese, Coppola, Stone), as the film industry was in complete chaos at the time. Then, in the 1980s, corporate monopolies took over studios. It was a big deal, and I think a sign of things to come, when Coca-Cola purchased Columbia Pictures (for a short while). From then on, movies wouldn't be made by those that liked them or even watched them. (Clearly, this ties in with the advent of neoliberalism and a larger shift in society.)

The system that eventually emerged was suffused with bullshit on every level. The process of "development" ("development hell," as writers prefer to call it) now ensures that each script has to pass through not just one but usually a half dozen clone-like executives with titles such as (Oscar lists some) "Managing Director of International Content and Talent, Executive Managing Director, Executive Vice President for Development, and, my favorite, Executive Creative Vice President for Television." Most are armed with MBAs in marketing and finance but know almost nothing about the history or technicalities of film or TV. Their professional lives, like that of Apollonia's boss, seem to consist almost entirely of writing emails and having ostensibly high-powered lunches with other executives bearing equally elaborate titles. As a result, what was once the fairly straightforward business of pitching and selling a script idea descends into a labyrinthine game of self-marketing that can go on for years before a project is finally approved.

It's important to emphasize that this happens not just when an independent writer tries to sell a script idea to a studio on "spec," but even in-house, for writers already inside a studio or production company. Oscar is obliged to work with an "incubator," who plays a role roughly equivalent to that of a literary agent, helping him prepare script proposals that the incubator will then pass to his own network of top executives, either within or outside the company. His example is of another television show, though he emphasizes the process is exactly the same for movies:

Oscar: So I "develop" a series project with this "incubator" . . . writing a "bible": a sixty-page document that details the project's concept, characters, episodes, plots, themes, etc. Once that's done comes the carnival of pitching. The incubator and I propose the project to a slew of broadcasters, financing funds, and production companies. These people are, purportedly, at the top of the food chain. You could spend months in the vacuum of communications with them—emails unanswered and so on. Phone calls are considered pushy, if not borderline harassment. Their jobs are to read and seek out projects—yet they couldn't be more unreachable if they worked from a shack in the middle of the Amazon Jungle.

Pitching is a strategic ballet. There is a ritual delay of at least a week between each communication. After a month or two, however, one executive might take enough of an interest to agree to a face-to-face meeting:

Oscar: In the meetings, they ask you to pitch them the project all over again (although they're supposed to have already read it). Once that's done, they usually ask you prewritten one-size-fits-all questions filled with buzzwords . . . It's always very noncommittal, and without exception, they tell you about all the other executives that would need to approve the project in case it would be decided to move forward.

Then you go, and they forget about you . . . and you have to follow up, and the loop begins anew. In fact, an executive will seldom tell you yes or no. If he says yes, and then the project goes nowhere or else gets made and bombs, it's his responsibility. If he says no and then it succeeds somewhere else, he will get blamed for the oversight. Above all, the executive loathes taking responsibility.

The game, then, is to keep the ball in the air as long as possible. Just to option an idea, which involves a mere token payment, typically requires approval from three other branches of the company. Once the option papers are signed, a new process of stalling begins:

Oscar: They will tell me the document they optioned is too long to send around; they need a shorter pitch document. Or suddenly they also want some changes to the concept. So we have a meeting, we talk it over, brainstorm.

A lot of this process is just them justifying their jobs. Everybody in the room will have a different opinion just for the sake of having a reason to be there. It's a cacophony of ideas, and they talk in the loosest, most conceptual terms possible. They pride themselves on being savvy marketers and incisive thinkers, but it's all generalities.

The executive loves to talk in metaphors, and he loves to expose his theories about how the audience thinks, what it wants, how it reacts to storytelling. Most fancy themselves corporatized Joseph Campbells[32]—with no doubt, here again, an influence from the corporate "philosophies" of Google, Facebook, and other such behemoths.

Or they'll say "I'm not saying you should do X, but maybe you should do X"; both tell you to do something and not to do it at the same time. The more you press for details, the blurrier it gets. I try to decipher their gibberish and tell them what I think they mean.

Alternately, the executive will totally, wholeheartedly agree with everything the writer proposes; then as soon as the meeting is over, he'll send out an email instructing her to do the opposite. Or wait a few weeks and inform her the entire project must be reconceived. After all, if all he did was shake the writer's hand and allow her to get to work, there'd be little point of having an Executive Creative Vice President to begin with—let alone five or six of them.

In other words, film and TV production is now not all that entirely different from the accountancy companies mis-training employees to stall the distribution of PPI payments, or Dickens's case of *Jarndyce and Jarndyce*. The longer the process takes, the greater the excuse for the endless multiplication of intermediary positions, and the more money is siphoned off before it has any chance to get to those doing the actual work.

Oscar: And *all this* for a (now) fifteen-page document. Now, extrapolate that to more people, a script, a director, producers, even more

187

executives, the shoot, the edit—and you have a picture of the insanity of the industry.

At this point, we are entering into what might be termed the airy reaches of the bullshit economy, and therefore, that part least accessible to study. We cannot know what Executive Creative Vice Presidents are really thinking. Even those who are secretly convinced their jobs are pointless—and for all we know, that's pretty much all of them—are unlikely to admit this to an anthropologist. So one can only guess.

But the effects of their actions can be observed every time we go to the cinema. "There's a reason," says Oscar, "why movies and TV series—to put it plainly—suck."

■ ■ ■

The rule of finance has seen the insertion of competitive games of this sort at every level of corporate life, or, for that matter, within institutions such as universities or charities that had previously been seen as the very antithesis of corporations. Perhaps in some it hasn't reached that zenith of bullshit which is Hollywood. But everywhere, managerial feudalism ensures that thousands of hours of creative effort will literally come to nothing. Take the domain of scientific research, or higher education once again. If a grant agency funds only 10 percent of all applications, that means that 90 percent of the work that went into preparing applications was just as pointless as the work that went into making the promo video for Apollonia's doomed reality TV show *Too Fat to Fuck*. (Even more so, really, since one can rarely make such an amusing anecdote out of it afterward.) This is an extraordinary squandering of human creative energy. Just to give a sense of the scale of the problem: one recent study determined that European universities spend roughly 1.4 billion euros a year on failed grant applications[33]—money that, obviously, might otherwise have been available to fund research.

Elsewhere, I have suggested that one of the main reasons for technological stagnation over the last several decades is that scientists, too, have to spend so much of their time vying with one another to convince potential donors they already know what they are going to discover.[34] Finally, the endless internal meeting rituals where Dynamic Brand Coordinators and East Coast Vision Managers[35] for private corporations display their PowerPoint presentations, mind maps, and graphics-rich glossy reports, are all essentially exercises in internal marketing as well.

We've already seen how, internally, large numbers of ancillary bullshit jobs tend to cluster around such internal marketing rituals: such as those hired to prepare, edit, copy, or provide graphics for the presentations or reports. It seems to me all this is an intrinsic feature of managerial feudalism. Where once universities, corporations, movie studios, and the like had been governed by a combination of relatively simple chains of command and informal patronage networks, we now have a world of funding proposals, strategic vision documents, and development team pitches— allowing for the endless elaborations of new and ever more pointless levels of managerial hierarchy, staffed by men and women with elaborate titles, fluent in corporate jargon, but who either have no firsthand experience of what it's like to actually do the work they are supposed to be managing, or who have done everything in their power to forget it.

conclusion, with a brief return to the question of three levels of causation

At this point, we can return to President Obama's remarks about health care reform and allow the pieces to fall together. The "one million, two million, three million jobs" that Obama was so concerned to preserve were created, specifically, by the very sorts of processes we have just been describing: the seemingly endless accrual of layer upon layer of unnecessary administrative and managerial positions resulting from the aggressive application of market principles, in this case, to the health care industry. It's a slightly different situation than most of those we've been looking at, since the US health care system, almost uniquely among those of wealthy countries, was always mainly private. Despite this—even more so after Obama, actually—it shows the exact same entanglement of public and private, economic and political, and the same role of government in guaranteeing private profits, as one is beginning to see in Canada or Europe with the partial privatization of national health systems. In every case (and in this case of US health care reform this was done quite self-consciously), ensuring that at least some of those profits are redistributed to creating well-paid, prestigious, but ultimately bullshit office jobs.

I began the chapter by speaking of different levels of causality. The reasons why individuals create, or accept, bullshit jobs are by no means the same as the reasons why such jobs will tend to proliferate in certain times and places rather than others. The deeper structural forces that drive such historical changes, in turn, are not the same as the cultural and political factors that determine how the public, and politicians, react to them. This chapter has been largely about structural forces. No doubt bullshit jobs have long been with us; but recent years have seen an enormous proliferation of such pointless forms of employment, accompanied by an ever-increasing bullshitization of real jobs—and despite a popular misconception that all this is somehow tied to the rise of the service sector, this proliferation appears to have everything to do with the growing importance of finance.

Corporate capitalism—that is, that form of capitalism in which production is largely carried out within large bureaucratically organized firms—first emerged in America and Germany in the late nineteenth century. During most of the twentieth century, large industrial corporations were very much independent of, and to some degree even hostile to, the interests of what was called "high finance." Executives in firms dedicated to producing breakfast cereals, or agricultural machinery, saw themselves as having far more in common with production-line workers in their own firms than they did with speculators and investors, and the internal organization of firms reflected this. It was only in the 1970s that the financial sector and the executive classes—that is, the upper echelons of the various corporate bureaucracies—effectively fused. CEOs began paying themselves in stock options, moving back and forth between utterly unrelated companies, priding themselves on the number of employees they could lay off. This set off a vicious cycle whereby workers, who no longer felt any loyalty to corporations that felt none toward them, had to be increasingly monitored, managed, and surveilled.

On a deeper level, this realignment set off a whole series of trends that had enormous implications on virtually everything that was to follow, from changes in political sensibilities to changes in directions of technological research. To take just one particularly revealing example: back in the 1970s, banks were still the only companies that were enthusiastic about the use of computers. There seems to be an intrinsic connection between the financialization of the economy, the blossoming of information industries, and the proliferation of bullshit jobs.[36]

The results were not just some sort of recalibration or readjustment of existing forms of capitalism. In many ways, it marked a profound break with what had come before. If the existence of bullshit jobs seems to defy the logic of capitalism, one possible reason for their proliferation might be that the existing system *isn't* capitalism—or at least, isn't any sort of capitalism that would be recognizable from the works of Adam Smith, Karl Marx, or, for that matter, Ludwig von Mises or Milton Friedman. It is increasingly a system of rent extraction where the internal logic—the system's "laws of motion," as the Marxists like to say—are profoundly different from capitalism, since economic and political imperatives have come to largely merge. In many ways, it resembles classic medieval feudalism, displaying the same tendency to create endless hierarchies of lords, vassals, and retainers. In other ways—notably in its managerialist ethos—it is profoundly different. And the whole apparatus, rather than replacing old-fashioned industrial capitalism, is instead superimposed on top of it, blending together in a thousand points in a thousand different ways. Hardly surprising, then, that the situation seems so confusing that even those directly in the middle don't really know quite what to make of it.

This was the structural level. In the next two chapters, I will turn to the cultural and political level. Here, of course, it is impossible to be neutral. Even to ask why it is that the existence of forms of pointless employment is not seen as a great social problem is to at least suggest that it really ought to be. Clearly, the original essay acted as a kind of catalyst in this regard—it seized on a broadly existing feeling that had not really found any other voice outside the corridors, a sense that something was very wrong with the organization of society, and it provided a series of frameworks for how one might begin to think about those issues in political terms. In what follows, I will expand on those suggestions, and think a little more systematically about what the larger political implications of the current division of labor actually are, and what might be done about the situation.

Chapter 6

Why Do We as a Society Not Object to the Growth of Pointless Employment?

How vain the opinion is of some certain people of the East Indies, who think that apes and baboons, which are with them in great numbers, are imbued with understanding, and that they can speak but will not, for fear they should be imployed and set to work.

—Antoine Le Grand, c. 1675

We have already considered the economic and social forces that have led to the proliferation of bullshit jobs, as well as the misery and distress those jobs cause for those who have to do them. Yet despite this evident and widespread distress, the fact that millions of people show up to work every day convinced they are doing absolutely nothing has not, until now, been considered a social problem. We have not seen politicians denouncing bullshit jobs, academic conferences dedicated to understanding the reasons for the rise of bullshit jobs, opinion pieces debating the cultural consequences of bullshit jobs, or protest movements campaigning to abolish them. To the contrary: if politicians, academics, editorialists, or social movements do weigh in on the matter, it's usually by acting directly or indirectly to make the problem worse.

The situation seems all the more extraordinary when we consider the larger social consequences of this proliferation. If it's really true that as much of half the work we do could be eliminated without any significant effect on overall productivity, why not just redistribute the remaining work in such a way that everyone is working four-hour days? Or four-day weeks with four months' yearly vacation time? Or some similarly easygoing arrangement? Why not start shutting down the global work machine? If nothing else, it would probably be the most effective thing we could do to put a break on global warming. A hundred years ago, many assumed that the steady advance of technology and labor-saving devices would have made this possible by now, and the irony is that they were probably right. We could easily all be putting in a twenty- or even fifteen-hour workweek. Yet for some reason, we as a society have collectively decided it's better to have millions of human beings spending years of their lives pretending to type into spreadsheets or preparing mind maps for PR meetings than freeing them to knit sweaters, play with their dogs, start a garage band, experiment with new recipes, or sit in cafés arguing about politics, and gossiping about their friends' complex polyamorous love affairs.

I think the easiest way to understand how this happened is to consider how difficult it is to imagine an opinion writer for a major newspaper or magazine writing a piece saying that some class of people is working too hard and might do well to cut it out. It's easy enough to find pieces complaining that certain classes of people (young people, poor people, recipients of various forms of public assistance, those of certain national or ethnic groups[1]) are work shy, entitled, lacking in drive or motivation, or unwilling to earn a living. The internet is littered with them. As Rachel put it in chapter 4, "I can barely scroll through Facebook without hitting some preachy think piece about my generation's entitlement and reluctance to just do a bloody day's work." Whenever there's a crisis, even an ecological crisis, there are calls for collective sacrifice. These calls always seem to involve everyone working more—despite the fact that, as noted, in ecological terms, a mass reduction of working hours is probably the quickest and easiest thing that could be done to save the planet.

Opinion writers are the moralists of our day. They are the secular equivalent of preachers, and when they write about work, their arguments reflect a very long theological tradition of valorizing work as a sacred duty, at once curse and blessing, and seeing humans as inherently sinful, lazy beings who can be expected to shirk that duty if they can. The discipline of economics itself emerged out of moral philosophy (Adam Smith was a professor of moral philosophy), and moral philosophy, in turn, was originally a branch of theology. Many economic concepts trace back directly to religious ideas. As a result, arguments about value always have something of a theological tinge. Some originally theological notions about work are so universally accepted that they simply can't be questioned. One cannot assert that hardworking people are *not*, generally speaking, admirable (regardless of what they might be working hard at), or that those who avoid work are not in any way contemptible, and expect to be taken seriously in public debate. If someone says a policy creates jobs, it is not considered acceptable to reply that some jobs aren't worth having. (I know this because I have occasionally done so to policy wonks, partly just to observe the shocked confusion that ensues.) Say any of these things, and anything else you might say will be written off as well as the effusions of a provocateur, a comedian, a lunatic—anyway, someone whose further arguments can now be automatically dismissed.

Still, while the voice of the moralists may be sufficient to convince us not to make a scandal of the proliferation of bullshit jobs (since in public debate, all work must be treated as sacred duty, and therefore any work is always preferable to none at all), when it comes to our own jobs, we tend to apply very different criteria. We expect a job to serve some purpose or have some meaning and are deeply demoralized if we find it does not. But this leads to another question: If work is not simply a value in itself, in what way is it a value to others? After all, when people say their jobs are "worthless" or "no good to anyone," they are making arguments about value. Of what sort?

■ ■ ■

The field of value is always contested territory. It seems that whenever there's a word for something everyone agrees to be desirable—"truth," "beauty," "love," "democracy"—then there will be no consensus as to what it really means. (Oddly enough, this is even true of money: economists are divided over what it is.) But in our own society, arguments about the value of work are particularly important to consider because they have led to what any outside observer would have to describe as weird, topsy-turvy effects. As we'll see, people do have a notion of the social value of their work; but our society has reached the point where not only is the social value of work usually in inverse proportion to its economic value (the more one's work benefits others, the less one is likely to be paid for it), but many people have come to accept this situation is morally right—they genuinely believe this is how things ought to be. That we *should* reward useless or even destructive behavior, and, effectively, punish those whose daily labors make the world a better place.

This is genuinely perverse. To understand how it happened, though, will require a bit of work on our own part.

on the impossibility of developing an absolute measure of value

When someone describes his job as pointless or worthless, he is necessarily operating within some sort of tacit theory of value: an idea of what would be a worthwhile occupation, and therefore what is not. It is notoriously difficult, however, to tease out exactly what that theory is in any given instance, let alone to come up with any reliable system of measurement that would make it possible to say that job X is more valuable or useful to society than job Y.

Economists measure value in terms of what they call "utility": the degree to which a good or service is useful in satisfying a want or need,[2] and many apply something like this to their own jobs. Do I provide something useful to the public? Sometimes the answer to the question is self-evident. If one is building a bridge, one considers it a worthwhile task if one anticipates that other people who wish to get across the river will find it useful. If workers are building a bridge no one is ever likely to use, such as the famous "bridges to nowhere" that local politicians in the United States will occasionally sponsor to direct federal money to their districts, they are likely to conclude they are engaged in a bullshit job.

Still, there's an obvious problem with the concept of utility. Saying that something is "useful" is just saying it's effective as a way of getting something else. If you buy a dress, the "utility" of that dress is partly that it protects you from the elements or ensures you don't violate laws against walking down the street naked, but it's largely the degree to which it makes you look or feel nice. So why would one dress achieve that and not another? Economists will usually say this is a matter of taste and therefore not their department. But any utility ultimately ends up in this kind of subjective problem if you push it back far enough, even something so relatively uncomplicated as a bridge. Yes, it can make it easier for people to get to the other side of a river, but why do they want to do that? To visit an aging relative? To go bowling? Even if it's just to shop for groceries. One does not buy groceries simply to maintain one's physical health: one also expresses one's personal taste, maintains an ethnic or family tradition, acquires the means to throw drinking parties with one's friends or to celebrate religious holidays. We can't really discuss any of these things in terms of a language of "needs." For much of human history—and this is still true in much of the world today—when poor people end up in crippling debt to local money-lenders, it's because they felt they had to borrow money to throw proper funerals for their parents or weddings for their children. Did they "need" to do this? Clearly, they felt strongly that they did. And since there's no scientific definition of what a "human need" actually is, beyond the body's minimal caloric and nutritional requirements, and a few other physical factors, such questions must always be subjective. To a large degree, needs are just other people's expectations. If you don't throw a proper wedding for your daughter, it would be a family disgrace.

Most economists conclude therefore that there's no point in sitting in judgment about what people *should* want; better to just accept that they *do* want, and then sit in judgment about how effectively ("rationally") they set about pursuing their desires. Most workers seem to agree. As I've noted, those who felt their jobs were pointless almost never said things such as "I produce selfie sticks. Selfie sticks are stupid. People shouldn't buy stupid things like that," or, "Who really needs a two-hundred-dollar pair of socks?" Even the one or two exceptions were revealing. Take Dietrich, who worked for a company that provided party supplies, mostly to local churches:

> Dietrich: I worked for years in the warehouse of a novelty store. I don't really know what to say other than it was complete and total BS. One doesn't know true degradation until one has spent a good portion of one's waking hours schlepping around boxes of clown noses, sneezing powders, plastic champagne flutes, cardboard cutouts of basketball play-ers, and all other manner of other pointless knickknacks and nonsense. Most of the time, we just sat in the back of the warehouse with little to nothing to do, musing on the total irrelevance of what we were doing, year after year, as the business proved more and more unsustainable.
>
> To add insult to injury, our paychecks were bright red and had clown faces on them, much to the amusement of bank tellers every-where—as if their jobs were any more meaningful!

One might speculate at length about why Dietrich found this particular collection of products so offensive. (What's wrong with a little silly fun?) My guess would be: because it wasn't Dietrich who decided he was working for purveyors of ephemeral junk; these products never claimed to be any-thing other than ephemeral junk, anti-utilities destined only to be thrown away, mockeries of "real" objects and "real" values. (Even the money was a joke.) Even more, novelty items do not reject "real" values in the name of anything in particular; they provide no actual challenge to what they claim to be making fun of. So one could say they aren't even genuine mockery; they're a mockery of a mockery, reduced to something with so little real subversive content that they can be embraced by even the most boring and stodgy members of society "for the sake of the children."

There's little more depressing than enforced gaiety. Still, even testimo-nies such as Dietrich's were rare.

In most cases, when employees assessed the social value of their work, they appealed to some variant of the position presented by Tom, the special effects artist we met in chapter 2: "I consider a worthwhile job to be one that fulfills a preexisting need, or even that creates a product or service that people hadn't thought of, that somehow enhances and improves their lives"—as opposed to, in Tom's case, his "beauty work", which involved manipulating images of celebrities so as to make audiences feel unattractive and then selling them cures that didn't really work. Telemarketers sometimes expressed similar concerns, but, again, much of what they were doing was simple fraud; you don't really need an elaborate theory of social value to tell you why cajoling retirees into buying subscriptions they can't afford to magazines they'll never read is problematic. Very few sat in judgment on their customers' tastes and preferences; it was more the aggressiveness and dishonesty of their own interventions that they felt proved they provided nothing of real value.

Other objections appealed to much older traditions of social critique. Take Rupert, the bank employee, who asserted that "the entire [banking] sector adds no value and is therefore bullshit," since finance was really just a matter of "appropriating labor through usury." The labor theory of value he's referencing here, which traces back at least to the European Middle Ages, starts from the assumption that the real value of a commodity is the work that has been invested in making its existence possible. So when we give money in exchange for a loaf of bread, what we are really paying for is the human effort that went into growing the wheat, baking the bread, and packing and transporting the loaves. If some loaves of bread are more expensive than others, it's either because it took more work to produce and transport them, or, alternately, because we consider some of that work to itself be of higher quality—to involve more skill, more artistry, more effort—than others, and therefore are willing to pay more for the resulting product. Similarly, if you're defrauding others of their wealth, as Rupert felt he was doing working for an international investment bank, you're really stealing the real, productive work that went into creating that wealth.

Now, of course, there's a long history of using arguments like this to challenge arrangements where some are—or at least can be said to be—living off the backs of others; but the very existence of bullshit jobs raises certain problems for any labor theory of value. True, saying all value comes from work[3] is obviously not the same thing as saying that all work produces value.

Rupert felt that most bank employees were in no sense idling about; actually, he felt most worked quite hard; only all their labor was ultimately accomplishing, in his estimation, was to come up with clever ways to appropriate the fruits of the *real* labor done by others. But that still leaves us with the same problem of how to distinguish "real" value-creating work from its opposite. If giving someone a haircut is providing a valuable service, why is providing advice on their investment portfolio not?

Yet Rupert's feelings were not unusual. He might have been unusual in framing them explicitly in terms of the labor theory of value, but he was expressing an uneasiness that many of those working in finance and related fields clearly do feel. Presumably, he had to turn to such theories because mainstream economics just didn't give him much to work with. According to the prevailing view among contemporary economists, since value is ultimately subjective, there's simply no way to justify such feelings. Everyone should therefore withhold judgment and operate on the assumption that, if there's a market for a given good or service (and in this, they would include financial services), then it's clearly valuable to someone, and that's all one needs to know. Up to a point, as we've seen, most workers would really appear to agree with the economists on principle, at least when it comes to the tastes and proclivities of the general public; but when it comes to their own jobs, their experience often glaringly contradicts the idea that the market can always be trusted in such matters. After all, there's a market in labor as well. If the market were always right, then someone being paid $40,000 to play computer games and gossip with old friends on WhatsApp all day would have to accept that the service he provides for the company by playing computer games and gossiping was actually worth $40,000. It clearly is not. So markets can't always be right. It follows that, if the market can get things so wrong in the one area the worker knows best, then surely she cannot just blandly assume the market can be trusted to assess the true value of goods and services in those areas where she lacks firsthand information.

Anyone who has a bullshit job, or knows someone who has a bullshit job, is aware, then, that the market is not an infallible arbiter of value. The problem is that nothing else is, either. Questions of value are always at least a little murky. Most people would agree that some companies might just as well not exist, but it's more likely to be based on some kind of gut instinct than anything they can articulate precisely. If I had to tease out the prevailing, unstated common sense, for a first pass, anyway, I would say that most people seem to operate with a combination of Tom's and Rupert's positions: that when a good or service answers a demand or otherwise improves people's lives, then it can be considered genuinely valuable, but when it merely serves to *create* demand, either by making people feel they are fat and ugly, or luring them into debt and then charging interest, it is not. This seems reasonable enough. But it still doesn't answer the question of what it means to "improve people's lives," and on that, of course, rests everything.

how most people in contemporary society do accept the notion of a social value that can be distinguished from economic value, even if it is very difficult to pin down what it is

So we are back, again, to theories of value. What can actually be said to improve people's lives?

In economics, theories of value have largely served as a way to explain commodity prices: the price of a loaf of bread will fluctuate according to the contingencies of supply and demand, but that price will always gravitate around some kind of center that seems the natural price a loaf of bread *should* have. In the Middle Ages, this was seen explicitly as a moral question: How can one determine the "just price" of a commodity? If a merchant raised prices during wartime, at what point was he paying himself legitimate hazard pay, and at what point was he just gouging? One popular example invoked by jurists at the time was a prisoner living on bread and water who traded his fortune to another prisoner for a boiled egg. Could this really be considered a free choice? Should such a contract be considered enforceable once both prisoners were released?

So the idea that the market can undervalue or overvalue things has been with us for a very long time. It's still an inherent part of our common sense, otherwise it would be impossible for anyone to ever say they were ripped off or got an especially good deal—even if no one has ever managed to come up with a reliable formula to calculate exactly what the "real" value of any given commodity should be, and therefore, just how badly one was ripped off or just how good a deal one really got. There are too many factors to take into consideration, and many—sentimental value, individual or subcultural taste—clearly can't be quantified. If anything is surprising, it's the dogged insistence of so many economists, amateur and otherwise, that it *should* be possible to do so.

Many hold that all those other forms of value are somehow illusory, or irrelevant to market concerns. Economists, for instance, will often take the position that, since value is ultimately just utility, commodity prices will gravitate around their real market value over time—even if this comes down to a purely circular proposition that whatever price a commodity tends to gravitate around over time must be its real market value. Marxists and other anticapitalists have often been known to take an even more extreme position, insisting that since capitalism is a total system, anyone who imagines she is operating outside it or pursuing values other than those created by the system is fooling herself. Often, when I present the concept of bullshit jobs in radical forums, someone awash in Marxist theory will instantly stand up to declare I have it wrong: maybe some workers think their work is useless, but that work must be producing profits for capitalism, which is all that matters under the present capitalist system.[4] Others, even more finely attuned to the niceties of such matters, will explain that clearly I am really talking about the difference between what Marx terms "productive" and "unproductive" labor—by which he meant labor that is either productive or unproductive *for capitalists*. Productive labor yields some kind of surplus value that capitalists can extract in profits; other labor is at best "reproductive"—that is, like housework or education (these are always put forward as the primary examples), such tasks perform the necessary second-order work of keeping workers alive and raising new generations of workers so that in the future they can, in turn, do the "real" work of being exploited.[5]

It is certainly true that capitalists themselves will often see things in this way. Business lobbies, for instance, are notorious for urging governments to treat schools primarily as places for training future employees. It might seem a little strange seeing the same logic coming from anticapitalists, but, in a way, it makes sense; it's a means of saying that half measures will never work. For instance, a well-meaning liberal who buys fair trade coffee and sponsors a float in the Gay Pride Parade isn't really challenging power structures of power and injustice in the world in any significant way, but, ultimately, just reproducing them on another level. This is an important point to make—sanctimonious liberals are irritating and deserve to be reminded of this—but the problem, at least for me, is the leap from saying that *from the perspective of capitalism*, a mother's love or a teacher's labors have no meaning except as a means of reproducing the labor force, and the assumption that therefore any other perspective on the matter is necessarily irrelevant, illusory, or incorrect. Capitalism is not a single totalizing system that shapes and embraces every aspect of our existence. It's not even clear it makes sense to speak of "capitalism" at all (Marx, for instance, never really did), implying as it does that "capitalism" is a set of abstract ideas that have somehow come to take material form in factories and offices. The world is more complicated and messy than that. Historically, the factories and offices emerged first, long before anyone knew quite what to call them, and to this day, they operate on multiple contradictory logics and purposes. Similarly, value itself is a constant political argument. No one is ever quite sure what it is.

■ ■ ■

In English, as currently spoken, we tend to make a distinction between "value" in the singular, as in the value of gold, pork bellies, antiques, and financial derivatives, and "values" in the plural: that is, family values, religious morality, political ideals, beauty, truth, integrity, and so on. Basically, we speak of "value" when talking about economic affairs, which usually comes down to all those human endeavors in which people are paid for their work or their actions are otherwise directed toward getting money. "Values" appear when that is not the case. For instance, housework and child care are, surely, the single most common forms of unpaid work. Hence, we constantly hear about the importance of "family values." But participating in church activities, charitable works, political volunteering, and most artistic and scientific pursuits are equally unremunerated. Even if a sculptor does end up becoming fabulously wealthy and marries a porn star, or a guru ends up in possession of a fleet of Rolls-Royces, most will consider his wealth legitimate only insofar as it is a kind of side effect, because originally, at least, he wasn't in it just for the money.

What money brings into the picture is the ability to make precise quantitative comparisons. Money makes it possible to say that this amount of pig iron is equivalent in value to that number of fruit drinks or pedicures or tickets to the Glastonbury music festival. This might sound obvious, but the implications are profound. It means the market value of a commodity is, precisely, the degree to which it can be compared to (and, hence, exchanged for) something else. This is exactly what is missing in the domain of "values"—it might sometimes be possible to argue that one work of art is more beautiful, or one religious devotee more pious than another, but it would be bizarre to ask how *much* more, to say that this monk is five times more pious than that one, or this Rembrandt is twice as lovely as that Monet.[6] It would be if anything even more absurd to try to come up with a mathematical formula to calculate just how much it would be legitimate to neglect one's family in pursuit of art, or break the law in the name of social justice. Obviously, people do make such decisions all the time, but by definition, they cannot be quantified.

In fact, one could even further say that is precisely the key to their value. Just as commodities have economic "value" *because* they can be compared precisely with other commodities, "values" are valuable because they cannot be compared with anything. They are each considered unique, incommensurable—in a word, priceless.

It seems to me that the words "value" and "values" have become our commonsense shorthand for how to think about such complicated questions. It's not a terrible one. Still, even this is more an ideal of how we like to think things should work than an accurate representation of how they actually do work. After all, it's not as if life is really divided between an "economy" where everyone thinks only about money and material self-interest, and a series of other spheres (politics, religion, family, and so on) where people behave entirely differently. Real motives are always mixed.

It's always important to emphasize here that for most of human history, it would never have occurred to anyone that it would be possible to even make such distinctions; the very idea of either pure self-interest, or pure selfless altruism, would have seemed equally bizarre—just as bizarre, in fact, as the idea of "selling one's time." Such concepts became possible only with the rise of impersonal markets across Eurasia roughly around 600 BC. The invention of coinage made it possible to create markets where strangers could interact with one another only with an eye to material advantage; wherever these cash markets appeared, whether in China, India, or the Mediterranean world, they were quickly followed by the birth of universal religions that in every case preached that material things were not important, and that the pious should give their goods selflessly to charity. But no attempt to create an absolute firewall between material selfishness and selfless idealism (value and values) has ever been successful; each always ends up leaking into the other. This leakage, it should be emphasized, is not just in one direction. Yes, it often turns out that artists, idealists, priests, and statesmen will turn out to be secretly pursuing some personal material advantage, or sometimes something even worse; but it is equally the case that businessmen will often take pride in their honor or integrity, or workers will agonize over whether their work actually does anyone any good.

This was certainly the primary consideration of those who wondered about the larger meaning of their jobs. In most of the testimonies I collected, "meaningful" was just a synonym for "helpful," and "valuable," for "beneficial." Let's take a glance at some of the ways people reflected on the value of their jobs:

> Car Salesman: I work for a large used-car finance company in the United States that caters to the subprime market. Oftentimes, I find myself wondering if my job really has any value at all besides to the owners of the company.
>
> Aerospace Engineer: The senior management are happy to work fifty to sixty hours a week (and encourage all their minions to do likewise) to be seen to be busy but without ever producing anything of value . . . True, if knowledge and new technology are created as

by-products, then one could argue that the job retains some value. In some instances of my job, this did occur, but it tended to be the exception rather than the rule.

Telemarketer: It's a job with no social value whatsoever. At least if you stack shelves at a supermarket, you are doing something that benefits people. Everybody needs groceries and the things supermarkets sell. In call center work, the calls are essentially time-wasting nuisance calls.

Freelance Academic Translator: Over the years, I have translated papers from just about every academic discipline—from ecology to corporate law, social science to computer science. The vast majority of it is of no discernible value to humanity whatsoever.

Pharmacist: I entered the medical profession under the assumption that my job would be meaningful and my work would be helpful. In reality, I've realized most of the medical field is a house of cards. I would contest the idea that doctors have genuinely helpful jobs.

Civil Servant: Neither of these jobs helped anyone in any way.[7]

None of this is likely to be news to most readers; this is the way pretty much anyone might talk about his job if he had to reflect on it in the abstract. As Eric's father remarked in chapter 3, after dutifully chewing Eric out as a "nonsensical idiot" for quitting such a high-paying job, "Well, what good could that job do for anyone anyway?"

The telemarketer cited above made an explicit appeal to the concept of "social value"—value to society as a whole. This concept came up periodically in other accounts as well:

Homeowner Association Manager: Managing homeowners associations is one hundred percent bullshit. Wealthy people buy a condo building with a bunch of other wealthy strangers, then hire someone else to manage and maintain it. The only reason this job exists is that the owners don't like or trust each other. I did this job for three years and never saw one hint of social value.

Or recall Nigel the Data Perfecter, already quoted in chapter 4, who spent hundreds of hours staring at company loyalty card information looking for nonexistent mistakes:

Data Perfecter: I really think that if we had been processing applications for something that had a more obvious social value—organ transplant registration, say, or tickets to Glastonbury—then it would have felt different.

It's interesting to juxtapose these two, because they show that for most people, "social value" isn't just about creating wealth or even leisure. It is equally about creating sociability. Organ donation allows people to save one another's lives; the Glastonbury music festival allows them to slog through the mud together smoking drugs and playing or listening to their favorite music—that is, to give one another joy and happiness. Such collective experiences can be considered of "obvious social value." In contrast, making it easier for rich people to avoid one another (it's a notorious thing that very wealthy people almost invariably dislike their neighbors), shows "not one hint of social value."

Now, "social value" of this sort clearly can't be measured, and undoubtedly if one were to sit down with any one of the workers whose testimonies I've cited, one would find that each had a slightly different idea of what was useful or valuable to society and what was not. Still, I suspect they would all have agreed on at least two things: first, that the most important things one gets out of a job are (1) money to pay the bills, and (2) the opportunity to make a positive contribution to the world. Second, that there is an inverse relation between the two. The more your work helps and benefits others, and the more social value you create, the less you are likely to be paid for it.

concerning the inverse relationship between the social value of work and the amount of money one is likely to be paid for it

Virtutum omnium pretium in ipsis est.

—Epictetus

I made this point in the original bullshit jobs article in 2013 because it had struck me during my experience with Occupy Wall Street two years earlier. One of the most frequently heard complaints from supporters of the movement—particularly the ones working too much to spend much time in the camps, but who could only show up for marches or to express support on the Web—ran along the lines of: "I wanted to do something useful with my life; work that had a positive effect on other people or, at the very least, wasn't hurting anyone. But the way this economy works, if you spend your working life caring for others, you'll end up so underpaid and so deeply in debt you won't be able to care for your own family." There was a deep and abiding sense of rage at the injustice of such arrangements.[8] I began to refer to it, mostly to myself, as the "revolt of the caring classes." At the same time, occupiers in Manhattan's Zuccotti Park regularly reported conversations with young Wall Street traders who'd drop by and say things to the effect of: "Look, I know you guys are right; I'm not contributing anything positive to the world, the system is corrupt, and I'm probably part of the problem. I'd quit tomorrow if you could show me how to live in New York on a less-than-six-figure salary."

Some of the testimonies we've already read echoed similar dilemmas: think here of Annie, who noted how many women taking care of preschoolers were ultimately forced to quit and find office jobs to pay the rent, or Hannibal, the medical researcher, who summed up his experience in the medical field with the formula "the amount of money I can charge for doing the work I do is almost perfectly inversely correlated with how useful it is."

That there's a real problem here can be demonstrated by a simple thought experiment proposed in the original 2013 piece: imagine if a certain class of people were to simply vanish. Let me expand on this for a moment. If we all woke up one morning and discovered that not only nurses, garbage collectors, and mechanics, but for that matter, bus drivers, grocery store workers, firefighters, or short-order chefs had been whisked away into another dimension, the results would be equally catastrophic. If elementary school teachers were to vanish, most schoolchildren would likely celebrate for a day or two, but the long-term effects would be if anything even more devastating. And while we can no doubt argue about the relative merits of death metal versus klezmer music, or romance novels versus science fiction, there's no doubt that even if the sudden disappearance of certain categories of authors, artists, or musicians left certain sectors of the population indifferent or even happy, for others the world would become a far more dismal and depressing place.[9]

The same cannot be said of hedge fund managers, political consultants, marketing gurus, lobbyists, corporate lawyers, or people whose job it is to apologize for the fact that the carpenter didn't come. As Finn said of his software licensing firm in chapter 4: "If I showed up on Monday and the building had disappeared, not only would society not care, I wouldn't, either." And there are certainly office buildings in the world—I'm sure anyone reading this book can think, just off the top of her head, of several—that, were they to simply vanish, would leave the world much better off.

Yet in many of these are precisely the people who get paid the very highest salaries.

In fact, it often happens that, at the very top of organizations, apparently crucial positions can go unfilled for long periods of time without there being any noticeable effect—even, on the organization itself. In recent years, Belgium has gone through a series of constitutional crises that have left it temporarily without a sitting government: no prime minister and no one in charge of health, transportation, or education. These crises have been known to continue for considerable periods of time—the record so far is 541 days—without there being any observable negative impact on health, transportation, or education. One has to imagine that if the situation were to endure for decades, it would make some sort of difference; but it's not clear how much of one or whether the positive effects would outweigh the negative ones.[10] Similarly, at time of writing, the Uber corporation, considered one of the world's most dynamic, has seen the resignation not only of its founder, Travis Kalanick, but a host of other top executives, with the result that it "is currently operating without a CEO, chief operating officer, chief financial officer, or chief marketing officer"— all without any apparent effect on day-to-day operations.[11]

Similarly, there's a reason why those who work in the financial sector, and who have extremely well-paid occupations more generally, almost never go on strike. As Rutger Bergman likes to point out, in 1970 there was a six-month bank strike in Ireland; rather than the economy grinding to a halt as the organizers had anticipated, most people simply continued to write checks, which began to circulate as a form of currency, but otherwise carried on much as they had before. Two years before, when garbage collectors had gone on strike for a mere ten days in New York, the city caved in to their demands because it had become uninhabitable.[12]

■ ■ ■

Very few economists have actually attempted to measure the overall social value of different professions; most would probably take the very idea as something of a fool's errand; but those who have tried tend to confirm that there is indeed an inverse relation between usefulness and pay. In a 2017 paper, US economists Benjamin B. Lockwood, Charles G. Nathanson, and E. Glen Weyl combed through the existing literature on the "externalities" (social costs) and "spillover effects" (social benefits) associated with a variety of highly paid professions, to see if it were possible to calculate how much each adds to or subtracts from the economy overall. They concluded that while in some cases—notably anything associated with creative industries—the values involved were just too subjective to measure, in other cases, a rough approximation was possible. Their conclusion: the most socially valuable workers whose contributions could be calculated are medical researchers, who add $9 of overall value to society for every $1 they are paid. The least valuable were those who worked in the financial sector, who, on average, subtract a net $1.80 in value from society for every $1 of compensation. (And, of course, workers in the financial sector are often compensated extremely well.)

Here was their overall breakdown:[13]

- researchers   +9
- schoolteachers   +1
- engineers   +.2
- consultants and IT professionals   0
- lawyers   −.2

- advertisers and marketing professionals   −.3
- managers   −.8
- financial sector   −1.5

This would certainly seem to confirm a lot of people's gut suspicions about the overall value of such professions, so it's nice to see it spelled out, but the authors' focus on the most highly paid professionals makes it of limited use for present purposes. Schoolteachers are probably the lowest-paid workers on the list, at least on average, and many researchers get by on very little, so the results certainly don't contradict a negative relation between pay and usefulness; but to get a real sense of the full gamut of employment, one needs a broader sample.

The closest I know to such a study that does use such a broader sample was one carried out by the New Economic Foundation in the United Kingdom, whose authors applied a method called "Social Return on Investment Analysis" to examine six representative occupations, three high-income, three low. Here's a summary of the results:

- city banker – yearly salary c. £5 million – estimated £7 of social value destroyed for every £1 earned;
- advertising executive – yearly salary c. £500,000, estimated £11.50 of social value destroyed per £1 paid;
- tax accountant – yearly salary c. £125,000, estimated £11.20 of social value destroyed per £1 paid;
- hospital cleaner – yearly income c. £13,000 (£6.26 per hour), estimated £10 of social value generated per £1 paid;
- recycling worker – yearly income c. £12,500 (£6.10 per hour) – estimated £12 in social value generated per £1 paid;
- nursery worker – salary c. £11,500 – estimated £7 in social value generated per £1 paid.[14]

The authors admit that many of their calculations are somewhat subjective, as all such calculations must be, and the study focuses only on the top and bottom of the income scale. As a result, it leaves out the majority of jobs discussed in this book, which are mostly midrange in pay, and in most cases, at least, the social benefit is neither positive nor negative but seems to hover around zero. Still, as far as it goes, it strongly confirms the general principle that the more one's work benefits others, the less one tends to be paid for it.

There are exceptions to this principle. Doctors are the most obvious. Physicians' salaries tend to the upper end of the scale, especially in America, yet they do seem to play an indisputably beneficial role. Yet even here, there are health professionals who would argue they're not as much exceptions as they might seem—such as the pharmacist cited a few pages back, who was convinced most doctors contribute very little to human health or happiness but are mainly just dispensers of placebos. This may or may not be the case; frankly, I don't have the competence to say; but if nothing else, the oft-cited fact that the overwhelming majority of improvement in longevity since 1900 is really due to hygiene, nutrition, and other public health improvements and not to improvements in medical treatment,[15] suggests a case could be made that the (very poorly paid) nurses and cleaners employed in a hospital are actually more responsible for positive health outcomes than the hospital's (very highly paid) physicians.

There are a smattering of other exceptions. Many plumbers and electricians, for instance, do quite well despite their usefulness; some low-paid work is fairly pointless—but in large measure, the rule does seem to hold true.[16]

The reasons for this inverse relation between social benefit and level of compensation, however, are quite another matter. None of the obvious answers seem to work. For instance: education levels are very important in determining salary levels, but if this were simply a matter of training and education, the American higher education system would hardly be in the state that it is, with thousands of exquisitely trained PhDs subsisting on adjunct teaching jobs that leave them well below the poverty line—even dependent on food stamps.[17] On the other hand, if we were simply talking about supply and demand, it would be impossible to understand why American nurses are paid so much less than corporate lawyers, despite the fact that the United States is currently experiencing an acute shortage of trained nurses and a glut of law school graduates.[18]

Whatever the reasons—and myself, I believe that class power and class loyalty have a great deal to do with it—what is perhaps most disturbing about the situation is the fact that so many people not only acknowledge the inverse relation but also feel this is how things ought to be. That virtue, as the ancient Stoics used to argue, should be its own reward.

Arguments like this have long been made about teachers. It's commonplace to hear that grade school or middle school teachers shouldn't be paid well, or certainly not as well as lawyers or executives, because one wouldn't want people motivated primarily by greed to be teaching children. The argument would make a certain amount of sense if it were applied consistently—but it never is. (I have yet to hear anyone make the same argument about doctors.)

One might even say that the notion that those who benefit society should not be paid too well is a perversion of egalitarianism.

Let me explain what I mean by this. The moral philosopher G. A. Cohen argued that a case could be made for equality of income for all members of society, based on the following logic (or, at least, this is my own bastardized summary): Why, he begins, might one pay certain people more than others? Normally, the justification is that some produce more or benefit society more than others. But then we must ask why they do so:

1. If some people are more talented than others (for example, have a beautiful singing voice, are a comic genius or a math whiz), we say they are "gifted." If someone has already received a benefit (a "gift"), then it makes no sense to give them an additional benefit (more money) for that reason.

2. If some people work harder than others, it is usually impossible to establish the degree to which this is because they have a greater *capacity* for work (a gift again), and the degree to which it is because they choose to work harder. In the former case, it would again make no sense to reward them further for having an innate advantage over others.

3. Even if it could be proved that some work harder than others purely out of choice, one would then have to establish whether they did so out of altruistic motives—that is, they produced more because they wished to benefit society—or out of selfish motives, because they sought a larger proportion for themselves.

4. In the former case, if they produced more because they were striving to increase social wealth, then giving them a disproportionate share of that wealth would contradict their purpose. It would only make moral sense to reward those driven by selfish motives.

5. Since human motives are generally shifting and confused, one cannot simply divide the workforce into egoists and altruists. One is left with the choice of either rewarding everyone who makes greater efforts, or not doing so. Either option means that some people's intentions will be frustrated. Altruists will be frustrated in their attempts to benefit society, while egoists will be frustrated in their attempts to benefit themselves. If one is forced to choose one or the other, it makes better moral sense to frustrate the egoists.

6. Therefore, people should not be paid more or otherwise rewarded for greater effort or productivity at work.[19]

The logic is impeccable. Many of the underlying assumptions could no doubt be challenged on a variety of grounds, but in this chapter, I'm not so much interested in whether there is, in fact, a moral case for equal distribution of income, as much as observing that in many ways, our society seems to have embraced in points 3 and 4—just without 1, 2, 5, or 6. Critically, it rejects the premise that it is impossible to sort workers by motives. One need only look at what sorts of careers a worker has chosen. Is there any reason a person might be doing this job *other* than the money? If so, then that person should be treated as if point 4 applies.

As a result, there is a sense that those who choose to benefit society, and especially those who have the gratification of *knowing* they benefit society, really have no business also expecting middle-class salaries, paid vacations, and generous retirement packages. By the same token, there is also a feeling that those who have to suffer from the knowledge they are doing pointless or even harmful work just for the sake of the money ought to be rewarded with more money for exactly that reason.

One sees this on the political level all the time. In the UK, for instance, eight years of "austerity" have seen effective pay cuts to almost all government workers who provide immediate and obvious benefits to the public: nurses, bus drivers, firefighters, railroad information booth workers, emergency medical personnel. It has come to the point where there are full-time nurses who are dependent on charity food banks. Yet creating this situation became such a point of pride for the party in power that Parliamentarians were known to give out collective cheers on voting down bills proposing to give nurses or police a raise. The same party took a notoriously indulgent view of the sharply rising compensation of those City bankers who had very nearly crashed the world economy a few years before. Yet that government remained highly popular. There is a sense, it would seem, that an ethos of collective sacrifice for the common good *should* fall disproportionately on those who are already, by their choice of work, engaged in sacrifice for the common good. Or who simply have the gratification of knowing their work is productive and useful.

This can make sense only if one first assumes that work—more specifically, paid work—is a value in itself; indeed, so much a value in itself that either the motives of the person taking the job, or the effects of the work, are at best secondary considerations. The flip side of the left-wing protest marchers waving signs demanding "More Jobs" is the right-wing onlooker muttering "Get a job!" as they pass by. There seems a broad consensus not so much even that work is good but that *not* working is very bad; that anyone who is not slaving away harder than he'd like at something he doesn't especially enjoy is a bad person, a scrounger, a skiver, a contemptible parasite unworthy of sympathy or public relief. This feeling is echoed as much in the liberal politician's protest against the sufferings of "hardworking people" (what about those who work with only moderate intensity?) as it is in conservative protests about skivers and "welfare queens." Even more strikingly, the same values are now applied at the top. No longer do we hear much about the idle rich—this is not because they don't exist, but because their idleness is no longer celebrated. During the Great Depression

215

of the 1930s, impoverished audiences liked to watch high society movies about the romantic escapades of playboy millionaires. Nowadays they are more likely to be regaled with stories of heroic CEOs and their dawn-to-midnight workaholic schedules.[20] In England, newspapers and magazines even write similar things about the royal family, who, we now learn, spend so many hours a week preparing for and executing their ritual functions that they barely have time to have a private life at all.

Many testimonies remarked on this work-as-an-end-in-itself morality. Clement had what he described as "a BS job evaluating grants at a public university in the Midwest." During his off-hours, which was most of them, he spent a lot of time on the Web familiarizing himself with alternative political perspectives and eventually came to realize much of the money flowing through his office was intimately tied to the US war efforts in Iraq and Afghanistan. He quit, and, to the surprise and consternation of his coworkers, took a significantly lower-paying job with the local municipality. There, he said, the work is harder, but "at least some of it is interesting and helpful to humans."

One of the things that puzzled Clement was the way that everyone at his old job felt they had to pretend to one another they were overwhelmed by their responsibilities, despite the obvious fact that they had very little to do:

> Clement: My colleagues often discussed how busy things would get and how hard they work, even though they would routinely be gone at two or three in the afternoon. What is the name for this kind of public denial of the crystal-clear reality?
>
> My mind keeps going back to the pressure to value ourselves and others on the basis of how hard we work at something we'd rather not be doing. I believe this attitude exists in the air around us. We sniff it into our noses and exhale it as a social reflex in small-talk; it is one of the guiding principles of social relations here: if you're not destroying your mind and body via paid work, you're not living right. Are we to believe that we are sacrificing for our kids, or something, who we don't get to see because we're at work all fucking day!?

Clement felt this kind of pressure was especially acute in what he described as the German-Protestant-inflected culture of the American Midwest. Others spoke of Puritanism, but the feeling does not appear to be limited to Protestant or North Atlantic environments. It exists everywhere; the differences are more a matter of varying degrees and intensities. And if the value of work is in part the fact that it's "something we'd rather not be doing," it stands to reason that anything we would wish to be doing is less like work and more like play, or a hobby, or something we might consider doing in our spare time, and therefore less deserving of material reward. Probably we shouldn't be paid for it at all.

This certainly resonates with my own experience. Most academics are first drawn to their careers because they love knowledge and are excited by ideas. After all, pretty much anyone capable of spending seven years earning a PhD knows that she could just as easily have spent three years in law school and come out with a starting salary many times higher. Yet despite that, when two academics in the same department hobnob over coffee, a love of knowledge or excitement about ideas is likely to be the last thing they express. Instead, they will almost invariably complain about how overwhelmed they are with administrative responsibilities. True, this is partly because academics actually are expected to spend less and less of their time reading and writing, and more and more time dealing with administrative problems,[21] but even if one is pursuing some exciting new intellectual discovery, it would be seen as inconsiderate to act as if one was enjoying one's work when others clearly aren't. Some academic environments are more anti-intellectual than others. But everywhere, at the very least, there is a sense that the pleasurable aspects of one's calling, such as thinking, were not really what one is being paid for; they were better seen as occasional indulgences one is granted in recognition of one's real work, which is largely about filling out forms.

Academics aren't paid for writing or reviewing research articles, but at least the universities that do pay them acknowledge, however reluctantly, that research is part of their job description. In the business world, it's worse. For instance, Geoff Shullenberger, a writing professor at New York University, reacted to my original 2013 essay with a blog pointing out that many businesses now feel that if there's work that's gratifying in any way at all, they really shouldn't have to pay for it:

> For Graeber, bullshit jobs carry with them a moral imperative: "If you're not busy all the time doing something, anything—doesn't really matter what it is—you're a bad person." But the flipside of that logic seems to be: if you actually like doing X activity, if it is valuable, meaningful, and carries intrinsic rewards for you, it is wrong for you to expect to be paid (well) for it; you should give it freely, even (especially) if by doing so you are allowing others to profit. In other words, we'll make a living from you doing what you love (for free), but we'll keep you in check by making sure you have to make a living doing what you hate.

Shullenberger gave the example of translation work. Translating a paragraph or document from one language to another—particularly from a dry business document—is not a task that many people would do for fun; still, one can imagine some reasons people might do it other than the money. (They are trying to perfect their language abilities, for example.) Therefore, most executives' first instinct, upon hearing that translation work is required, is to try to see if they can't find some way to make someone do it for free. Yet these very same executives are willing to shell out handsome salaries for "Vice Presidents for Creative Development" and the like, who do absolutely nothing. (In fact, such executives might themselves *be* Vice Presidents for Creative Development, and do nothing at all other than trying to figure out how to get others to do work for free.)

Shullenberger speaks of an emerging "voluntariat," with capitalist firms increasingly harvesting the results not of paid labor but of unpaid interns, internet enthusiasts, activists, volunteers, and hobbyists, and "digitally sharecropping" the results of popular enthusiasm and creativity to privatize and market the results.[22] The free software industry, perversely enough, has become a paradigm in this respect. The reader may recall Pablo, who introduced the notion of duct taping in chapter 2: software engineering work was divided between the interesting and challenging work of developing core technologies, and the tedious labor of "applying duct tape" to allow different core technologies to work together, because the designers had never bothered to think about their compatibility. His main point, though, was that, increasingly, open source means that all the really engaging tasks are done for free:

> Pablo: Where two decades ago, companies dismissed open source software and developed core technologies in-house, nowadays companies rely heavily on open source and employ software developers almost entirely to apply duct tape on core technologies they get for free.
>
> In the end, you can see people doing the nongratifying duct-taping work during office hours and then doing gratifying work on core technologies during the night.
>
> This leads to an interesting vicious circle: given that people choose to work on core technologies for free, no company is investing in those technologies. The underinvestment means that the core technologies are often unfinished, lacking quality, have a lot of rough edges, bugs, etc. That, in turn, creates need for duct tape and thus proliferation of duct-taping jobs.

Paradoxically, the more that software engineers collaborate online to do free creative labor simply for the love of doing it, as a gift to humanity, the less incentive they have to make them compatible with other such software, and the more those same engineers will have to be employed in their day jobs fixing the damage—doing the sort of maintenance work that no one would be willing to do for free. He concludes:

> Pablo: My guess is that we are going to see the same dynamics in other industries as well. E.g., if people are willing to write news articles for free, nobody would pay professional journalists. Instead, the money will be redirected to the PR and advertisement industries. Eventually the quality of news will decrease because of lack of funding.

One could argue that this has already begun to happen, as fewer and fewer newspapers and news services employ actual reporters. My purpose here, though, is not to unravel the complex and often arcane labor arrangements that grow out of this ethos, but simply to document the existence of the ethos itself. Attitudes toward labor have changed. Why? How have so many humans reached the point where they accept that even miserable, unnecessary work is actually morally superior to no work at all?

Here we must consider the history of changing ideas about work itself.

on the theological roots of our attitudes toward labor

Man is made to be in the visible universe an image and likeness of God Himself, and he is placed in it in order to subdue the earth . . . Only man is capable of work, and only man works, at the same time by work occupying his existence on earth.

—Pope John Paul II, *Laborem Exercens* (*On Human Labor*), 1981

We may define labor as any exertion of mind or body undergone partly or wholly with a view to some good other than the pleasure derived from the work.

—Alfred Marshall, *Principles of Economics*, 1890

What is "work"? Normally we see it as the opposite of play. Play, in turn, is defined most often as action that one does for its own sake, for pleasure, or just for the sake of doing it. Work, therefore, is activity—typically, onerous and repetitive—that one does not carry out for its own sake, and that one probably would never carry out for its own sake, or if one did certainly not for very long, but engages in only to accomplish something else (to obtain food, for example, or build a mausoleum).

Most languages have some word that translates at least roughly as "work," but the precise borders between what we'd designate "work," "play," "teaching," "learning," "ritual," or "nurturance" tend to vary a great deal from one culture to another. The particular tradition that has come to shape sensibilities about work in most parts of the world today harkens back to the Eastern Mediterranean, where it is first documented in the early chapters of the book of Genesis, and in the works of the Greek epic poet Hesiod. In both the story of the Garden of Eden and in the myth of Prometheus, the fact that humans have to work is seen as their punishment for having defied a divine Creator, but at the same time, in both, work itself, which gives humans the ability to produce food, clothing, cities, and ultimately our own material universe, is presented as a more modest instantiation of the divine power of Creation itself. We are, as the existentialists liked to put it, condemned to be free, forced to wield the divine power of creation against our will, since most of us would really rather be naming the animals in Eden, dining on nectar and ambrosia at feasts on Mount Olympus, or watching cooked geese fly into our waiting gullets in the Land of Cockaygne, than having to cover ourselves with cuts and calluses to coax sustenance from the soil.

Now, one could argue that this is simply in each case a poetic extrapolation of the two key aspects of what has become our common definition of work: first, that it is something no one would ordinarily wish to be doing for its own sake (hence, punishment); second, that we do it anyway to accomplish something beyond the work itself (hence, creation). But the fact that this "something beyond" should be conceived as "creation" is not self-evident. In fact, it's somewhat odd. After all, most work can't be said to "create" anything; most of it is a matter of maintaining and rearranging things.[23] Consider a coffee cup. We "produce" it once. We wash it a thousand times. Even work we think of as "productive"—growing potatoes, forging a shovel, assembling a computer—could just as easily be seen as tending, transforming, reshaping, and rearranging materials and elements that already exist.

This is why I would insist our concept of "production," and our assumption that work is defined by its "productivity," is essentially theological. The Judeo-Christian God created the universe out of nothing. (This in itself is slightly unusual: most Gods work with existing materials.) His latter-day worshippers, and their descendants, have come to think of themselves as cursed to imitate God in this regard. The sleight of hand involved, the way that most human labor, which cannot in any sense be considered "production," is thus made to disappear, is largely effected through gender. In the familiar lines from the story of the Fall, from the book of Genesis, God condemns men to till the soil ("By the sweat of your brow you will eat your food") and women to bear children in similarly unhappy circumstances ("I will make your pains in childbearing very severe; with painful labor you will give birth to children".)[24] Male "productive" labor is thus being framed here as the equivalent of childbirth, which, from a male point of view (not so much from a female one, but it is very much a male point of view being presented here), can seem about as close to pure creation ex nihilio—the infant appearing fully formed apparently out of nowhere—that human beings can perform.

Yet it is also painful "labor."

This conception is still with us, for instance, in the way social scientists speak of "production" and "reproduction." Etymologically, the English verb "produce" derives from the Latin *producere*, "to bring forth," or "put out," as one might still say "She produced a wallet from her handbag." Both the words "production" and "reproduction" are based on the same core metaphor: in the one case, objects seem to jump, fully formed, out of factories; in the other, babies seem to jump, fully formed, out of women's bodies. In neither case, of course, is this actually true. But as in so many patriarchal social orders, men like to conceive of themselves as doing socially, or culturally, what they like to think of women as doing naturally. "Production" is thus simultaneously a variation on a male fantasy of childbirth, and of the action of a male Creator God who similarly created the entire universe through the sheer power of his mind and words, just as men see themselves as creating the world from their minds and brawn, and see that as the essence of "work," leaving to women most of the actual labor of tidying and maintaining things to make this illusion possible.

on the origins of the northern european notion of paid labor as necessary to the full formation of an adult human being

It's essential to emphasize the theological origins of this sort of thought. Most of the core assumptions of modern economics originally trace back to theological arguments: for instance, Saint Augustine's argument that we are cursed with infinite desires in a finite world and thus naturally in a situation of competition with one another—which reappears in secular form in the seventeenth century in Thomas Hobbes—has become the basis for the assumption that rational human action is largely a matter of "economizing," the optimal allocation of scarce resources by rational actors in a competitive world.

Of course, in the European Middle Ages, when economic matters fell under the jurisdiction of church law, no one really pretended these questions were not theological. Still, that period introduced a further element, not explicitly theological, the importance of which for later conceptions of labor can hardly be overstated. This is the notion of "service."[25] It is very much a Northern European idea.

In theory, feudal society was a vast system of service: not only serfs but also lower-ranking feudal lords "served" higher ones, just as higher ones provided feudal service to the king. However, the form of service that had the most important and pervasive influence on most people's lives was not feudal service but what historical sociologists have called "life-cycle" service. Essentially, almost everyone was expected to spend roughly the first seven to fifteen years of his or her working life as a servant in someone else's household. Most of us are familiar with how this worked itself out within craft guilds, where teenagers would first be assigned to master craftsmen as apprentices, and then become journeymen, but only when they achieved the status of master craftsmen would they have the means to marry and set up their own households and shops, and take apprentices of their own. In fact, the system was in no sense limited to artisans. Even peasants normally expected to spend their teenage years onward as "servants in husbandry" in another farm household, typically, that of someone just slightly better off. Service was expected equally of girls and boys (that's what milkmaids were: daughters of peasants during their years of service), and was usually expected even of the elite. The most familiar example here would be pages, who were apprentice knights, but even noblewomen, unless they were at the very top of the hierarchy, were expected to spend their adolescence as ladies-in-waiting—that is, servants who would "wait upon" a married noblewoman of slightly higher rank, attending to her privy chamber, toilette, meals, and so forth, even as they were also "waiting" for such time as they, too, were in a position to marry and become the lady of an aristocratic household themselves. Royal courts similarly had "gentleman waiters," who attended to the privy chamber of the king.[26]

In the case of young nobles, "waiting" largely meant waiting for an inheritance—or for one's parents to decide one was old and sufficiently well groomed to merit a transfer of title and property. This might be the case for servants in husbandry as well, but generally speaking, among commoners, servants were paid and expected to save a good share of their wages. So they were acquiring both the knowledge and experience needed to manage a household, shop, or farm, and also the wealth needed to acquire one—or, in the case of women, to be able to offer a dowry to a suitor able to do the same. As a result, medieval people married late, usually around thirty, which meant that "youth"—adolescence, a time when one was expected to be at least a little wild, lustful, and rebellious—would often last a good fifteen to twenty years.

The fact that servants were paid is crucial because it meant that while wage labor did exist in Northern Europe, centuries before the dawn of capitalism, almost everyone in the Middle Ages assumed that it was something respectable people engaged in only in the first phase of their working life. Service and wage labor were largely identified; even in Oliver Cromwell's time, day laborers could still be referred to as "servants." Service, in turn, was seen above all as the process whereby young people learned not only their trade, but the "manners," the comportment appropriate to a responsible adult. As one oft-quoted account by a Venetian visitor to England put it around 1500:

> The want of affection in the English is strongly manifested toward their children; for after having kept them at home till they arrive at the age of seven or nine years at the utmost, they put them out, both males and females, to hard service in the households of other people, binding them generally for seven or nine years.[27] And these are called

apprentices, and during that time they perform all the most menial offices; and few are born who are exempted from this fate, for everyone, however rich he may be, sends away his children into the houses of others, whilst he, in return, receives those of strangers into his own. And on inquiring their reason for this severity, they answered that they did it in order that their children learn better manners.[28]

Manners, in the medieval and Early Modern sense, went well beyond etiquette; the term referred to one's manner of acting and being in the world more generally, one's habits, tastes, and sensibilities. Young people were expected to work for wages in the households of others because— unless one was intending to join the clergy and become a scholar—what we would consider paid work, and what we would consider education, were seen as largely the same thing, and both were a process of learning self-discipline, about "achiev[ing] mastery of one's baser desires"[29] and learning how to behave like a proper self-contained adult.

This is not to say that medieval and Early Modern culture had no place for the rambunctiousness of youth. To the contrary. Young people, even though in service in others' households, typically also created an alternative culture of their own, centered on youth lodges with names such as the Lords of Misrule and Abbots of Unreason, which sometimes were even allowed to take temporary power during the popular festivals. Yet ultimately, disciplined work under the direction of an adult head of a household was to transform the young into self-disciplined adults, at which point they would no longer have to work for others but would be self-employed.

■ ■ ■

As a result of such arrangements, attitudes toward work in medieval Northern Europe look quite different from those that prevailed in the classical world, or even, as we've seen, the later Mediterranean. (The Venetian ambassador was scandalized by English practices.) Most of our sources from Greek and Roman antiquity are male aristocrats who saw physical labor or service as fit only for women or slaves. Work, Aristotle insisted, in no sense makes you a better person; in fact, it makes you a worse one, since it takes up so much time, thus making it difficult to fulfill one's social and political obligations. As a result, the punishment aspect of work tended to be emphasized in classical literature, while the creative and godlike aspect was largely seen as falling to those male heads of household rich enough that they didn't actually have to get their hands dirty but could tell others what to do. In Northern Europe in the Middle Ages and the Renaissance, almost everyone was expected to get their hands dirty at some point or another.[30] As a result, work, especially paid work, was seen as transformative. This is important because it means that certain key aspects of what was to become known as the Protestant work ethic were already there, long before the emergence of Protestantism.

how, with the advent of capitalism, work came to be seen in many quarters either as a means of social reform or ultimately as a virtue in its own right, and how laborers countered by embracing the labor theory of value

> No adequate history of the meanings of work has been written.
> —C. Wright Mills, *White Collar: The American Middle Classes*, 1951

All this was to change with the advent of capitalism. By "capitalism," here I am referring not to markets—these had long existed—but to the gradual transformation of relations of service into permanent relations of wage labor: that is, a relation between some people who owned capital, and others who did not and thus were obliged to work for them. What this meant in human terms was, first of all, that millions of young people found themselves trapped in permanent social adolescence. As the guild structures broke down, apprentices could become journeymen, but journeymen could no longer become masters, which meant that, in traditional terms, they would not be a position to marry and start families of their own. They were expected to live their entire lives effectively as unfinished human beings.[31] Inevitably, many began to rebel, give up on the interminable waiting, and began marrying early, abandoning their masters to set up cottages and families of their own—which, in turn, set off a wave of moral panic among the emerging employing class very reminiscent of later moral panics about teenage pregnancy. The following is from *The Anatomie of Abuses*, a sixteenth-century manifesto by a Puritan named Phillip Stubbes:

> And besides this, you shall have every saucy boy, of ten, fourteen, sixteen, or twenty years of age, catch up a woman, and marry her, without any fear of God at all . . . or, which is more, without any respect how they may live together, with sufficient maintenance for their callings and estate. No, no! It maketh no matter for these things, so he have his pretty pussy to huggle withall, for that is the only thing he desireth. Then build they up a cottage, though but of elder poles, in every lane end almost, where they live as beggers all their life after. This filleth the land with such store of mendicants . . . that in short time it is like to grow to great poverty and scarceness.[32]

It was at this moment that one can speak of the birth of the proletariat as a class—a term derived appropriately enough from a Latin word for "those who produce offspring," since in Rome, the poorest citizens who did not have enough wealth to tax were useful to the government only by producing sons who could be drafted into the army.

Stubbes's *Anatomie of Abuses* might be considered the very manifesto of the Puritan "Reformation of Manners," as they called it, which was very much a middle-class vision, with an equally jaundiced view of both the carnality of court life, and the "heathenish rioting" of popular entertainment. It also shows it's impossible to understand debates about Puritanism and the origins of the Protestant work ethic without understanding this larger context of the decline of life-cycle service and creation of a proletariat. English Calvinists (actually they were only called "Puritans" by those who disliked them) tended to be drawn from the class of master craftsmen and "improving" farmers who were employing this newly created proletariat, and their "Reformation of Manners" took special aim at popular festivals, gaming, drinking, "and all the annual rites of misrule when youth temporarily inverted the social order."[33] The Puritan ideal was for all such "masterless men" to be rounded up, and placed under the stern discipline of a pious household whose patriarch could direct them in work and prayer. But this was just the first of a long history of attempts to reform the manners of the lower classes that has followed, from Victorian workhouses where the poor were taught proper time discipline, to workfare and similar government programs today.

Why, starting in the sixteenth century, did the middle classes suddenly develop such an interest in reforming the moral comportment of the poor—a subject they had not previously found of much interest one way or the other? This has always been something of a historical mystery. In the context of life-cycle service, though, it actually makes perfect sense. The poor were seen as frustrated adolescents. Work—and specifically, paid labor under the eye of a master—had traditionally been the means by which such adolescents learned how to be proper, disciplined, self-contained adults. While in practical terms Puritans and other pious reformers could no longer promise much to the poor—certainly not adulthood as it used to be conceived, as freedom from the need to work under the orders of others—they substituted charity, discipline, and a renewed infusion of theology. Work, they taught, was both punishment and redemption. Work was self-mortification and as such had value in itself, even beyond the wealth it produced, which was merely a sign of God's favor (and not to be enjoyed too much.)[34]

After the industrial revolution, the celebration of work was taken up with renewed vigor by the Methodists, but even more, if anything, in educated middle-class circles that didn't see themselves as particularly religious. Perhaps its greatest advocate was Thomas Carlyle, an enormously popular essayist, who, concerned with the decline of morality in the new Age of Mammon, proposed what he called a Gospel of Work. Carlyle insisted that labor should not be viewed as a way to satisfy material needs, but as the essence of life itself; God had intentionally created the world unfinished so as to allow humans the opportunity to complete His work through labor:

> A man perfects himself by working . . . Consider how, even in the meanest sorts of Labour, the whole soul of man is composed into a kind of real harmony, the instant he sets himself to work! Doubt, Desire, Sorrow, Remorse, Indignation, Despair itself, all these like hell-dogs lie beleaguering the soul of the poor day-worker, as of every man; but he bends himself with free valour against his task, and all these are stilled, all these shrink murmuring far off into their caves. The man is now a man. The blessed glow of Labour in him, is it not purifying fire, wherein all poison is burnt up?
>
> All true Work is sacred; in all true Work, were it but true hand-labour, there is something of divineness . . . Oh brother, if this is not "worship," then I say, the more the pity for worship; for this is the noblest thing yet discovered under God's sky. Who art thou that complainest of thy life of toil? Complain not. Look up, my wearied brother; see thy fellow Workmen there, in God's Eternity, sacred Band of the Immortals, celestial Bodyguard of the Empire of Mankind.[35]

Carlyle was ultimately led to the conclusion so many reach today: that if work is noble, then the most noble work should *not* be compensated, since it is obscene to put a price on something of such absolute value ("the 'wages' of every noble Work do yet lie in Heaven or else nowhere")[36]— though he was generous enough to allow that the poor did need to be afforded "fair wages" in order to obtain the means to live.

Such arguments were immensely popular in middle-class circles. Unsurprisingly, the worker's movement beginning to form in Europe around Carlyle's time was less impressed. Most workers involved in Luddism, Chartism, Ricardian Socialism, and the various early strains of English radicalism would probably have agreed there was something divine in work, but that divine quality lay not in its effect on the soul and body—as laborers, they knew better than that—but that it was the source of wealth; everything that made rich and powerful people rich and powerful was, in fact, created by the efforts of the poor. Adam Smith and David Ricardo, the founders of British economic science, had embraced the labor theory of value—as did many of the new industrialists, since it allowed them to distinguish themselves from the landed gentry, whom they represented as mere idle consumers—but the theory was almost instantly taken up by Socialists and labor organizers and turned against the industrialists themselves. Before long economists began seeking for alternatives on explicitly political grounds. Already in 1832—that is, thirty-five years before the appearance of Marx's *Capital*—we encounter warnings like the following: "That labor is the sole source of wealth seems to be a doctrine as dangerous as it is false, as it unhappily affords a handle to those who would represent all property as belonging to the working classes, and the share which is received by others as a robbery or fraud upon them."[37]

By the 1830s, many were, in fact, proclaiming exactly that. It is important to emphasize just how universally accepted the labor theory of value became in the generations immediately following the industrial revolution—even before the dissemination of Marx's works, which gave such arguments a renewed energy and a more sophisticated theoretical language. It was particularly powerful in Britain's American colonies. The mechanics and tradesmen who became the foot soldiers of the American War of Independence represented themselves as producers of the wealth that they saw the British crown as looting, and after the Revolution, many turned the same language against would-be capitalists. "The solid rock on which their idea of the good society rested," as one historian put it, "was that labor created all wealth."[38] The word "capitalist" at that time was largely a term of abuse. When US President Abraham Lincoln delivered his first annual message to Congress in 1861, for instance, he included the following lines, which, radical though they seem to a contemporary ear, where really just a reflection of the common sense of the time:[39] "Labor is prior to and independent of capital. Capital is only the fruit of labor, and could never have existed if labor had not first existed. Labor is the superior of capital, and deserves much the higher consideration."

Still, Lincoln went on to insist, what made the United States different from Europe, indeed what made its democracy possible, was that it lacked a permanent population of wage laborers:

"There is not of necessity any such thing as the free hired laborer being fixed to that condition for life. Many independent men everywhere in these States a few years back in their lives were hired laborers. The prudent, penniless beginner in the world labors for wages a while, saves a surplus with which to buy tools or land for himself, then labors on his own account another while, and at length hires another new beginner to help him."

In other words, even though he didn't put it quite this way, Lincoln argued that, owing to America's rapid economic and territorial expansion, it was possible there to maintain something like the old medieval system, in which everyone started out working for others, then used the proceeds of wage labor to set up shop, or buy a farm (on land seized from its indigenous inhabitants), and then eventually themselves play the capitalist, employing young people as laborers in their own right.

This was definitely the ideal in pre–Civil War America—though Lincoln was from Illinois, not too far from the frontier; workingmen's associations in the old cities of the Eastern Seaboard were already taking issue with arguments like this.[40] What's significant here is that Lincoln felt he had to accept the labor theory of value as the framework of debate. Everyone did. This remained the case at least until the end of the century. It was true even along the Western frontier, where one might have imagined European-style class tensions were least likely to flare up. In 1880 a Protestant "home missionary" who had spent some years traveling along the Western frontier reported that: "You can hardly find a group of ranchmen or miners from Colorado to the Pacific who will not have on their tongue's end the labor slang of Denis Kearney, the infidel ribaldry of [atheist pamphleteer] Robert Ingersoll, the Socialistic theories of Karl Marx."[41]

Certainly a detail left out of every cowboy movie I ever saw! (The notable exception being *The Treasure of the Sierra Madre*, which does indeed begin with a scene where John Huston, as a miner, explains the labor theory of value to Humphrey Bogart.)[42]

concerning the key flaw in the labor theory of value as it became popular in the nineteenth century, and how the owners of capital exploited that flaw

> Virtually any form of labor can be described as "caring" in the sense that it results in activities that help meet the needs of others.
> —Nancy Folbre

I turned to America for a reason. The United States plays a key role in our story. Nowhere was the principle that all wealth derives from labor more universally accepted as ordinary common sense, yet nowhere, too, was the counterattack against this common sense so calculated, so sustained, and so ultimately effective. By the early decades of the twentieth century, when the first cowboy movies were being made, this work was largely complete, and the idea that ranch hands had once been avid readers of Marx would have seemed as ridiculous as it would to most Americans today. Even more important, this counteroffensive laid the groundwork for the apparently bizarre attitudes toward work, largely emanating from North America, that we can still observe spreading across the world, with pernicious results.

Lincoln was no doubt overstating his case, but it is nonetheless true that in the "Artisans Republic" that existed before the Civil War, something roughly like the older tradition of life-cycle service did endure—with the notable difference that most hired laborers were not called "servants" and did not live in their employers' homes. Politicians did see this as the ideal and legislated accordingly. Would-be capitalists were not granted the right to create limited-liability corporations unless they could prove doing so would constitute a clear and incontestable "public benefit" (in other words, the notion of social value not only existed but was inscribed in law)—this usually meant, in practice, only if they were proposing to dig a canal or build a railroad.[43] Apart from the atheists along the frontier, much of this anticapitalist feeling was justified on religious grounds; popular Protestantism, drawing on its Puritan roots, not only celebrated work, but embraced the belief that, as my fellow anthropologists Dimitra Doukas and Paul Durrenberger have put it, "work was a sacred duty and a claim to moral and political superiority over the idle rich"—a more explicitly religious version of Carlyle's "gospel of work" (most historians simply call it "producerism"), which insisted that work was both a value in itself *and* the only real producer of value.

In the immediate wake of the Civil War all this began to change with the first stirrings of large-scale bureaucratic, corporate capitalism. The "Robber Barons," as the new tycoons came to be called, were at first met (as the name given them implies) with extraordinary hostility. But by the 1890s they embarked on an intellectual counteroffensive, proposing what Doukas and Durrenberger call, after an essay by Andrew Carnegie, a "Gospel of Wealth":

> The fledgling corporate giants, their bankers, and their political allies objected to producerist moral claims and, starting in the 1890s, reached out with a new ideology that claimed, to the contrary, that capital, not labor, creates wealth and prosperity. Powerful coalitions of corporate interests made concerted efforts to transform the message of schools, universities, churches, and civic groups, claiming that "business had solved the fundamental ethical and political problems of industrial society."
>
> Steel magnate Andrew Carnegie was a leader of this cultural campaign. To the masses, Carnegie argued for what we'd now call consumerism: the productivity of "concentrated" capital, under the wise stewardship of the fit, would so lower the price of commodities that the workers of tomorrow would live as well as the kings of the past. To the elite, he argued that coddling the poor with high wages was not good for "the race."[44]

The promulgation of consumerism also coincided with the beginnings of the managerial revolution, which was, especially at first, largely an attack on popular knowledge. Where once hoopers and wainwrights and seamstresses saw themselves as heirs to a proud tradition, each with its secret knowledge, the new bureaucratically organized corporations and their "scientific management" sought as far as possible to literally turn workers into extensions of the machinery, their every move predetermined by someone else.

The real question to be asked here, it seems to me, is: Why was this campaign so successful? Because it cannot be denied that, within a generation, "producerism" had given way to "consumerism," the "source of status," as Harry Braverman put it, was "no longer the ability to make things but simply the ability to purchase them,"[45] and the labor theory of value—which had, meanwhile, been knocked out of economic theory by the "marginal revolution"—had so fallen away from popular common sense that nowadays, only graduate students or small circles of revolutionary Marxist theorists are likely to have heard of it. Nowadays, if one speaks of "wealth producers," people will automatically assume one is referring not to workers but to capitalists.

This was a monumental shift in popular consciousness. What made it possible? It seems to me that the main reason lies in a flaw in the original labor theory of value itself. This was its focus on "production"—a concept which, as earlier noted, is basically theological, and bears in it a profound patriarchal bias. Even in the Middle Ages, the Christian God was seen as a craftsman and an artificer,[46] and human work—which was always conceived primarily as male work—as a matter of making and building things, or perhaps coaxing them from the soil, while for women "labor" was seen primarily and emblematically as a matter of producing babies. Most real women's labor disappeared from the conversation. Obviously, the startling, unprecedented increases in productivity that followed in the wake of the industrial revolution played a role here, too: they could only have had led to arguments about the relative importance of machines, and the people operating them, and indeed those arguments remained at the center of political and economic debate throughout the nineteenth century.

But even when it comes to factory labor, there is something of a darker story. The initial instinct of most early factory owners was not to employ men in the mills at all, but women and children: the latter were, after all, considered more tractable, and women especially, more inured to monotonous, repetitive work. The results were often brutal and horrific. The situation also left traditional male craftsmen in a particularly distressing situation; not only were they thrown out of work by the new factories, their wives and children, who used to work under their direction, were now the breadwinners. This was clearly a factor in the early wave of machine-breaking during the Napoleonic Wars that came to be known as Luddism, and a key element in allaying that rebellion seems to have been a tacit social compromise whereby it came to be understood that it would be primarily adult men who would be employed in factory work. This, and the fact that for the next century or so labor organizing tended to focus on factory workers (partly simply because they were the easiest to organize), led to the situation we have now, where simply invoking the term "working class" instantly draws up images of men in overalls toiling on production lines, and it's common to hear otherwise intelligent middle-class intellectuals suggest that, with the decline of factory work, the working class in, say, Britain or America no longer exists—as if it were actually ingeniously constructed androids that were driving their buses, trimming their hedges, installing their cables, or changing their grandparents' bedpans.

In fact, there was never a time most workers worked in factories. Even in the days of Karl Marx, or Charles Dickens, working-class neighborhoods housed far more maids, bootblacks, dustmen, cooks, nurses, cabbies, schoolteachers, prostitutes, caretakers, and costermongers than employees in coal mines, textile mills, or iron foundries. Are these former jobs "productive"? In what sense and for whom? Who "produces" a soufflé? It's because of these ambiguities that such issues are typically brushed aside when people are arguing about value; but doing so blinds us to the reality that most working-class labor, whether carried out by men or women, actually more resembles what we archetypically think of as women's work, looking after people, seeing to their wants and needs, explaining, reassuring, anticipating what the boss wants or is thinking, not to mention caring for, monitoring, and maintaining plants, animals, machines, and other objects, than it involves hammering, carving, hoisting, or harvesting things.

This blindness has consequences. Let me give an illustration. In 2014 there was a transit strike when London's mayor threatened to close perhaps a hundred London Underground ticket offices, leaving only machines. This sparked an online debate among certain local Marxists about whether the workers threatened with redundancy had "bullshit jobs"—the logic put forward by some being that, either a job produced value for capitalism, which the capitalists clearly no longer thought these jobs did, or else it served a social function that would be necessary even if capitalism did not exist, which clearly these did not since under full communism, transport would be free. Needless to say I was drawn in. Asked to respond, I eventually referred my interlocutors to a circular put out by the strikers themselves, called "Advice to Passengers Using the Future London Underground." It included lines like these:

> Please ensure you are thoroughly familiar with London Underground's 11 lines and 270 stations before traveling . . . Please ensure that there are no delays in your journey, or any accidents, emergencies, incidents, or evacuations. Please do not be disabled. Or poor. Or new to London. Please avoid being too young or too old. Please do not be harassed or assaulted while traveling. Please do not lose your property or your children. Please do not require assistance in any way.

It apparently never having occurred to many advocates of proletarian revolution to investigate what it is that transit workers actually did, they appear to have lapsed into something very like the right-wing tabloid stereotype of city employees as overpaid idlers lounging about on the public dime.

What tube workers actually do, then, is something much closer to what feminists have termed "caring labor." It has more in common with a nurse's work than a bricklayer's. It's just that, in the same way as women's unpaid caring labor is made to disappear from our accounts of "the economy," so are the caring aspects of other working-class jobs made to disappear as well. One might make a case, perhaps, that British working-class traditions of caring labor do make themselves known in popular culture, which is largely a working-class product, with all the characteristic gestures, manners, and cadences by which working-class people cheer one another up reflected in British music, British comedy, and British children's literature. But it is not recognized as value-creating labor in itself.

"Caring labor" is generally seen as work directed at other people, and it always involves a certain labor of interpretation, empathy, and understanding. To some degree, one might argue that this is not really work at all, it's just life, or life lived properly—humans are naturally empathetic creatures, and to communicate with one another at all, we must constantly cast ourselves imaginatively into each other's shoes and try to understand what others are thinking and feeling, which usually means caring about them at least a little—but it very much becomes work when all the empathy and imaginative identification is on one side. The key to caring labor as a commodity is not that some people care but that others don't; that those paying for "services" (note how the old feudal term is still retained) feel no need to engage in interpretive labor themselves. This is even true of a bricklayer, if that bricklayer is working for someone else. Underlings have to constantly monitor what the boss is thinking; the boss doesn't have to care. That, in turn, is one reason, I believe, why psychological studies regularly find that people of working-class background are more accurate at reading other people's feelings, and more empathetic and caring, than those of middle-class, let alone wealthy, backgrounds.[47] To some degree, the skill at reading others' emotions is just an effect of what working-class work actually consists of: rich people don't have to learn how to do interpretive labor nearly as well because they can hire other people to do it for them. Those hirelings, on the other hand, who have to develop a habit of understanding other's points of view, will also tend to care about them.[48]

By this token, as many feminist economists have pointed out, all labor can be seen as caring labor, since—to turn to an example from the beginning of the chapter—even if one builds a bridge, it's ultimately because one cares about people who might wish to cross the river. As the examples I cited at the time make clear, people do really think in these terms when they reflect on the "social value" of their jobs.[49]

To think of labor as valuable primarily because it is "productive," and productive labor as typified by the factory worker, effecting that magic transformation by which cars or teabags or pharmaceutical products are "produced" out of factories through the same painful but ultimately mysterious "labor" by which women are seen to produce babies, allows one to make all this disappear. It also makes it maximally easy for the factory owner to insist that no, actually, workers are really no different from the machines they operate. Clearly, the growth of what came to be called "scientific management" made this easier; but it would never have been possible had the paradigmatic example of "worker" in the popular imagination been a cook, a gardener, or a masseuse.

■ ■ ■

Most economists nowadays see the labor theory of value as a curiosity from the formative days of the discipline; and it's probably true that, if one's primary interest is to understand patterns of price formation, there are better tools available. But for the worker's movement—and arguably, for revolutionaries like Karl Marx—that was never the real point. The real point is philosophical. It is a recognition that the world we inhabit is something we made, collectively, as a society, and therefore, that we could also have made differently. This is true of almost any physical object likely to be within reach of us at any given moment. Every one was grown or manufactured by someone on the basis of what someone imagined we might be like, and what they thought we might want or need. It's even more true of abstractions like "capitalism," "society," or "the government." They only exist because we produce them every day. John Holloway, perhaps the most poetic of contemporary Marxists, once proposed to write a book entitled *Stop Making Capitalism*.[50] After all, he noted, even though we all act as if capitalism is some kind of behemoth towering over us, it's really just something we produce. Every morning we wake up and re-create capitalism. If one morning we woke up and all decided to create something else, then there wouldn't be capitalism anymore. There would be something else.

One might even say that this is the core question—perhaps ultimately the only question—of all social theory and all revolutionary thought. Together we create the world we inhabit. Yet if any one of us tried to imagine a world we'd like to live in, who would come up with one exactly like the one that currently exists? We can all imagine a better world. Why can't we just create one? Why does it seem so inconceivable to just stop making capitalism? Or government? Or at the very least bad service providers and annoying bureaucratic red tape?

Viewing work as production allows us to ask such questions. This couldn't be more important. It's not clear, however, if it gives us the means to answer them. It strikes me that recognizing that a great deal of work is not strictly speaking productive but caring, and that there is always a caring aspect even to the most apparently impersonal work, does suggest one reason why it's so difficult to simply create a different society with a different set of rules. Even if we don't like what the world looks like, the fact remains that the conscious aim of most of our actions, productive or otherwise, is to do well by others; often, very specific others. Our actions are caught up in relations of caring. But most caring relations require we leave the world more or less as we found it. In the same way that teenage idealists regularly abandon their dreams of creating a better world and come to accept the compromises of adult life at precisely the moment they marry and have children, caring for others, especially over the long term, requires maintaining a world that's relatively predictable as the grounds on which caring can take place. One cannot save to ensure a college education for one's children unless one is sure in twenty years there will still be colleges—or for that matter, money. And that, in turn, means that love for others—people, animals, landscapes—regularly requires the maintenance of institutional structures one might otherwise despise.

how, over the course of the twentieth century, work came to be increasingly valued primarily as a form of discipline and self-sacrifice

> We keep inventing jobs because of this false idea that everyone has to be employed at some sort of drudgery because, according to Malthusian Darwinian theory, he must justify his right to exist.
> —Buckminster Fuller

However this may be, the "Gospel of Wealth" counteroffensive has been successful, and the captains of industry, first in America, then increasingly everywhere, have been able to convince the public that they, and not those they employ, are the real creators of prosperity. Their very success, however, created an inevitable problem. How are workers supposed to find meaning and purpose in jobs where they are effectively being turned into robots? Where they are actually being *told* they are little better than robots, even as at the same time they are increasingly expected to organize their lives around their work?

The obvious answer is to fall back on the old idea that work forms character; and this is precisely what seems to have happened. One could call it a revival of Puritanism, but as we've seen this idea goes much further back: to a fusion of the Christian doctrine of the curse of Adam with the Northern European notion that paid labor under a master's discipline is the only way to become a genuine adult. This history made it very easy to encourage workers to see their work not so much as wealth-creation, or helping others, or at least not primarily so, but as self-abnegation, a kind of secular hair-shirt, a sacrifice of joy and pleasure that allows us to become an adult worthy of our consumerist toys.

A great deal of contemporary research has confirmed this assessment. True, people in Europe or America have not historically seen their avocation as what should mark them in the eyes of eternity. Visit a graveyard; you will search in vain for a tombstone inscribed with the words "steam-fitter," "executive vice president," "park ranger," or "clerk." In death, the essence of a soul's being on earth is seen as marked by the love they felt for, and received from, their husbands, wives, and children, or sometimes also by what military unit they served with in time of war. These are all things which involve both intense emotional commitment, and the giving and taking of life. While alive, in contrast, the first question anyone was likely to have asked on meeting any of those people was, "What do you do for a living?"

This continues to be the case. The fact that it does remains something of a stubborn paradox because the "Gospel of Wealth" and subsequent rise of consumerism was supposed to have changed all that. No longer were we to think of ourselves as expressing our being through what we produced, but rather, through what we consumed: what sorts of clothes we wear, music we listen to, sports teams we follow. Especially since the seventies, everyone has been expected to sort themselves out into tribal subcultures as sci-fi geeks, dog lovers, paintball enthusiasts, stoners, or supporters of the Chicago Bulls or Manchester United but definitely not as longshoremen or Catastrophe Risk Analysts. And it is true that on one level, most of us do prefer to think of ourselves as being defined by anything other than our jobs.[51] Yet somehow, paradoxically, people regularly report that work is what gives the ultimate meaning to their lives, and that unemployment has devastating psychological effects.

There have been an enormous number of surveys, studies, inquests, and ethnographies of work over the course of the twentieth century. Work about work has become a kind of minor industry in its own right. The conclusions reached by this body of research—and what follows appears to hold true, with only minor variations, for both blue- and white-collar workers virtually anywhere in the world—might be summarized as follows:

1. Most people's sense of dignity and self-worth is caught up in working for a living.
2. Most people hate their jobs.

We might refer to this as "the paradox of modern work." The entire discipline of the sociology of work, not to mention industrial relations, has largely been concerned with trying to understand how both these things can be true at the same time. As two paragons of the field, Al Gini and Terry Sullivan, put it in 1987:

> In well over a hundred studies in the last twenty-five years, workers have regularly depicted their jobs as physically exhausting, boring, psychologically diminishing or personally humiliating and unimportant.
>
> [But at the same time] they want to work because they are aware at some level that work plays a crucial and perhaps unparalleled psychological role in the formation of human character. Work is not just a course of livelihood, it is also one of the most significant contributing factors to an inner life . . . To be denied work is to be denied far more than the things that work can buy; it is to be denied the ability to define and respect one's self."[52]

After many years of research on the topic, Gini finally came to the conclusion that work was coming to be considered less and less a means to an end—that is, a way of obtaining resources and experiences that make it possible to pursue projects (as I've put it, values other than the economic: family, politics, community, culture, religion)—and more and more as an end in itself. Yet at the same time it was an end in itself that most people found harmful, degrading, and oppressive.

How to reconcile these two observations? One way might be to return to the arguments I made in chapter 3 and to acknowledge that human beings essentially *are* a set of purposes, so that without any sense of purpose, we would barely be said to exist at all. There is surely truth in this. In some sense we are all in the situation of the inmate who prefers working in the prison laundry to sitting in the cell watching TV all day. But one possibility the sociologists generally overlook is that, if work is a form of self-sacrifice or self-abnegation, then the very awfulness of modern work *is* what makes it possible to see it as an end in itself. We have returned to Carlyle: work *should* be painful, the misery of the job is itself what "forms character."

Workers, in other words, gain feelings of dignity and self-worth *because* they hate their jobs.

This is the attitude that, as Clement observed, seems to remain in the air all around us, implicit in office small-talk. "The pressure to value ourselves and others on the basis of how hard we work at something we'd rather not be doing . . . If you're not destroying your mind and body via paid work, you're not living right." It is, to be sure, more common among middle-class office workers like Clement than among migrant farm workers, parking lot attendants, or short-order chefs. But even in working-class environments, the attitude can be observed through its negation, since even those who do not feel they have to validate their existence, on a day-to-day basis, by boasting how overworked they are will nonetheless agree that those who avoid work entirely should probably drop dead.

In America, stereotypes of the lazy and undeserving poor have long been tied up in racism: generations of immigrants learned what it means to be a "hardworking American" by being taught to despise the imagined indiscipline of the descendants of slaves, just as Japanese workers were taught to disdain Koreans, or English workers, Irish.[53] Nowadays mainstream media is usually obliged to be more subtle, but there is an endless drumbeat of vilification of the poor, the unemployed, and especially those on public relief—and most people do seem to accept the basic logic of the contemporary moralists: that society is besieged by those who want something for nothing, that the poor are largely poor because they lack the will and discipline to work, that only those who do or have worked harder than they'd like to at something they would rather not be doing, preferably under a harsh taskmaster, deserve respect and consideration from their fellow citizens. As a result, the sadomasochistic element in work described in chapter 4, rather than being an ugly, if predictable, side effect to top-down chains of command in the workplace, has actually become central to what validates work itself. Suffering has become a badge of economic citizenship. It's not that much different than a home address. Without it, you have no right to make any other claim.

We have come full circle, then, to the situation with which we began; but at least now we can understand it in its full historical context. Bullshit jobs proliferate today in large part because of the peculiar nature of managerial feudalism that has come to dominate wealthy economies—but to an increasing degree, all economies. They cause misery because human happiness is always caught up in a sense of having effects on the world; a feeling which most people, when they speak of their work, express through a language of social value. Yet at the same time they are aware that the greater the social value produced by a job, the less one is likely to be paid to do it. Like Annie, they are faced with the choice between doing useful and important work like taking care of children but being effectively told that the gratification of helping others should be its own reward, and it's up to them to figure out how to pay their bills, or accepting pointless and degrading work that destroys their mind and body for no particular reason, other than a widespread feeling that if one does not engage in labor that destroys the mind and body, whether or not there is a reason to be doing it, one does not deserve to live.

Perhaps we should leave the last word to Carlyle, who includes in his celebration of work one chapter that consists entirely of a peculiar diatribe against happiness. Here he was responding to the utilitarian doctrines of men like Jeremy Bentham, who had proposed that human pleasure could be precisely quantified, and therefore all morality reduced to calculating what would provide "the greatest happiness for the greatest number."[54] Happiness, Carlyle objected, is an ignoble concept. "The only happiness a brave man ever troubled himself with asking much about was, happiness enough to get his work done. It is, after all, the one unhappiness of a man that he cannot work, that he cannot get his destiny as man fulfilled."[55]

Bentham and the Utilitarians, who saw no purpose of human life other than the pursuit of pleasure, can be seen as the philosophical ancestors of modern consumerism, which is still justified by an economic theory of "utility." But Carlyle's perspective isn't really the negation of Bentham's; or if it is, then only in the dialectical sense, where two apparent opposites remain permanently at war with one another, their advocates unaware that in their struggle, they constitute a higher unity which would be impossible without both. The belief that what ultimately motivates human beings has always been, and must always be, the pursuit of wealth, power, comforts, and pleasure, has always and must always be complemented by a doctrine of work as self-sacrifice, as valuable precisely *because* it is the place of misery, sadism, emptiness, and despair. As Carlyle put it:

"All work, even cotton-spinning, is noble; work is alone noble, be that here said and asserted once more. And in like manner too, all dignity is painful. A life of ease is not for any man . . . Our highest religion is named the Worship of Sorrow. For the son of man there is no noble crown, well worn or even ill worn, but there is a crown of thorns!"[56]

What Are the Political Effects of Bullshit Jobs, and Is There Anything That Can Be Done About This Situation?

I believe that this instinct to perpetuate useless work is, at bottom, simply fear of the mob. The mob (the thought runs) are such low animals that they would be dangerous if they had leisure; it is safer to keep them too busy to think.

—George Orwell, *Down and Out in Paris and London*

If someone had designed a work regime perfectly suited to maintaining the power of finance capital, it's hard to see how they could have done a better job. Real, productive workers are relentlessly squeezed and exploited. The remainder are divided between a terrorized stratum of the, universally reviled, unemployed and a larger stratum who are basically paid to do nothing, in positions designed to make them identify with the perspectives and sensibilities of the ruling class (managers, administrators, etc.)—and particularly its financial avatars—but, at the same time, foster a simmering resentment against anyone whose work has clear and undeniable social value.

—from "On the Phenomenon of Bullshit Jobs"

I would like to end this book with a few thoughts about the political implications of the current work situation, and one suggestion about a possible way out. What I have described over the last two chapters are the economic forces driving the proliferation of bullshit jobs—what I've called managerial feudalism—and the cosmology, the overall way of imagining the place of human beings in the universe, that allows us to put up with this arrangement. The more the economy becomes a matter of the mere distribution of loot, the more inefficiency and unnecessary chains of command actually make sense, since these are the forms of organization best suited to soaking up as much of that loot as possible. The less the value of work is seen to lie either in what it produces, or the benefits it provides to others, the more work comes to be seen as valuable primarily as a form of self-sacrifice, which means that anything that makes that work less onerous or more enjoyable, even the gratification of knowing that one's work benefits others, is actually seen to lower its value—and as a result, to justify lower levels of pay.

All this is genuinely perverse.

In a sense, those critics who claim we are not working a fifteen-hour week because we have chosen consumerism over leisure are not entirely off the mark. They just got the mechanisms wrong. We're not working harder because we're spending all our time manufacturing PlayStations and serving one another sushi. Industry is being increasingly robotized, and the real service sector remains flat at roughly 20 percent of overall employment. Instead, it is because we have invented a bizarre sadomasochistic dialectic whereby we feel that pain in the workplace is the only possible justification for our furtive consumer pleasures, and, at the same time, the fact that our jobs thus come to eat up more and more of our waking existence means that we do not have the luxury of—as Kathi Weeks has so concisely put it—"a life," and that, in turn, means that furtive consumer pleasures are the only ones we have time to afford. Sitting around in cafés all day arguing about politics or gossiping about our friends' complex polyamorous love affairs takes time (all day, in fact); in contrast pumping iron or attending a yoga class at the local gym, ordering out for Deliveroo, watching an episode of *Game of Thrones*, or shopping for hand creams or consumer electronics can all be placed in the kind of self-contained predictable time-slots one is likely to have left over between spates of work, or else while recovering from it. All these are examples of what I like to call "compensatory consumerism." They are the sorts of things you can do to make up for the fact that you don't have a life, or not very much of one.

on how the political culture under managerial feudalism comes to be maintained by a balance of resentments

Now at the time of which I was speaking, as the voters were inscribing their ostraka [to determine which politician would be expelled from the city], it is said that an unlettered and utterly boorish fellow handed his ostrakon to Aristides, whom he took to be one of the ordinary crowd, and asked him to write Aristides on it. He, astonished, asked the man what possible wrong Aristides had done him. "None whatever," was the answer, "I don't even know the fellow, but I am tired of hearing him everywhere called 'The Just.'" On hearing this, Aristides made no answer, but wrote his name on the ostrakon and handed it back.

—Plutarch, *Life of Aristides the Just*

No doubt I am overstating my case. People in consumer societies, even those in bullshit jobs, do eke out some kind of a life—though one might ask how viable such forms of life really are in the long term, considering that the stratum of the population most likely to be trapped in pointless employment would also appear to be the most likely to have lives marked by episodes of clinical depression or other forms of mental illness, not to mention, to fail to reproduce. At least, I suspect that this is the case. Such suspicions could only be affirmed by empirical research.

Even if none of this turned out to be the case, though, one thing is inescapable: such work arrangements foster a political landscape rife with hatred and resentment. Those struggling and without work resent the employed. The employed are encouraged to resent the poor and unemployed, who they are constantly told are scroungers and freeloaders. Those trapped in bullshit jobs resent workers who get to do real productive or beneficial labor, and those who do real productive or beneficial labor, underpaid, degraded, and unappreciated, increasingly resent those who they see as monopolizing those few jobs where one can live well while doing something useful, high-minded, or glamorous—who they refer to as "the liberal elite." All are united in their loathing for the political class, who they see (correctly) as corrupt, but the political class, in turn, finds these other forms of vacuous hatred extremely convenient, since they distract attention from themselves.

Some of these forms of resentment are familiar enough, and will be instantly recognizable by the reader; others are less discussed, and might seem at first puzzling. It's easy to imagine how someone working in a French tea factory might resent the flock of useless new middle managers imposed on them (even before those middle managers decided to fire them all). It's not nearly so clear why those middle managers should resent the factory workers. But often middle managers, and even more, those managers' administrative assistants, clearly do resent factory workers, for the simple reason that the latter have legitimate reason to take pride in their work. A key part of the justification of underpaying such workers is simple envy.

Moral envy is an undertheorized phenomenon. I'm not sure that anyone has ever written a book about it. Still, it's clearly an important factor in human affairs. By "moral envy," I am referring here to feelings of envy and resentment directed at another person, not because that person is wealthy, or gifted, or lucky, but because his or her behavior is seen as upholding a higher moral standard than the envier's own. The basic sentiment seems to be "How dare that person claim to be better than me (by acting in a way that I do indeed acknowledge is better than me)?" I remember first encountering this attitude in college, when a lefty friend once told me that he no longer had any respect for a certain famous activist since he had learned the activist in question kept an expensive apartment in New York for his ex-wife and child. "What a hypocrite!" he exclaimed. "He could have given that money to the poor!" When I pointed out the activist in question gave almost all his money to the poor, he was unmoved. When I pointed out the critic, while not exactly poor himself, appeared to give nothing to charity, he was offended. In fact I'm not sure he ever spoke to me again. I've run into this attitude repeatedly ever since. Within a community of do-gooders, anyone who exemplifies shared values in too exemplary a way is seen as a threat; ostentatiously good behavior ("virtue signaling" is the new catchword) is often perceived as a moral challenge; it doesn't matter if the person in question is entirely humble and unassuming—in fact, that can even make it worse, since humility can be seen as itself a moral challenge to those who secretly feel they aren't humble enough.

Moral envy of this sort is rife in activist or religious communities; what I would like to suggest here is that it is also, more subtly, present in the politics surrounding work. Just as anger at immigrants often involves the simultaneous accusation that newcomers work both too much and too little, so does resentment against the poor focus simultaneously on those who don't work, since they are imagined to be lazy, and those who do work, since (unless they've been dragooned into some kind of work-fare) at least they don't have bullshit jobs. Why, for instance, have conservatives in the United States been so successful at whipping up popular resentment against unionized hospital or autoworkers? During the 2008 bailout of the financial industry, while there was a public outcry against bankers' million-dollar bonuses, no actual sanctions followed; however, the consequent bailout of the auto industry did involve sanctions: on assembly line workers. They were widely denounced as coddled for having union contracts that allowed them generous health and pension plans, vacations, and $28-per-hour wages, and forced into massive give-backs. Those working in the financial offices of the same companies who (insofar as they were not just sitting around doing nothing at all) were the ones who had actually caused the problems and were not expected to make similar sacrifices. As a local paper recalled:

The bank bailout would be followed in February by a bailout of auto companies. Here, it was assumed that thousands of jobs must be shed for those companies to regain profitability. There had long been envy of auto-workers' job protection and health benefits; now they became a scapegoat. As once-proud Michigan manufacturing cities all but shut down, right-wing radio commentators asserted that workers—instrumental, historically, through their labor struggles in obtaining seven-day work weeks and forty-hour days for everyone—were getting their just desserts.[1]

One reason American autoworkers had such relatively generous plans, compared with other blue-collar workers, was first and foremost because they played such an essential role in creating something their fellow citizens actually needed, and what's more, something recognized as culturally important (indeed, central to their sense of themselves as Americans).[2] It's hard to escape the impression that this was precisely what others resented about them. "They get to make cars! Shouldn't that be enough for them? I have to sit around filling out stupid forms all day, and these bastards want to rub it in by threatening to go on strike to demand a dental plan, or two weeks off to take their kids to see the Grand Canyon or the Colosseum, on top of that?"

It's quite the same with the otherwise inexplicable drum-beat of animosity directed, in the United States, against primary and secondary school teachers. Schoolteachers, of course, are the very definition of those who chose a socially important and high-minded vocation in the full knowledge that it would involve low pay and stressful conditions. One becomes a teacher because one wants to have a positive impact on others' lives. (As a New York subway recruiting ad used to say, "No one ever called someone up twenty years later to thank them for being such an aspiring insurance claims adjuster.") Yet again, this seems to be what makes them fair game in the eyes of all those who denounce them as spoiled, entitled, overpaid spouters of secular humanist anti-Americanism. Granted, one can understand why Republican activists target teachers' unions. Teachers' unions are one of the mainstays of support for the Democratic Party. But teachers' unions include both teachers and school administrators, the latter being those actually responsible for most of the policies most

Republican activists object to. So why not focus on them? It would have been much easier for them to make a case that the school administrators are overpaid parasites than that teachers are coddled and spoiled. As Eli Horowitz noted:

> What's remarkable about this is that Republicans and other conservatives actually *did* complain about school administrators—but then they stopped. For whatever reason, those voices (which were few and quiet to begin with) dwindled to nonexistence almost as soon as the conversation began. In the end, *the teachers themselves* turned out to be the more valid political targets, even though they do the more valuable work.[3]

Again, I think this can only be put down to moral envy. Teachers are seen as people who have ostentatiously put themselves forward as self-sacrificing and public-spirited, as wanting to be the sort of person who gets a call twenty years later saying "Thank you, thank you for all you did for me." For people like that to form unions, threaten strikes, and demand better working conditions is considered almost hypocritical.

■ ■ ■

There is one major exception to the rule that anyone pursuing a useful or high-minded line of work, but who also expects comfortable levels of pay and benefits, is a legitimate target of resentment. The rule does not apply to soldiers, or anyone else who works directly for the military. To the contrary, soldiers must never be resented. They are above critique.

I've written about this curious exception before, but it might be helpful to recall the argument very briefly, because I think it's impossible to really understand right-wing populism without it.[4] Let me again take the case of America because it's the one I'm most familiar with (though I'm assured the argument, in its broad outlines, does apply anywhere from Brazil to Japan). For right-wing populists, in particular, military personnel are the ultimate good guys. One must "support the troops"; this is an absolute injunction; anyone who would compromise on it in any way is a traitor pure and simple. The ultimate bad guys in contrast are the intelligentsia. Most working-class conservatives, for instance, don't have much use for corporate executives, but they usually don't feel especially passionate about their dislike for them. Their true hatred is directed at the "liberal elite" (this divides into various branches: the "Hollywood elite," the "journalistic elite," "university elite," "fancy lawyers," or "the medical establishment")—that is, the sort of people who live in big coastal cities, watch public television or public radio, or even more, who might be involved in producing or appearing in same. It seems to me there are two perceptions that lie behind this resentment: (1) the perception that members of this elite see ordinary working people as a bunch of knuckle-dragging cavemen, and (2) the perception that these elites constitute an increasingly closed caste; one which the children of the working class would actually have far more difficulty breaking into than the class of actual capitalists.

It also seems to me that both these perceptions are largely accurate. The first is pretty much self-evidently true if reactions to the 2016 election of Donald Trump are anything to go by. The white working class in particular is the one identity group in America toward which statements that might otherwise be immediately denounced as bigoted (for instance, that a certain class of people are ugly, violent, or stupid) are accepted without remark in polite society. The second is also true if you really think about it. We might again look to Hollywood for an illustration. Back in the thirties and forties, even the name "Hollywood" would tend to evoke images of magical social advance: Hollywood was a place where a simple farm girl could go to the big city, be discovered, find herself a star. For present purposes, it doesn't really matter how often this actually happened (it clearly did now and then); the point is at the time, Americans did not see the fable as inherently implausible. Look at a list of the lead actors of a major motion picture nowadays and you are likely to find barely a single one that can't boast at least two generations of Hollywood actors, writers, producers, and directors in their family tree. The film industry has come to be dominated by an in-marrying caste. Is it surprising, then, that Hollywood celebrities' pretensions to egalitarian politics tend to ring a bit hollow in the ears of most working-class Americans? Neither is Hollywood in any way an exception in this regard. If anything it's emblematic of what has happened to all the liberal professions (if, perhaps, a trifle more advanced).

Conservative voters, I would suggest, tend to resent intellectuals more than they resent rich people, because they can imagine a scenario in which they or their children might become rich, but cannot possibly imagine one in which they could ever become a member of the cultural elite. If you think about it that's not an unreasonable assessment. A truck driver's daughter from Nebraska might not have very much chance of becoming a millionaire—America now has the lowest social mobility in the developed world—but it *could* happen. There's virtually no way that same daughter will ever become an international human rights lawyer, or drama critic for the *New York Times*. Even if she could get into the right schools, there would certainly be no possible way for her to then go on to live in New York or San Francisco for the requisite years of unpaid internships.[5] Even if the son of glazier got a toehold in a well-positioned bullshit job, he would likely, like Eric, be unable or unwilling to transform it into a platform for the obligatory networking. There are a thousand invisible barriers.

If we return to the opposition of "value" versus "values" laid out in the last chapter, we might put it this way: if you just want to make a lot of money, there might be a way to do it; on the other hand, if your aim is to pursue any other sort of value—whether that be truth (journalism, academia), beauty (the art world, publishing), justice (activism, human rights), charity, and so forth—and you actually want to be paid a living wage for it, then if you do not possess a certain degree of family wealth, social networks, and cultural capital, there's simply no way in. The "liberal elite," then, are those who have placed an effective lock on any position where it's possible to get paid to do anything that one might do for any reason other than the money. They are seen as trying, and largely succeeding, in constituting themselves as a new American nobility—in the same sense as the Hollywood aristocracy, monopolizing the hereditary right to all those jobs where one can live well, and still feel one is serving some higher purpose—which is to say, feel noble.

In the United States, of course, all this is very much complicated by the country's legacy of slavery and inveterate racism. It's largely the white working class that expresses class resentment by focusing on intellectuals; African Americans, migrants, and the children of migrants tend to reject anti-intellectual politics, and still see the educational system as the most likely means of social advancement for their children. This makes it easier for poor whites to see them as unfairly in alliance with rich white liberals.

But what does all this have to do with supporting the troops? Well if that truck driver's daughter was absolutely determined to find a job that would allow her to pursue something unselfish and high-minded, but still paid the rent and guaranteed access to adequate dental care, what options does she really have? If she's of a religious temperament there might be some possibility in her local church. But such jobs are hard to come by. Mainly, she can join the army.

The reality of the situation first came home to me over a decade ago when attending a lecture by Catherine Lutz, an anthropologist who has been carrying out a project studying the archipelago of US overseas military bases. She made the fascinating observation that almost all of these bases organize outreach programs, in which soldiers venture out to repair schoolrooms or to perform free dental checkups in nearby towns and villages. The ostensible reason for the programs was to improve relations with local communities, but they rarely have much impact in that regard; still, even after the military discovered this, they kept the programs up because they had such an enormous psychological impact on the soldiers, many of whom would wax euphoric when describing them: for example, "This is why I joined the army," "This is what military service is really all about—not just defending your country, it's about helping people!" Soldiers allowed to perform public service duties, they found, were two or three times more likely to reenlist. I remember thinking, "Wait, so most of these people really want to be in the Peace Corps?" And I duly looked it up and discovered: sure enough, to be accepted into the Peace Corps, you need to already have a college degree. The US military is a haven for frustrated altruists.

■■■

A case could be made that the great historical difference between what we call the Left and the Right largely turns on the relation between "value" and "values." The Left has always been about trying to collapse the gulf between the domain dominated by pure self-interest and the domain traditionally dominated by high-minded principles; the Right has always been about prising them even farther apart, and then claiming ownership of both. They stand for *both* greed *and* charity. Hence, the otherwise inexplicable alliance in the Republican Party between the free market libertarians and the "values voters" of the Christian Right. What this comes down to in practice has usually been the political equivalent of a strategy of good-cop-bad-cop: first unleash the chaos of the market to destabilize lives and all existing verities alike; then, offer yourself up as the last bastion of the authority of church and fatherhood against the barbarians they have themselves unleashed.

By juxtaposing the call to "support the troops" with condemnations of the "liberal elite" the Right is effectively calling out the Left as hypocrites. They're saying, "Sixties campus radicals claimed they were trying to create a new society in which everyone could be happy idealists living in material prosperity, where under Communism the distinction between value and values would be annihilated and all would work for the common good—but all they really ended up doing was to guarantee any jobs which allow one to feel like one is doing that are set aside exclusively for their own spoiled children."

This has some very important implications for the nature of the societies we live in. One thing it suggests about capitalism more generally, is that societies based on greed, even that say that human beings are inherently selfish and greedy and that attempt to valorize this sort of behavior, don't really believe it, and secretly dangle out the right to behave altruistically as a reward for playing along. Only those who can prove their mettle at selfishness are to be afforded the right to be selfless. Or, that's how the game is supposed to work. If you suffer and scheme and by doing so manage to accumulate enough economic value, then you are allowed to cash in and turn your millions into something unique, higher, intangible, or beautiful—that is, turn value into values. You assemble a collection of Rembrandts, or classic racing cars. Or you set up a foundation and devote the rest of your life to charity. To skip straight to the end is obviously cheating.

We are back to Abraham Lincoln's version of medieval life-cycle service, with the proviso that now, the overwhelming majority of us can only expect to experience anything like full adulthood on retirement, if at all.

Soldiers are the one legitimate exception because they "serve" their country; and—I suspect—because usually, they don't get much out of it in the long run. This would explain why right-wing populists, so unconditional in their support for the troops during their term of service, seem so strangely indifferent to the fact that a large percentage of them end up spending the rest of their lives homeless, jobless, impoverished, addicted, or begging with no legs. A poor kid might tell himself he's joining the Marines for the educational and career opportunities; but everyone knows that's at best a crapshoot. Such is the nature of his sacrifice; hence, of his true nobility.

All the other objects of resentment I've mentioned so far can be seen as ostentatious violations of the principle of inverse relation of compensation and social benefit. Unionized autoworkers and teachers perform a vitally necessary function, yet have the temerity to demand middle-class lifestyles. They are objects of a special ire, I suspect, by those trapped in soul-destroying low- and middle-level bullshit jobs. Members of the "liberal elite" of the Bill Maher or Angelina Jolie variety are seen as having skipped to the front of every line they've ever been asked to stand on, so as to be able to monopolize the few jobs that do exist that are simultaneously fun, well paid, and make a difference in the world—while at the same time, presuming to represent themselves as the voice of social justice. They are the particular objects of resentment of the working class, whose painful, difficult, body-destroying, but equally socially useful labor never seems to strike such paragons of liberalism as of much interest or importance.

At the same time, that indifference would seem to overlap with the outright envious hostility of those members of the "liberal classes" trapped in higher-order bullshit jobs, toward those same working classes for their ability to make an honest living.

how the current crisis over robotization relates to the larger problem of bullshit jobs

Puritanism: the haunting fear that someone, somewhere, may be happy.

—H. L. Mencken

A crisscrossing of resentments increasingly defines the politics of wealthy countries. This is a disastrous state of affairs.

It seems to me all this makes the old leftist question—"every day we wake up and collectively make a world together; but which one of us, left to our own devices, would ever decide they wanted to make a world like this one?"—more relevant than ever. In many respects, the science-fiction fantasies of the early twentieth century have become possible. We can't teleport or place colonies on Mars, it's true, but we could easily rearrange matters in such a way that pretty much everyone on earth lived lives of relative ease and comfort. In material terms this would not be very difficult. While the pace at which scientific revolutions and technological breakthroughs occur has slowed considerably since the heady pace the world came to be familiar with from roughly 1750 to 1950, improvements in robotics continue, largely because they are a matter of improved application of existing technological knowledge. Combined with advances in materials science, they are ushering in an age where a very large proportion of the most dreary and tiresome mechanical tasks can indeed be eliminated. What this means is that work, as we know it, will less and less resemble what we think of as "productive" labor, and more and more resemble "caring" labor—since, after all, caring consists mainly of the sorts of things most of us would least like to see done by a machine.[6]

There has been a lot of scare literature of late about the perils of mechanization. Most of it follows along the lines that Kurt Vonnegut had already developed in his very first novel, *Player Piano*, in 1952: with most forms of manual labor eliminated, society, these critics warn, will necessarily divide into two classes, a wealthy elite who own and design the robots, and a haggard and disconsolate former working class who spend their days shooting pool and drinking because they have nothing else to do. (The middle class would split between them.) This obviously not only completely ignored the caring aspects of real labor, it also assumed property relations were unalterable, and that human beings—at least, those who were not, say, science-fiction writers—were so completely unimaginative that even with unlimited free time, they would be unable to come up with anything particularly interesting to do.[7] The 1960s counterculture challenged the second and third assumptions (though not so much the first one), with many sixties revolutionaries embracing the slogan "Let the machines do all the work!" This in turn led to a renewed backlash of moralizing about work as a value in itself of the sort we've already encountered in chapter 6—at the same time as an export of many factory jobs to poor countries where labor was cheap enough it could still be performed by human beings. It was in the wake of this reaction to the sixties counterculture, in the seventies and eighties, that the first wave of managerial feudalism, and the extreme bullshitization of employment, began to make itself felt.

The latest wave of robotization has caused the same moral crises and moral panics as the sixties. The only real difference is that, since any significant change in economic models, let alone property regimes, is now treated as definitively off of the table, it's simply assumed the only possible result will be to convey even more wealth and power to the 1 percent. Martin Ford's recent *The Rise of the Robots*, for example, documents how, after making most blue-collar workers redundant, Silicon Valley is in the process of taking aim at health care, education, and the liberal professions as well. The likely outcome, he predicts, is "techno-feudalism." Throwing workers out of work, or impoverishing them by forcing them to compete with machines, will be deeply problematic, he argues: particularly since, without paychecks, how exactly is anyone going to afford all the shiny toys and efficient services the robots will provide? This may be a cruelly simplified summary, but it helps to underline what I think to be missing from such accounts—that predictions of robots replacing humans always go just so far, and then stop. It's possible for futurologists to imagine robots replacing sports editors, sociologists, or real estate agents, for example, yet I have yet to see one suggest that the basic functions that capitalists are supposed to perform, which mainly consist of figuring out the optimal way to invest resources in order to answer current or potential future consumer demand, could possibly be performed by a machine. Why not? One could easily make a case that the main reason the Soviet economy worked so badly was because they never were able to develop computer technology efficient enough to coordinate such large amounts of data automatically. But the Soviet Union only made it to the 1980s. Now it would be easy. Yet no one dares suggest this. The famous Oxford study by engineer Michael Osborne and economist Carl Frey, which sizes up 702 different professions in terms of their susceptibility for being replaced by robots,[8] for instance, considers hydrologists, makeup artists, and travel guides, but makes no mention whatsoever of the possibility of automated entrepreneurs, investors, or financiers.

At this point, my own instinct is to turn for inspiration from Vonnegut to a different science-fiction writer, Stanislaw Lem, whose space voyager Ijon Tichy describes a visit to a planet inhabited by a species to which the author gives the rather unsubtle name of Phools. At the time of his arrival the Phools were experiencing a classic Marxian overproduction crisis. Traditionally, they had been divided into Spiritors (Priests), Eminents (Aristocrats), and Drudgelings (Workers). As one helpful native explained:

"Through the ages inventors built machines that simplified work, and where in ancient times a hundred Drudgelings had bent their sweating backs, centuries later a few stood by a machine. Our scientists improved the machines, and the people rejoiced at this, but subsequent events show how cruelly premature was that rejoicing."

The factories, ultimately, became a little too efficient, and one day an engineer created machines that could operate with no supervision at all:

"When the New Machines appeared in the factories, hordes of Drudgelings lost their jobs; and, receiving no salary, they faced starvation."

"Excuse me, Phool," I asked, "but what became of the profits the factories made?"

"The profits," he replied, "went to the rightful owners, of course. Now, then, as I was saying, the threat of annihilation hung—"

"But what are you saying, worthy Phool!" I cried. "All that had to be done was to make the factories common property, and the New Machines would have become a blessing to you!"

The minute I say this the Phool trembled, blinked his ten eyes nervously, and cupped his ears to ascertain whether any of his companions milling about the stairs had overheard my remark.

"By the Ten Noses of the Phoo, I implore you, O stranger, do not utter such vile heresy, which attacks the very foundations of our freedom! Our supreme law, the principle of Civic Initiative, states that no one can be compelled, constrained, or even coaxed to do what he does not wish. Who, then, would dare expropriate the Eminents' factories, it being their will to enjoy possession of same? That would be the most horrible violation of liberty imaginable. Now, then, to continue, the New Machines produced an abundance of extremely cheap goods and excellent food, but the Drudgelings bought nothing, for they had not the wherewithal—"[9]

Before long, the Drudgelings, though—as Tichy's interlocutor insisted, entirely free to do what they wanted provided they did not interfere in anyone else's property rights—were dropping like flies. Much heated debate ensued, and a succession of failed half measures. The Phools' high council, the Plenum Moronicum, attempted to replace the Drudgelings as consumers as well, by creating robots that would eat, use, and enjoy all the products the New Machines produced far more intensely than any living being could possibly do, while also materializing money to pay for it. But this was unsatisfying. Finally, realizing a system where both production and consumption were being done by machines was rather pointless, they concluded the best solution would be for the entire population to render itself—entirely voluntarily—to the factories to be converted into beautiful shiny disks and arranged in pleasant patterns across the landscape.

This might seem heavy-handed,[10] but sometimes, I think, a dose of heavy-handed Marxism is exactly what we need. Lem is right. It's hard to imagine a surer sign that one is dealing with an irrational economic system than the fact that the prospect of eliminating drudgery is considered to be a *problem*.

Star Trek solved the problem with replicators, and young radicals here in the United Kingdom sometimes talk about a future of "fully automated luxury communism," which is basically the same thing. A case could easily be made that any future robots and replicators should be the common property of humanity as a whole, since they would be the fruit of a collective mechanical intelligence that goes back centuries, in much the same way as a national culture is the creation of, and thus belongs to, everyone. Automated public factories would make life easier. Still, they wouldn't actually eliminate the need for Drudgelings. Lem's story, and others like it, still assume that "work" means factory work, or, anyway, "productive" work, and ignore what most working-class jobs actually consist of—for instance, the fact noted in the last chapter, that workers in "ticket offices" in the London Underground aren't there to take tickets but to find lost children and talk down drunks. Not only are robots that could perform such functions very far away, but even if they did exist, most of us would not want such tasks performed in the way a robot would perform them anyway.

So the more automation proceeds, the more it should be obvious that actual value emerges from the caring element of work. Yet this leads to another problem. The caring value of work would appear to be precisely that element in labor that *cannot* be quantified.

Much of the bullshitization of real jobs, I would say, and much of the reason for the expansion of the bullshit sector more generally, is a direct result of the desire to quantify the unquantifiable. To put it bluntly, automation makes certain tasks more efficient, but at the same time, it makes other tasks *less* efficient. This is because it requires enormous amounts of human labor to render the processes, tasks, and outcomes that surround anything of caring value into a form that computers can even recognize. It is now possible to build a robot that can, all by itself, sort a pile of fresh fruits or vegetables into ripe, raw, and rotten. This is a good thing because sorting fruit, especially for more than an hour or two, is boring. It is not possible to build a robot that can, all by itself, scan over a dozen history course reading lists and decide which is the best course. This isn't such a bad thing, either, because such work is interesting (or at least, it's not hard to locate people who would find it so). One reason to have robots sorting fruit is so that real human beings can have more time to think about what history course they'd prefer to take, or some equally unquantifiable thing like who's their favorite funk guitarist or what color they'd like to dye their hair. However—and here's the catch—if we did for some reason wish to pretend that a computer *could* decide which is the best history course, say, because we decided we need to have uniform, quantifiable, "quality" standards to apply across the university for funding purposes, there's no way that computer could do the task by itself. The fruit you can just roll into a bin. In the case of the history course, it requires enormous human effort to render the material into units that a computer would even begin to know what to do with.

To get even the most minimal sense of what happens when you try, consider the following diagrams, which illustrate the difference between what's required to print an exam, or upload a syllabus, in Queensland, a contemporary managerial university in Australia (where all course materials have to be in a uniform format), as compared with a traditional academic department (see figures 8.1–8.4).

Figure 8.1 Creation of Course Profile/Syllabus (Managerial)

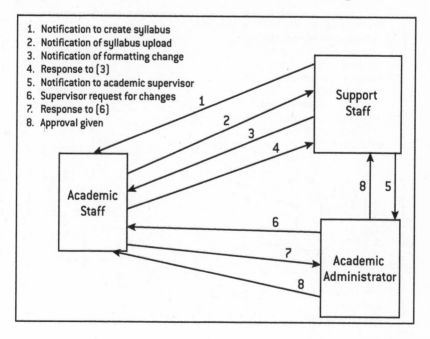

Figure 8.2 Creation of Course Profile/Syllabus (Non-Managerial)

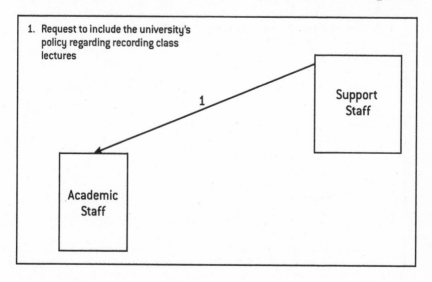

Figure 8.3   Creation of Exam (Managerial)

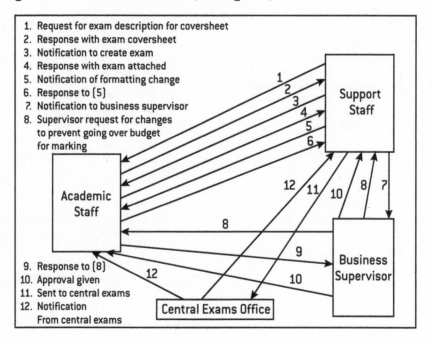

1. Request for exam description for coversheet
2. Response with exam coversheet
3. Notification to create exam
4. Response with exam attached
5. Notification of formatting change
6. Response to (5)
7. Notification to business supervisor
8. Supervisor request for changes
    to prevent going over budget
    for marking

9. Response to (8)
10. Approval given
11. Sent to central exams
12. Notification
    From central exams

Support Staff

Academic Staff

Business Supervisor

Central Exams Office

Figure 8.4   Creation of Exam (Non-Managerial)

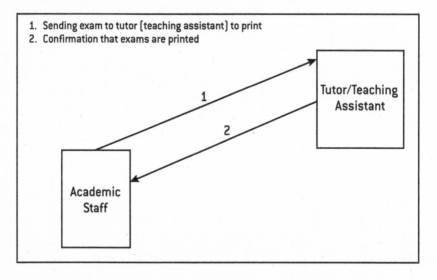

1. Sending exam to tutor (teaching assistant) to print
2. Confirmation that exams are printed

Tutor/Teaching Assistant

Academic Staff

The critical thing about this diagram is that each of those additional lines represents an action that has to be performed, not by a computer, but by an actual human being.

on the political ramifications of bullshitization and consequent decline of productivity in the caring sector as it relates to the possibility of a revolt of the caring classes

Since at least the Great Depression, we've been hearing warnings that automation was or was about to be throwing millions out of work—Keynes at the time coined the term "technological unemployment," and many assumed the mass unemployment of the 1930s was just a sign of things to come—and while this might make it seem such claims have always been somewhat alarmist, what this book suggests is that the opposite was the case. They were entirely accurate. Automation *did*, in fact, lead to mass unemployment. We have simply stopped the gap by adding dummy jobs that are effectively made up. A combination of political pressure from both right and left, a deeply held popular feeling that paid employment alone can make one a full moral person, and finally, a fear on the part of the upper classes, already noted by George Orwell in 1933, of what the laboring masses might get up to if they had too much leisure on their hands, has ensured that whatever the underlying reality, when it comes to official unemployment figures in wealthy countries, the needle should never jump too far from the range of 3 to 8 percent. But if one eliminates bullshit jobs from the picture, and the real jobs that only exist to support them, one could say that the catastrophe predicted in the 1930s really did happen. Upward of 50 percent to 60 percent of the population has, in fact, been thrown out of work.

Except of course, there's absolutely no reason it should have been a catastrophe. Over the course of the last several thousand years there have been untold thousands of human groups that might be referred to as "societies," and the overwhelming majority of them managed to figure out ways to distribute those tasks that needed to be done to keep them alive in the style to which they were accustomed in such a fashion that most everyone had some way to contribute, and no one had to spend the majority of their waking hours performing tasks they would rather not be doing, in the way that people do today.[11] What's more, faced with the "problem" of abundant leisure time, people in those societies seem to have had little trouble figuring out ways to entertain themselves or otherwise pass the time.[12] From the perspective of anyone born in one of those past societies, we'd probably look just as irrational as the Phools to Ijon Tichy.

The reason the current allocation of labor looks the way it does, then, has nothing to do with economics or even human nature. It's ultimately political. There was no reason we had to try to quantify the value of caring labor. There is no real reason we have to continue to do so. We could stop. But before we launch a campaign to reconstitute work and how we value it, I think we would do well to once again consider carefully the political forces at play.

■ ■ ■

One way to think about what's happened is to return to the opposition between "value" and "values," through which perspective, of course, what we are seeing is an attempt to force one to submit to the logic of the other.

Before the industrial revolution, most people worked at home. It's only since perhaps 1750 or even 1800 that it's made any sense to talk about society as we typically do today, as if it were made up of a collection of factories and offices ("workplaces") on the one hand, and a collection of homes, schools, churches, waterparks, and the like on the other—presumably, with a giant shopping mall placed somewhere in between. If work is the domain of "production" then home is the domain of "consumption," which is also, of course, the domain of "values" (which means that what work people do engage in, in this domain, they largely do for free). But you could also flip the whole thing around and look at society from the opposite point of view. From the perspective of business, yes, homes and schools are just the places we produce and raise and train a capable workforce, but from a human perspective, that's about as crazy as building a million robots to consume the food that people can no longer afford to eat, or warning African countries (as the World Bank has occasionally been known to do) that they need to do more to control HIV because if everyone is dead it will have adverse effects on the economy. As Karl Marx once pointed out: prior to the industrial revolution, it never seems to have occurred to anyone to write a book asking what conditions would create the most overall wealth. Many, however, wrote books about what conditions would create the best people—that is, how should society be best arranged to produce the sort of human beings one would like to have around, as friends, lovers, neighbors, relatives, or fellow citizens? This is the kind of question that concerned Aristotle, Confucius, and Ibn Khaldun, and in the final analysis it's still the only really important one. Human life is a process by which we, as humans, create one another; even the most extreme individualists only become individuals through the care and support of their fellows; and "the economy" is ultimately just the way we provide ourselves with the necessary material provisions with which to do so.

If so, talking about "values"—which are valuable *because* they can't be reduced to numbers—is the way that we have traditionally talked about the process of mutual creation and caring.[13]

Now, clearly, if we assume this to be true, then the domain of value has been systematically invading the domain of values for at least the last fifty years, and it's hardly surprising that political arguments have come to take the form they do. For instance, in many major American cities, the largest employers are now universities and hospitals. The economy of such cities, then, centers on a vast apparatus of production and maintenance of human beings—divided, in good Cartesian fashion, between educational institutions designed to shape the mind, and medical institutions designed to maintain the body. (In other cities such as New York, universities and hospitals come in second and third as employers, the biggest employers being banks. I'll get back to banks in a moment.) Where once left-wing political parties at least claimed to represent factory workers, nowadays, all such pretense has been discarded, and they have come to be dominated by the professional-managerial classes that run institutions like schools and hospitals. Right-wing populism has taken systematic aim

at the authority of those institutions in the name of a different set of religious or patriarchal "values"—for instance, challenging the authority
of universities by rejecting climate science or evolution, or challenging
the authority of the medical system by campaigns against contraception
or abortion. Or it has dabbled in impossible fantasies about returning to
the Industrial Age (Trump). But really this is something of a bitter-ender
game. Realistically, the likelihood of right populists in America wresting
control of the apparatus of human production from the corporate Left is
about as great as the likelihood of a Socialist party taking power in America and collectivizing heavy industry. For the moment, it would appear
to be a stand-off. The mainstream Left largely controls the production of
humans. The mainstream Right largely controls the production of things.

It's in this context that the financialization and bullshitization of both
the corporate sector, and particularly the caring sector, are taking place—
leading to ever-higher social costs, even at the same time as those who
are doing the actual frontline caring are finding themselves increasingly
squeezed. Everything seems to be in place for a revolt of the caring classes.
Why has none yet taken place?

Well, one obvious reason is the way that right-wing populism and
divide-and-conquer racism have placed many of the caring classes in opposite camps. But on top of that, there's the even stickier problem that in many
areas of dispute, both sides are supposed to be in the "same" political camp.
This is where banks come in. The entanglement of banks, universities, and
hospitals has become truly insidious. Finance works its way into everything,
from car loans to credit cards, but it's significant that the principal cause of
bankruptcy in America is medical debt, and the principal force drawing
young people into bullshit jobs is the need to pay student loans. Yet since
Clinton in the United States and Blair in the United Kingdom, it's been the
ostensibly left parties that have most embraced the rule of finance, received
the largest contributions from the financial sector, and worked the most
closely with financial lobbyists to "reform" the laws to make all this possible.[14] It was exactly at the same time that these same parties self-consciously
rejected any remaining elements of their old working-class constituencies,
and instead became, as Tom Frank has so effectively demonstrated, the par-

ties of the professional-managerial class: that is, not just doctors and lawyers, but the administrators and managers actually responsible for the bullshit-ization of the caring sectors of the economy.[15] If nurses were to rebel against the fact that they have to spend the bulk of their shifts doing paperwork, they would have to rebel against their own union leaders, who are firmly allied with the Clintonite Democratic Party, whose core support comes from the hospital administrators responsible for imposing the paperwork on them to begin with. If teachers were to rebel they'd have to rebel against school administrators who are actually represented, in many cases, by the exact same union. If they protest too loudly, they will simply be told they have no choice but to accept bullshitization, because the only alternative is to surrender to the racist barbarians of the populist Right.

I have myself smashed my head against this dilemma repeatedly. Back in 2006, when I was being kicked out of Yale for my support of grad students engaged in a teacher unionization drive (the Anthropology Department had to get special permission to change the reappointment rules for my case, and my case only, in order to get rid of me), union strategists considered a campaign on my behalf on MoveOn.org and similar left liberal mailing lists—until reminded that the Yale administrators behind my dismissal were probably active on those lists themselves. Years later, with Occupy Wall Street, which might be considered the first great rising of the caring classes, I watched those same "progressive" professional-managerials first attempt to co-opt the movement for the Democratic Party, then, when that proved impossible, sit idly by or even collude while a peaceful movement was suppressed by military force.

on universal basic income as an example of a program that might begin to detach work from compensation and put an end to the dilemmas described in this book

I don't usually like putting policy recommendations in my books. One reason for this is that it has been my experience that if an author is critical of existing social arrangements, reviewers will often respond by effectively asking "so what are you proposing to do about it, then?" search the text until they find something that looks like a policy suggestion, and then act as if that is what the book is basically about. So if I were to suggest that a mass reduction of working hours or a policy of universal basic income might go far in solving the problems described here, the likely response will be to see this as a book about reducing working hours or about universal basic income, and to treat it as if it stands and falls on the workability of that policy—or even, the ease by which it could be implemented.

That would be deceptive. This is not a book about a particular solution. It's a book about a problem—one that most people don't even acknowledge exists.

Another reason I hesitate to make policy suggestions is that I am suspicious of the very idea of policy. Policy implies the existence of an elite group—government officials, typically—that gets to decide on something ("a policy") that they then arrange to be imposed on everybody else. There's a little mental trick we often play on ourselves when discussing such matters. We say, for instance, "What are we going to do about the problem of X?" as if "we" were society as a whole, somehow acting on ourselves, but, in fact, unless we happen to be part of that roughly 3 percent to 5 percent of the population whose views actually do affect policy makers, this is all a game of make-believe; we are identifying with our rulers when, in fact, we're the ones being ruled. This is what happens when we watch a politician on television say "What shall we do about the less fortunate?" even though at least half of us would almost certainly fit that category ourselves. Myself, I find such games particularly pernicious because I'd prefer not to have policy elites around at all. I'm personally an anarchist, which means that, not only do I look forward to a day sometime in the future when governments, corporations, and the rest will be looked at as historical curiosities in the same way as we now look at the Spanish Inquisition or nomadic invasions, but I prefer solutions to immediate problems that do not give more power to governments or corporations, but rather, give people the means to manage their own affairs.

It follows that when faced with a social problem my impulse is not to imagine myself in charge, and ponder what sort of solutions I would

then impose, but to look for a movement already out there, already trying to address the problem and create its own solutions. The problem of
bullshit jobs, though presents unusual challenges in this regard. There are
no anti–bullshit job movements. This is partly because most people don't
acknowledge the proliferation of bullshit jobs to be a problem, but also because even if they did, it would be difficult to organize a movement around
such a problem. What local initiatives might such a movement propose?
One could imagine unions or other worker organizations launching
anti-bullshit initiatives in their own workplaces, or even across specific
industries—but they would presumably call for the de-bullshitization of
real work rather than firing people in unnecessary positions. It's not at all
clear what a broader campaign against bullshit jobs would even look like.
One might try to shorten the working week and hope things would sort
themselves out in response. But it seems unlikely that they would. Even a
successful campaign for a fifteen-hour week would be unlikely to cause
the unnecessary jobs and industries to be spontaneously abandoned; at the
same time, calling for a new government bureaucracy to assess the usefulness of jobs would inevitably itself turn into a vast generator of bullshit.

So would a guaranteed jobs program.

I've only been able to identify one solution currently being promoted
by social movements, that would reduce rather than increase the size and
intrusiveness of government. That's Universal Basic Income.

Let me end with a final testimony, from an activist friend whose political purpose in life is to render her own bullshit job unnecessary, and one
of her fellow activists. Leslie is a Benefits Advisor in the United Kingdom,
that is, she works for an NGO whose purpose is to guide citizens through
the elaborate obstacle course successive governments have set up to make
it as difficult as possible for those out of work, or otherwise in material
need, to get access to the money the government claims it has set apart for
them. Here is the testimony she sent in:

Leslie: My job shouldn't be necessary, but it is, because of the whole
long train of bullshit jobs invented to keep people who need money
from having it. As if claiming any kind of benefit were not Kafkaesque,

intrusive and humiliating enough, they also make it incredibly complicated. Even when someone is entitled to something, the process of applying is so complex most need help to understand the questions and their own rights.

Leslie has had to deal for years with the insanity that ensues when one tries to reduce human caring to a format that can be recognized by computers—let alone computers designed to keep caring precisely limited. As a result she ends up in much the same position as Tania in chapter 2, who had to spend hours rewriting job applicants' CVs and coaching them on which keywords to use to "make it past the computer":

> Leslie: There are now certain words which have to be used on the forms, I call it the catechism, which if not used can result in a failed claim—but these are only known by those like myself who have had training and access to the handbooks. And even then, especially for disability claims, the claimant often ends up having to fight through to a tribunal to get their entitlement recognized. I do get a little thrill every time we win through for someone. But this doesn't make up for the anger I feel about the colossal waste of everyone's time this is. For the claimant, for me, for the various bods at the DWP [Department of Works and Pensions] who deal with the claim, for the judges at the tribunals, the experts called in to support either side. Isn't there something more constructive we could all be doing, like, I don't know, installing solar panels or gardening? I also often wonder about whoever made up these rules. How much did they get paid for it? How long did it take them? How many people were involved? To their minds I guess they were ensuring that the noneligible don't get money ... And then I think of visiting aliens laughing at us, humans inventing rules to prevent other humans from getting access to tokens of a human concept, money—which is by its nature not scarce.

On top of all that, since she is a do-gooder, Leslie can expect to make only a minimal living herself and the money to run her office itself involves satisfying an endless chain of self-satisfied paper pushers.

Leslie: To add insult to injury, my work is funded by charity trusts, a whole other long chain of BS jobs, from me applying for money up to the CEOs who claim their organizations fight poverty, or "make the world a better place." At my end this starts with hours searching for relevant funds, reading their guidelines, spending time learning how to best approach them, filling out forms, making phone calls. If successful, I'll next have to spend hours every month compiling statistics and filling out monitoring forms. Each trust has its own catechism and its own sets of indicators, each wants their own set of evidence that we are "empowering" people, or "creating change" or innovation, when, in fact, we're juggling rules and language on behalf of people who just need help to fill out the paperwork, so they can get on with their lives.

Leslie told me of studies that demonstrate that any system of means testing, no matter how it's framed, will necessarily mean at least 20 percent of those who legitimately qualify for benefits give up and don't apply. That's almost certainly more than the number of "cheats" who might be detected by the rules—in fact, even counting those who are honestly mistaken the number still only comes to 1.6 percent. The 20 percent figure would apply even if no one actually was formally denied benefits at all. But of course the rules are designed to deny as many claimants as can plausibly be denied: between sanctions and capricious applications of the rules, we've gotten to the point now where 60 percent of those eligible for unemployment benefits in the United Kingdom don't get them. In other words, everyone she describes, the entire archipelago that starts with the bureaucrats who write the rules, and includes the DWP, enforcement tribunals, advocates, and employees who work for the funding bodies that process applications for the NGOs that employ those advocates, all of them, are part of a single vast apparatus that exists to maintain the illusion that people are naturally lazy and don't really want to work—and therefore, that even if society does have a responsibility to ensure they don't literally starve to death, it is necessary to make the process of providing them with the means of continued existence as confusing, time-consuming, and humiliating as possible.

The job, then, is essentially a kind of horrific combination of box ticking and duct taping, making up for the inefficiencies of a system of caregiving intentionally designed not to work. Thousands of people are maintained on comfortable salaries in air-conditioned offices simply in order to ensure that poor people continue to feel bad about themselves.

Leslie knew this better than anyone because she'd spent time on both sides of the desk. She had been on benefits herself for years as a single mother; she knew exactly what things looked like on the receiving end. Her solution? Eliminate the apparatus entirely. She is involved in the movement for Universal Basic Income, which calls for replacing all means-tested social welfare benefits with a flat fee to be paid to everyone, equally, residing in the country.

Candi, a fellow Basic Income activist—who also held a useless job in the system whose details she preferred not to disclose—told me she originally became interested in such issues when she first moved to London in the 1980s and became part of the International Wages for Housework Movement:

Candi: I got involved in Wages for Housework because I felt that my mother needed it. She was trapped in a bad marriage, and she would have left my dad a lot earlier if she'd had her own money. That's something really important for anyone in an abusive or even just boring relationship: to be able to get out of it without being financially impacted.

I'd just been in London for a year. I'd been trying to get involved in some form of feminism back in the States. One of my formative memories was my mother taking me to a consciousness raising group in Ohio when I was nine. We ripped out pages from St. Paul's Gospel where he was talking about how terrible women are and made a pile of them. And because I was the youngest member of the group they told me to light the pile. I remember I wouldn't do it at first because I'd been taught not to play with matches.

David: But you did eventually light it?

Candi: I did. My mother gave me permission. Not long after that she got a job that paid enough to live on, and immediately, she left my dad. That was kind of proof in the pudding for me.

In London, Candi found herself drawn to Wages for Housework—then widely seen by most other feminists as an annoying if not dangerous fringe group—because she saw it as providing an alternative to sterile debates between liberals and separatists. Here at least was an economic analysis of the real-life problems women faced. Some at the time were beginning to speak of a "global work machine," a planetwide wage-labor system designed to pump more and more effort out of more and more people, but what feminist critics had begun pointing out was that same system also defined what was to be considered "real" labor—the kind that could be reduced to "time" and could thus be bought and sold—and what wasn't. Most women's labor was placed in the latter category, despite the fact that without it, the very machine that stamped it as "not really work" would grind to a halt immediately.

Wages for Housework was essentially an attempt to call capitalism's bluff, to say, "Most work, even factory work, is done for a variety of motives; but if you want to insist that work is only valuable as a marketable commodity, then at least you can be consistent about the matter!" If women were to be compensated in the same way as men then a huge proportion of the world's wealth would instantly have to be handed over to them; and wealth, of course, is power. What follows is from a conversation with both of them:

David: So inside Wages for Housework, were there many debates about the policy implications—you know, the mechanisms through which the wages would actually be paid?

Candi: Oh, no, it was much more a perspective—a way to expose the unpaid work that was being done that nobody was supposed to talk about. And for that it did a really good job. Few were talking about the work women were already doing for free in the 1960s, but it became an issue when Wages for House-work was established in the 1970s—and now it's standard to take it into account when working out divorce settlements, for example.

David: So the demand itself was basically a provocation?

Candi: It was much more a provocation than it was ever a plan, "this is how we could actually do it"—anything like that. We did talk about where the money would come from. At first, it was all about getting money out of capital. Then in the later eighties, Wilmette Brown's book *Black Women and the Peace Movement* came out,[16] all about how war and the war economy affects women and particularly Black women more than anyone else, so we started using the slogan "pay women not soldiers." Actually you still hear that, "wage caring not killing."

So we certainly targeted where the money was. But we never much got into the mechanics.

David: Wait, "wage caring not killing"—whose slogan is that?

Leslie: Global Women's Strike. That's the contemporary successor to Wages for Housework. When we came out with the first European UBI [Universal Basic Income] petition back in 2013, that was Global Women's Strike's response: two months later, they put out a petition to wage carers instead. Which myself, I wouldn't have a problem with, if they were willing to admit that everyone is a carer in one form or another. If you're not looking after someone else then at the very least you're looking after yourself, and this takes time and energy the system is less and less willing to afford people. But then recognizing that would just lead back to UBI again: if everyone's a carer, then you might as well just fund everybody, and let them decide for themselves who they want to care for at any given time.

Candi had come around from Wages for Housework to UBI for similar reasons. She and some of her fellow activists started asking themselves: Say we did want to promote a real, practical program, what would that be?

> Candi: The reaction we used to get on the street when we leafleted for Wages for Housework was, either women would say, "Great! Where can I sign up?" or they'd say, "How dare you demand money for something I do for love?" That second reaction wasn't entirely crazy, these women were understandably resistant to commodifying all human activity in the way that getting a wage for housework might imply.

Candi was particularly moved by the arguments of the French Socialist thinker André Gorz. When I offered my own analysis on the inherently unquantifiable nature of caring, she told me Gorz had anticipated it forty years ago:

> **Candi:** Gorz's critique of Wages for Housework was that if you kept emphasizing the importance of care to the global economy in strictly financial terms, then there was the danger that you'd end up putting a dollar value on different forms of caring, and saying, that's its real "value." But in that case, you are running the risk of more and more of that caring becoming monetized, quantified, and therefore, kind of fucked up, because monetizing those activities often decreases the qualitative value of the care, especially if it's done, as it is usually, as a list of specific tasks with set time limits. He was already saying that in the seventies, and now, of course, that's exactly what's transpired. Even in teaching, nursing.[17]

Leslie: Let alone what I do.

David: Yeah, I know. "Bullshitization" is my phrase.

Candi: Yes, it's been bullshitized, absolutely.

277

Leslie: Whereas UBI . . . Didn't Silvia [Federici] write or talk in an interview recently about how the UN and then all sorts of world bodies kind of glommed onto feminism as a way to resolve the capitalist crisis of the seventies? They said, sure, let's bring women and carers into the paid workforce (most working-class women were already doing a "double day"), not to empower women but as a way of disciplining men. Because insofar as you see an equalization of wages since then, it's mainly because in real terms, working-class men's wages have gone *down*, not because women are necessarily getting that much more. They're always trying to set us against each other. And that's what all these mechanisms for assessing the relative value of different kinds of work are necessarily going to be about.

That's why for me, the pilot study of Basic Income carried out in India is so exciting. Well a lot of things are exciting about it—for instance, domestic violence goes way down. (This makes sense because I think some 80 percent of domestic disputes that lead to violence turn out to be about money.) But the main thing is, it starts to make social inequalities dissolve. You start by giving everyone an equal amount of money. That in itself is important, because money has a certain symbolic power: it's something that's the same for everyone, and when you give everyone, men, women, old, young, high caste, low caste, exactly the same amount, those differences start to dissolve. This happened in the Indian pilot where they observed that the girls were given the same amount of food as boys unlike before, disabled people were more accepted in village activities, and young women dropped the social convention that said they were supposed to be shy and modest and started hanging around in public like boys . . . Girls started participating in public life.[18]

And any UBI payment would have to be enough to live on, all by itself, and it would have to be completely unqualified. Everyone has to get it. Even people who don't need it. It's worth it, just to establish the principle that when it comes to what's required to live, everyone deserves that, equally, without qualification. This makes it a human right, not just charity or duct tape for lack of other forms of income. Then if there are further needs on top of that, say someone is disabled, well, then you address that, too. But only *after* you establish the right of material existence for all people.

This is one of the elements that startles and confuses a lot of people when they first hear about the concept of Basic Income. Surely you aren't going to give $25,000 a year (or whatever it is) to Rockefellers, too? The answer is yes. Everyone is everyone. It's not like there are so many billionaires this will come to a particularly large amount of money; rich people could be taxed more anyway; if one wanted to start means-testing, even for billionaires, then one would have to set up a bureaucracy to start means-testing again, and if history tells us anything, it's that such bureaucracies tend to expand.

What Basic Income ultimately proposes is to detach livelihood from work. Its immediate effect would be to massively reduce the amount of bureaucracy in any country that implemented it. As Leslie's case shows, an enormous amount of the machinery of government, and that half-government corporate NGO penumbra that surrounds it in most wealthy societies, is just there to make poor people feel bad about themselves. It's an extraordinarily expensive moral game played to prop up a largely useless global work machine.

Candi: Let me give an example. Recently I was thinking maybe I'd foster a kid. So I looked into the package. It's quite generous. You get a council flat, and on top of that you get £250 a week to look after the child. But then I realized: wait a minute. They're talking about £13,000 a year and an apartment, for one child. Which the child's parents in probably most cases didn't have. If we'd just given the same thing to the parents so they didn't get into so many problems they'd never have had to foster the child to begin with.

And, of course, that's not even counting the cost of the salaries of the civil servants who arrange and monitor fosterage, the building and upkeep of the offices in which they work, the various bodies that monitor and control those civil servants, the building and upkeep of the offices in which *they* work, and so forth.

This is not the place to enter into arguments about how a Basic Income program might actually work.[19] If it seems implausible to most ("But where would the money come from?"), it's largely because we've all grown up with largely false assumptions about what money is, how it's produced, what taxes are really for, and a host of other issues that lie far beyond the scope of this volume. Waters are further muddied by the fact that there are radically different visions of what a universal income is and why it would be good to have one: ranging from a conservative version that aims to provide a modest stipend as a pretext to completely eliminate existing welfare state provisions like free education or health care, and just submit everything to the market, to a radical version such as Leslie and Candi support, which assumes existing unconditional guarantees like the British National Health Service will be left in place.[20] One sees Basic Income as a way of contracting, the other sees it as a way of expanding the zone of unconditionality. This latter is the kind that I would myself be able to get behind. I do this despite my own politics, which is quite explicitly antistatist: as an anarchist, I look forward to seeing states dismantled entirely, and in the meantime, have no interest in policies that will give states more power than they have already.

But oddly, this is why I can get behind Basic Income. Basic Income might seem like it is a vast expansion of state power, since presumably it's the government (or some quasi-state institution like a central bank) that would be creating and distributing the money, but, in fact, it's the exactly the reverse. Huge sections of government—and precisely, the most intrusive and obnoxious ones, since they are most deeply involved in the moral surveillance of ordinary citizens—would be instantly made unnecessary and could be simply closed down.[21] Yes, millions of minor government officials and benefit advisors like Leslie would be thrown out of their current jobs, but they'd all receive basic income too. Maybe some of them will come up with something genuinely important to do, like installing solar panels, as Leslie suggests, or discovering the cure for cancer. But it wouldn't matter if they instead formed jug bands, devoted themselves to restoring antique furniture, spelunking, translating Mayan hieroglyphics, or trying to set the world record for having sex at an advanced age. Let them do what they like! Whatever they end up doing, they will almost certainly be happier than they are now, imposing sanctions on the unemployed for arriving late at CV-building seminars or checking to see if the homeless are in possession of three forms of ID; and everybody else will be better off for their newfound happiness.

Even a modest Basic Income program could become a stepping-stone toward the most profound transformation of all: to unlatch work from livelihood entirely. As we saw in the last chapter, a strong moral case can be made for paying everyone the same regardless of their work. Yet the argument cited in that chapter did assume people were being paid *for* their work, and this would at the very least require some kind of monitoring bureaucracy to ensure that people were, in fact, working, even if it did not have to measure how hard or how much they produced. A full Basic Income would eliminate the compulsion to work, by offering a reasonable standard of living to all, and then either leaving it up to each individual to decide whether they wished to pursue further wealth, by doing a paying job, or selling something, or whether they wished to do something else with their time. Alternately, it might open the way to developing better ways of distributing goods entirely. (Money is after all a rationing ticket, and in an ideal world, one would presumably wish to do as little rationing as possible.) Obviously, all this depends on the assumption that human beings don't have to be compelled to work, or at least, to do something that they feel is useful or beneficial to others. As we've seen, this is a reasonable assumption. Most people would prefer not to spend their days sitting around watching TV and the handful who really are inclined to be total parasites are not going to be a significant burden on society, since the total amount of work required to maintain people in comfort and security is not that formidable. The compulsive workaholics who insist on doing far more than they really have to would more than compensate for the occasional slackers.[22]

Finally, the concept of unconditional universal support is directly relevant to two issues that have come up repeatedly over the course of this book. The first is the sadomasochistic dynamic of hierarchical work arrangements—a dynamic that tends to be sharply exacerbated when everyone knows the work to be pointless. A lot of the day-to-day misery in working people's lives springs directly from this source. In chapter 4, I cited Lynn Chancer's notion of sadomasochism in everyday life, and particularly the point that, unlike actual BDSM play, where there's always a safe-word, when "normal" people fall into the same dynamic, there's never such an easy way out.

"You can't say 'orange' to your boss."

It's always occurred to me this insight is important and could even become the basis for a theory of social liberation. I like to think that Michel Foucault, the French social philosopher, was moving in this direction before his tragic death in 1984. Foucault, according to people who knew him, underwent a remarkable personal transformation on discovering BDSM, turning from a notoriously cagey and standoffish personality to one suddenly warm, open, and friendly[23]—but his theoretical ideas also entered into a period of transformation that he was never able to fully bring to fruit. Foucault, of course, is famous mainly as a theorist of power, which he saw as flowing through all human relationships, even as the basic substance of human sociality, since he once defined it as simply a matter of "acting on another's actions."[24] This always created a peculiar paradox because while he wrote in such a way as to suggest he was an antiauthoritarian opposed to power, he defined power in such a way that social life would impossible without it. At the very end of his career, he seems to have aimed to resolve the dilemma by introducing a distinction between what he called power and domination. The first, he said, was just a matter of "strategic games." Everyone is playing power games all the time, we can hardly help it, but neither is there anything objectionable about our doing so. So in this, his very last interview:

Power is not an evil. Power is strategic games. We know very well that power is not an evil. Take for example, sexual relationship or love relationships. To exercise power over another, in a sort of open strategic game, where things could be reversed, that is not evil. That is part of love, passion, of sexual pleasure . . .

It seems to me we must distinguish the relations of power as strategic games between liberties—strategic games that result from the fact that some people try to determine the conduct of others—and the states of domination, which are what we ordinarily call "power."[25]

Foucault isn't quite explicit on how we are to distinguish one from the other, other than to say that in domination, things are not open and cannot be reversed—otherwise fluid relations of power become rigid and "congealed." He gives the example of the mutual manipulation of teacher and student (power-good), versus the tyranny of the authoritarian pedant (domination-bad). I think Foucault is circling around something here, and never quite gets to the promised land: a safe-word theory of social liberation. Because this would be the obvious solution. It's not so much that certain games are fixed—some people like fixed games, for whatever reasons—but that sometimes, you can't get out of them. The question then does indeed become: What *would* be the equivalent of saying "orange" to one's boss? Or to an insufferable bureaucrat, obnoxious academic advisor, or abusive boyfriend? How do we create only games that we actually feel like playing, because we can opt out at any time? In the economic field, at least, the answer is obvious. All of the gratuitous sadism of workplace politics depends on one's inability to say "I quit" and feel no economic consequences. If Annie's boss knew Annie's income would be unaffected even if she did walk off in disgust at being called out yet again for a problem she'd fixed months ago, she would know better than to call her into the office to begin with. Basic Income in this sense would, indeed, give workers the power to say "orange" to their boss.

Which leads to the second theme: it's not just that Annie's boss would have to treat her with at least a small degree of dignity and respect in a world of guaranteed incomes. If Universal Basic Income was instituted, it's very hard to imagine jobs like Annie's long continue to exist. One could well imagine people who didn't *have* to work to survive still choosing to become dental assistants, or toymakers, or movie ushers, or tugboat operators, or even sewage treatment plant inspectors. It's even easier to imagine them choosing to become some combination of several of these. It's extremely difficult to imagine someone living without financial constraints choosing to spend any significant amount of their time highlighting forms for a Medical Care Cost Management company—let alone in an office where underlings were not allowed to speak. In such a world, Annie would have no reason to give up on being a preschool teacher, unless she actually decided she was no longer interested in being a preschool teacher, and if Medical Care Cost Management companies continued to exist, they would have to figure out another way to highlight their forms.

It's unlikely Medical Care Cost Management companies would exist for long. The need for such firms (if you can even call it a "need") is a direct result of a bizarre and labyrinthine US health care system which overwhelming majorities of Americans see as idiotic and unjust, and which they wish to see replaced by some kind of public insurance or public health provider. As we have seen, one of the main reasons this system has not been replaced—at least, if President Obama's own account is to be believed—is precisely because its inefficiency creates jobs like Annie's. If nothing else, Universal Basic Income would mean millions of people who recognize the absurdity of this situation will have the time to engage in political organizing to change it, since they will no longer be forced to highlight forms for eight hours a day, or (if they insist on doing something useful with their lives) scramble around for an equivalent amount of time trying to figure out a way to pay the bills.

It's hard to escape the impression that for many of those who, like Obama, defend the existence of bullshit jobs, that's one of the most appealing things about such arrangements. As Orwell noted, a population busy working, even at completely useless occupations, doesn't have time to do much else. At the very least, this is further incentive not to do anything about the situation.

Be this as it may, however, it opens the way to my second and final point. The first objection typically raised when someone suggests guaranteeing everyone a livelihood regardless of work is that if you do so, people simply won't work. This is just obviously false and at this point I think we can dismiss it out of hand. The second, more serious objection is that most will work, but many will choose work that's of interest only to themselves. The streets would fill up with bad poets, annoying street mimes, and promoters of crank scientific theories, and nothing would get done. What the phenomenon of bullshit jobs really brings home is the foolishness of such assumptions. No doubt a certain proportion of the population of a free society would spend their lives on projects most others would consider to be silly or pointless; but it's hard to imagine how it would go much over 10 or 20 percent. But already right now, 37 to 40 percent of workers in rich countries *already* feel their jobs are pointless. Roughly half the economy consists of, or exists in support of, bullshit. And it's not even particularly interesting bullshit! If we let everyone decide for themselves how they were best fit to benefit humanity, with no restrictions at all, *how could they possibly end up with a distribution of labor more inefficient than the one we already have?*

This is a powerful argument for human freedom. Most of us like to talk about freedom in the abstract, even claim that it's the most important thing for anyone to fight or die for, but we don't think a lot about what being free or practicing freedom might actually mean. The main point of this book was not to propose concrete policy prescriptions, but to start us thinking and arguing about what a genuine free society might actually be like.

Acknowledgments

I would like to thank the hundreds of people who shared their stories of workplace woe, but cannot be named. You know who you are.

I would like to thank Vyvian Raoul at *Strike!* for commissioning the original essay and everyone else at *Strike!* (especially The Special Patrol Group) for making all this possible.

This book wouldn't exist without the hard work of my team at Simon & Schuster: editor Ben Loehnen, Erin Reback, Jonathan Karp, and Amar Deol, and without the encouragement of my agent, Melissa Flashman at Janklow & Nesbit.

And, of course, much gratitude to my friends who put up with me and my colleagues at LSE, for their patience and support, and particularly to the administrative staff: Yanina and Tom Hinrichsen, Renata Todd, Camilla Kennedy Harper, and Andrea Elsik. Sophie Carapetian and Rebecca Coles provided excellent research assistance and support.

I think I should also thank Megan Laws, the indefatigable LSE anthropology graduate student whose entire job is to monitor my "impact." I can only hope this book will facilitate her efforts.

Notes

Preface: On the Phenomenon of Bullshit Jobs

1. I've got a lot of push-back about the actuaries, and now think I was being unfair to them. Some actuarial work does make a difference. I'm still convinced the rest could disappear with no negative consequences.
2. David Graeber, "The Modern Phenomenon of Bullshit Jobs," *Canberra (Australia) Times* online, last modified September 3, 2013, www.canberratimes .com.au/national/public-service/the-modern-phenomenon-of-bullshit -jobs-20130831-2sy3j.html.
3. To my knowledge, only one book has ever been written on the subject of bullshit jobs, *Boulots de Merde!*, by Paris-based journalists Julien Brygo and Olivier Cyran (2015)—and the authors told me it was directly inspired by my article. It's a good book but covers a rather different range of questions than my own.

Chapter 1: What Is a Bullshit Job?

1. "Bullshit Jobs," LiquidLegends, www.liquidlegends.net/forum/general /460469-bullshit-jobs?page=3, last modified October 1, 2014.
2. "Spanish Civil Servant Skips Work for 6 Years to Study Spinoza," Jewish Telegraphic Agency (JTA), last modified February 26, 2016, www.jta.org

/2016/02/26/news-opinion/world/spanish-civil-servant-skips-work-for-6-years-to-study-spinoza.

3. Jon Henley, "Long Lunch: Spanish Civil Servant Skips Work for Years Without Anyone Noticing," *Guardian* (US), last modified February 26, 2016, www.theguardian.com/world/2016/feb/12/long-lunch-spanish-civil-servant-skips-work-for-years-without-anyone-noticing. Perhaps he was inspired by Spinoza's argument that all beings strive to maximize their power, but that power consists equally of the ability to have effects on other beings, but also, to be affected by them. From a Spinozan perspective, having a job where you affect and are affected by no one would be the worst possible employment situation.

4. Post carriers are clearly not bullshit jobs but the implication of the story seems to be that since 99 percent of the mail they chose not to deliver was junk mail, they might as well have been. This seems unlikely to have actually been the case but the story reflects on public attitudes. For shifting attitudes toward postal workers, see my *Utopia of Rules* (2015), 153–163.

5. http://news.bbc.co.uk/1/hi/world/europe/3410547.stm?a, accessed April 7, 2017.

6. "Vier op tien werknemers noemt werk zinloos," http://overhetnieuwewerken .nl/vier-op-tien-werknemers-noemt-werk-zinloos/, accessed July 10, 2017.

7. Typical remark, from Rufus: "I'd love to tell you that my most worthless job was making lattes for very particular and peculiar people, but in retrospect, I understand I played a vital role in helping them through their day."

8 I should observe that the following is drawn mainly from pop culture representations of hit men, rather than any ethnographic or sociological analysis of real ones.

9. Interestingly enough, "bull" is not an abbreviation for "bullshit," but "bullshit" is an early-twentieth-century elaboration on "bull." The term is ultimately derived from the French *bole*, meaning "fraud or deceit." The term "bullshit" is first attested in an unpublished poem by T. S. Eliot. "Bollocks" is another derivation from "bole."

10. I would have said "lying" but the philosopher Harry Frankfurt (2005) famously argued that bullshitting is not the same as lying. The difference between them is analogous to the difference between murder and manslaughter; one is intentional deception, the other, reckless disregard for the truth. I'm not sure the distinction entirely works in this context but

I didn't think entering a debate on the subject would be particularly helpful.

11. To fully appreciate the feudal connection, the reader might consider the name "Corleone." This was the name of the fictional Mafia family in Mario Puzo's novel and Francis Ford Coppola's film *The Godfather* but, in fact, it's the name of a town in Sicily that is notorious for being the home of many famous mafiosi. In Italian it means "lion-heart." The reason for this appears to be that the Normans who conquered England in 1066 had also conquered previously Arab-held Sicily, and imported many features of Arabic administration. Readers will recall in most Robin Hood stories, the archvillain is the Sheriff of Nottingham, and the distant king away at the crusades is "Richard the Lion-Hearted." The word "sheriff" is just an anglicization of the Arabic *sharif* and was one of those positions inspired by the administration of Sicily. The exact connection between Corleone and the British king is debated, but some connection definitely exists. So however indirectly, the Marlon Brando character in *The Godfather* is named after Richard the Lion-Hearted.

12. Many burgle in their spare time. An apartment complex in which I once lived was once plagued by a series of burglaries, that always took place on a Monday. It was eventually determined that the burglar was a hairdresser, who generally get Mondays off.

13. Many thieves, ranging from art thieves to ordinary shoplifters, will hire out their services, but as such they are still just independent contractors, hence, self-employed. The case of the hit man is more ambiguous. Some might argue that if one is a long-standing but subordinate member of a criminal organization that does qualify as a "job," but it's not my impression (I don't really know, of course) that most people in such positions see it quite that way.

14. I do not say such a job is "a form of paid employment that *feels* so completely pointless, unnecessary, or pernicious that even the employee cannot justify its existence," I say it's "a form of paid employment that *is* so completely pointless, unnecessary, or pernicious that even the employee cannot justify its existence." In other words, I am not just saying that the employee believes his work to be bullshit, but that his belief is both valid and correct.

15. Let me take my own situation as an example. I am currently employed as a professor of anthropology at the London School of Economics. There are people who consider anthropology to be the very definition of a bullshit

subject. In 2011 Governor Rick Scott of Florida even singled out the discipline as his prime example of one his state's universities would be better off without (Scott Jaschik, "Florida GOP Vs. Social Science," *Inside Higher Education*, last modified October 12, 2011, www.insidehighered.com/news/2011/10/12/florida_governor_challenges_idea_of_non_stem_degrees).

16. I've been told that inside Countrywide Financial, one of the key players in the subprime mortgage scandals of 2008, there were basically two ranks in the company—the lowly "nerds," and the insiders—the insiders being those who had been told about the scams. I encountered an even more extreme example in my own research: one woman wrote to me that she had worked for almost a year selling advertising for an in-flight magazine that she gradually realized did not exist. She became suspicious when she realized she had never once seen a copy of the magazine in the office, or on an airplane, despite the fact she was a fairly frequent flyer. Eventually her coworkers quietly confirmed that the entire operation was a fraud.

17. There are exceptions to this as to all rules. In many large organizations like banks, as we will see, top-level managers will hire consultants or internal auditors to figure out what it is that people actually do; one bank analyst told me about 80 percent of bank workers are engaged in unnecessary tasks and most he felt were unaware of it, since they were kept in the dark about their role in the larger organization. Still, he said, their supervisors didn't know much better, and his suggestions for reform were invariably rejected. It's important to emphasize here, too, it's not that people mistakenly believed their jobs to be bullshit, but quite the other way around.

18. Even here one can imagine objections. What about Scientologists? Most of those who provide e-meter sessions to allow people to discover traumas in their past lives seem to be convinced their work has enormous social value, even as the great majority of the population is convinced they are delusional, or frauds. But again this isn't really relevant as no one is really saying "faith-healer" is a bullshit job.

19. A case could be made that often propaganda which is ostensibly aimed at tricking outsiders is really primarily aimed at assuaging the consciences of the propagandists themselves.

20. The remarks were extempore and not written down. The quotation is reconstructed partly from the passages cited in John Adam Byrne, "Influential Economist Says Wall Street Is Full of Crooks," *New York Post* online, April 28, 2013, http://nypost.com/2013/04/28/influential-economist-says

-wall-streets-full-of-crooks, partly from a partial transcript in a *Business Insider* article by Janet Tavakoli, www.businessinsider.com/i-regard-the-wall-street-moral-environment-as-pathological-2013-9?IR=T, accessed April 21, 2017), and partly from my own notes taken at the time.

21. In fact, over the course of my research, I've run into a surprising number of people (well, three) with college educations who, frustrated by the pointlessness of the office work available to them, actually did become cleaners simply to feel they were doing an honest day's work.

22. I really shouldn't have to point this out but since I find there will always be some readers who have a hard time with basic logic: saying shit jobs tend to be useful and productive is not saying that all useful and productive jobs tend to be shit.

23. *House of the Dead*, 1862, trans. Constance Garnett (Mineola, NY: Dover, 2004), 17–18. My friend Andrej Grubacic tells me this was actually done to his grandfather as a form of torture in a Titoist reeducation camp in Yugoslavia in the 1950s. The jailers had evidently read the classics.

24. The three-part list is not meant to be comprehensive. For instance, it leaves out the category of what's often referred to as "guard labor," much of which (unnecessary supervisors) is bullshit, but much of which is simply obnoxious or bad.

25. In David Graeber, *The Utopia of Rules: On Technology, Stupidity, and the Secret Joys of Bureaucracy* (Brooklyn, NY: Melville House, 2015), 9, I refer to this as "the Iron Law of Liberalism": that "any market reform, any government initiative intended to reduce red tape and promote market forces will have the ultimate effect of increasing the total number of regulations, the total amount of paperwork, and the total number of bureaucrats the government employs."

26. In fact, that's largely what making someone wear a uniform means, since uniforms are often placed on people (say, those working in a hotel laundry) who are never seen by the public at all. It's a way of saying "you should think of yourself as being under military discipline."

27. Oddly, the survey did break down the results by political voting preferences (Tory voters were least, and UKIP voters most likely to think their jobs were bullshit) and region (Southern England outside London was highest at 42 percent bullshit rate, Scotland lowest at 27 percent). Age and "social grade" seemed relatively insignificant.

28. *The Restaurant at the End of the Universe* (Hitchhiker's Guide to the Galaxy, book #2) (London: Macmillan Pan Books, 1980), 140.

29. There has been some debate as one might imagine among Douglas Adams fans on this topic but the consensus seems to be that while some jobs in the 1970s involved cleaning phones and other electronic equipment, "telephone sanitizer" as a separate profession did not exist. This did not stop Adams from collaborating with Graham Chapman of Monty Python in creating a TV special starring Ringo Starr called *The Telephone Sanitisers of Navarone*, which, sadly, was never produced.

30. To be fair, we learn later that the joke was on the Golgafrinchams, since they all eventually die from a plague that started from an improperly sanitized telephone. But no one ever seems to remember that part.

31. Hair salons in immigrant communities will often serve a similar role for both men and women. I even had some friends who became the in-house barbers for a big London squat who found this started happening to them as well: anyone new to town would stop in for a trim to find out what was going on.

32. Not to mention, she added, the fact that the amount of money invested in keeping them dancing on boxes could, if redirected, easily suffice to head off the threat of climate change. "The sex industry makes it evident that the most valuable thing that many women can offer is their bodies as sexual commodities when they are very young. It determines that many women earn more at eighteen to twenty-five than they ever do again in their lives. This is definitely the case in my own life"—the author being a successful academic and author who still doesn't make as much a year as she once might have in three months' stripping.

33. As evidence for this generalization: if telemarketers or useless middle managers were to be made illegal, a black market would be unlikely to emerge to replace them. Obviously, historically this has tended to happen in the case of sex work. This is why one might say the problem is patriarchy itself—the concentration of so much wealth and power in the hands of males who are then kept sexually unfulfilled or taught to seek out certain forms of gratification rather than others—and therefore something much more essential to the nature of society itself.

34. "L'invasion des «métiers à la con», une fatalité économique?," Jean-Laurent Cassely, *Slate*, August 26, 2013, www.slate.fr/story/76744/metiers-a-la-con. Accessed 23 September, 2013.

Chapter 2: What Sorts of Bullshit Jobs Are There?

1. I did this by creating an email account ("doihaveabsjoborwhat@gmail
.com"), and asking for input on Twitter. Gmail, rather quaintly, does not
allow the word "bullshit" in addresses.

2. The names therefore are all made up, and I have avoided naming any specific employers, or geographic information that might give identities away:
for instance, "a famous university in New Haven, Connecticut," or "a small
publishing firm based in Devon County, England, owned by a consortium in
Berlin." In some cases, such details are changed; in other cases, simply left out.

3. The quotations that follow are all drawn from this database unless otherwise indicated. I have kept them largely as I received them, except for some
light editing—changing abbreviations into full words, adjusting punctua-
tion, minor grammatical or stylistic tweaks, and so forth.

4. One BBC video that has been drawn to my attention divides "pointless
jobs" into three types, "No Work at Work," "Managers of Management that
Manage Managers," and "Negative Social Value." See "Do You Have a Pointless Job?," BBC online, last modified April 20, 2017, www.bbc.com/capital
/story/20170420-do-you-have-a-pointless-job.

5. So in 1603 one William Perkins wrote "it is required that such as are commonly called serving-men should have beside the office of waiting, some
other particular calling, unless they tend on men of great place and state . . .
For waiting-servants, by reason they spend most of their time in eating
and drinking, sleeping and gaming after dinner and after supper, do prove
the most unprofitable members both in Church and Commonwealth. For
when either their good masters die, or they be turned out of their office for
some misdemeanour, they are not fit for any calling, being unable to labor,
and thus they give themselves either to beg or to steal" (in Thomas 1999:
418). On the history of the term "waiter" see chapter 6. I should also emphasize that I am not saying *real* feudal retainers were "bullshit jobs" in the
modern sense, since they rarely felt obliged to claim to be anything other
than what they were; insofar as they misrepresented themselves, it was by
pretending to do less than they actually did, not more.

6. They also ran occasional errands. One gets a sense of how common such
characters used to be by how many different words for them there were: not
just footmen, but flunkies, henchmen, gofers, minions, lackeys, cronies,
menials, attendants, hirelings, knaves, myrmidons, retainers, and valets—

and these are just those that most immediately come to mind. All these are not to be confused with toadies, cronies, sidekicks, sycophants, parasites, stooges, yes-men, and the like, who are more in the order of independent hangers-on. It's worthy of pointing out that in European courts it was really the courtiers who performed no useful function; the uniformed attendants actually did all sorts of odd jobs when they weren't standing around during ceremonial events. But the whole point was to look as if they didn't.

7. I recognize that it is extremely rare for the rate of extraction to be that high, but as I say, this is just a thought experiment to bring out the dynamics that tend to emerge in such situations.

8. One might even say it's one of those things of which what we call "honor" historically consisted of.

9. The number of domestic servants in North Atlantic countries has declined precipitously since the First World War, but to a large extent their ranks have been replaced, first by what are called "service workers" ("waiter," for instance, was originally the name for a kind of household servant), and second by ever-growing legions of administrative assistants and other such underlings in the corporate sector. For an example of old feudal styles of unnecessary labor bleeding into the present day, consider this account: "My friend is working on a film set at an old manor house in Hertfordshire, where he runs errands and ensures that the crew don't mess up the nice old building. At the end of every day he has to spend two solid hours 'candle watching.' The Lord and Lady of the house told the crew that after the candles are extinguished in the main hall someone must watch them for at least TWO hours to make sure they don't spontaneously burst into flames again and burn the house down. My friend is not allowed to douse the candles in water or 'cheat' it any way." When asked *why* he wasn't allowed to stick the candles in water, he replied, "They gave no explanation."

10. Just to be absolutely clear: there are plenty of receptionists who serve a necessary function. I am referring here to those who do not.

11. The same remains true today, incidentally. I am personally acquainted with one young woman who, despite having no military experience whatsoever, ended up, as personal assistant to a NATO official, actually writing many strategic plans for operations in a war zone (neither do I have any reason to believe her plans weren't just as good or better than any NATO general would have come up with).

12. At the very least this is true of high-tech weaponry. One might argue that

most countries also maintain armies to suppress real or potential civil unrest, but this rarely involves a need for fighter jets, submarines, or MX mis-
siles. Historically, Mexico has had an explicit policy of not wasting money
on such expensive toys, arguing that owing to their geographic position,
the only countries they'd be likely to enter into hostilities with would be either the USA, or Guatemala. If they went to war with the USA, they'd lose,
pretty much regardless of armament; if they went to war with Guatemala,
they'd win, with or without fighter jets. Hence, Mexico merely maintains
such equipment as would suffice to suppress domestic dissent.

13. Such conversations are particularly challenging to me since in the 1980s
academics such as myself largely abandoned the idea that consumer demand was the product of marketing manipulation, and took up the idea
that consumers were basically patching together crazy-quilt identities by
using consumer goods in ways that had never really been intended (as if
everyone in America had turned into Snoop Dogg, or RuPaul). Granted I
was always pretty suspicious of that narrative. But it's clear that many of
those who work in the industry are quite certain that they really are what
everyone thought they were in the sixties and seventies.

14. A crude natural language script dating back to the late 1960s.

15. I have personal experience of this: lecturers at LSE are expected to fill out
elaborate time-allocation reports, with an hour-by-hour breakdown of
weekly professional activities. The forms offer endless fine distinctions between different sorts of administrative activity but no explicit category for
"reading and writing books." When I pointed this out I was told I could place
such activities under "LSE-funded research," that is, what was important
about research from the school's perspective was 1. that I had not got myself
outside funding to pay for this reading and writing activity, and 2. that therefore they were paying me to do it when I could be doing my real job.

16. A fairly typical testimony from within the IT industry: "I have often seen
projects designed to obscure responsibility. For example, to evaluate an IT
system. The purpose is not to affect the decision, which is taken somewhere
in the corridors, but to claim that everyone was heard and all concerns were
taken seriously. Since the project is only a pretense all work on the project is
wasted, and people soon realize and stop taking it seriously." This kind of false
consensus-seeking is common in ostensibly collegial institutions like universities or NGOs, but is quite common in the more hierarchical corporations
as well.

17. To give a sense of the scale of this industry, Citigroup announced in 2014 that by the next year, it would have thirty thousand employees working in compliance, or about 13 percent of the total staff. Sital S. Patel, "Citi Will Have Almost 30,000 Employees in Compliance by Year-end," *The Tell* (blog), MarketWatch, July 14, 2014, http://blogs.marketwatch.com/thetell/2014/07/14/citi-will-have-almost-30000-employees-in-compliance-by-year-end.

18. Except, of course, by trying to make some special arrangement that would allow someone else to do the paperwork for her, this was considered, for some reason, quite out of the question.

19. Another good example of a public/private box-ticking industry is in construction. Consider the following testimony:

> Sophie: I'm in this lucrative 'consultant' line of work for planning permissions. Back in the sixties just about the only consultant who submitted information for a planning permission was the architect. Now a planning permission for a large-ish building is accompanied by a long list of reports by consultants (including me!):
>
> Environmental impact assessment
> Landscape and visual impact assessment
> Transport report
> Wind microclimate assessment
> Sunlight/daylight analysis
> Heritage setting assessment
> Archaeology assessment
> Landscape maintenance management report
> Tree impact assessment
> Flood risk assessment . . .
> . . . and there's more than that!
>
> Each report is about 50 to 100 pages, and yet the strange thing is, the resulting buildings are ugly boxes remarkably similar to the ones we built in the sixties, so I don't think the reports are serving any purpose!"

20. Or only ostensible role.

21. One corporate consultant wrote: "I look forward to the day that someone in my industry steps up and goes full Sokal affair—i.e., submits a consulting

report that is entirely made up of vague business buzzwords, and doesn't actually contain any structured information at all. Although I suspect this has already happened many times, just without the consultants in question being conscious of it."

22. This made sense, in retrospect, because if you are a medical researcher, you already have all these journals in the library or have access to digitized versions; there would be no reason to fall back on interlibrary loan.

23. It's interesting to compare corporate magazines with the ones that Labor unions put out, which I suspect predate them as a literary form. They certainly have their share of puff pieces, but also discuss serious problems. My father was a member of Amalgamated Lithographers Local 1 in New York, a printers' union, and I remember as a child taking pride in the fact that their in-house magazine, *Lithopinion*, was by far the most beautiful magazine I'd ever seen, owing to their eagerness to show off new graphic techniques. It also contained real hard-hitting political analysis.

24. For instance, a recent survey determined that 80 percent of employees feel their managers are useless and that they could do their job just as well without them. It does not appear to document how many managers agree, but one has to assume the number is substantially lower ("Managers Can be Worse than Useless, Survey Finds," *Central Valley Business Times*, December 5, 2017, http://www.centralvalleybusinesstimes.com/stories/001/?ID= 33748, accessed December 18, 2017.

25. As we shall see, this is no less true of America, or anywhere else.

26. Here Chloe seems to be responding to the title of a version of my original essay that had run on evonomics.com under the title "Why Capitalism Creates Pointless Jobs." I didn't make up the title. Normally I avoid attributing agency to abstractions.

27. This must be assumed unless there is some reason to believe that pointless occupations require either more or less support work than useful ones.

28. This figure is obviously inexact. On the one hand, a very large percentage of cleaners, electricians, builders, etc., work for private individuals and not for firms at all. On the other hand, I am counting the 13 percent who say they aren't sure if their jobs are bullshit or nonbullshit jobs. The 50 percent figure (actually 50.3 percent) is based on the assumption these two factors would roughly cancel each other out.

Chapter 3: Why Do Those in Bullshit Jobs Regularly Report Themselves Unhappy? (On Spiritual Violence, Part 1)

1. And as we'll see even these tended to be highly ambivalent.

2. After writing this I presented my analysis to Eric, who confirmed it and added details: "I could definitely see that the middle- and upper-middle-class kids in the lower rungs of that job were seeing it as a path to career advancement—partly in terms of how they socialized around work (watching the rugby on a weekend in someone's suburban Bovis-home conservatory; cocktails in tacky wine bars but always networking, networking), and that for some it was merely a stop-gap that filled in an otherwise-blank spot on the CV until a family member found them a better opportunity." He added, "It's interesting that you mention the idea of the caring classes. My father's first remark when I quit that position was to say that I was a nonsensical idiot to turn down such a good paycheck. His second was to ask, 'What good could that job do for anyone anyway?'"

   On the other hand, Eric pointed out he does now have two advanced degrees, a research fellowship, and a successful career—he attributes much of this to the knowledge of social theory he gained while living in the squat.

3. Rufus more or less confirmed this when I asked about his father's motivations: he said his father couldn't stand the company, either, felt he was basically in a bullshit job himself, and just wanted his son to have something to put on his CV. The question remains why, as VP, he couldn't just have lied.

4. It is interesting to note that the British welfare state, like most post–World War II welfare states, was consciously constructed against the principle that the poor need to be compelled to labor. This started to change almost everywhere starting in the 1970s.

5. Since the seventies, surveys have regularly revealed that 74 percent to 80 percent of workers claim that, if they won the lottery or came into some similar fortune, they would continue working. The first study was by Morse and Weiss (1966), but it has been replicated frequently since.

6. Classic source on this: Robert D. Atkinson. 2002. "Prison Labor: It's More than Breaking Rocks." *Policy Report*, Washington, DC, Progressive Policy Institute—though by citing I am in no sense supporting his policy conclusions that prison labor should be made generally available to industry!

7. And also, crucially, that they might just as easily *not* have done it. Hence, Groos defined the attendant joy as being the feeling of freedom.

8. So, for instance, another psychoanalyst, G. A. Klein, writes, "[W]hen the baby starts to grasp articles, sits up, tries to walk, he begins a process that eventually yields the sense that the locus and origins of these achievements is in himself. When the child thus feels the change as originating within himself, he begins to have a sense of being himself, a psychologically, not simply physically, autonomous unit" (1976: 275).

    Francis Broucek, "The Sense of Self," *Bulletin of the Menninger Clinic* 41 (1977): 86, feels this doesn't go far enough: "The sense of efficacy is at the core of the primitive sense of self and not a property of some already defined self. This primitive feeling of efficacy is what the psychoanalytic literature refers to as infantile omnipotence—a sense of efficacy, the limits of which are not yet apprehended . . . The primary sense of self emerges from effectance pleasure associated with the successful correspondence of intention and effect." There is thus a fundamental joy in the knowledge of one's own existence that is tied to one's freedom to have effects on the world around you, including others, at first regardless of what those may be.

9. Francis Broucek, "Efficacy in Infancy: A Review of Some Experimental Studies and Their Possible Implications to Clinical Theory," *International Journal of Psycho-Analysis* 60 (January 1, 1979): 314. "The total inner separation from the environment in response to such traumata may foreshadow later schizophrenic, depressive, narcissistic or phobic behaviour, depending on the frequency, severity and duration of the experiences of failed influence or invalidated expectancy, the age at which such traumata occur, and how much of a sense of self based on efficacy experiences has been established prior to the traumata."

10. I am, of course, offering an extremely simplified version of Schiller's philosophy.

11. In legal terms, most slaveholding societies justify the institution by the legal fiction that slaves are prisoners of war—and, in fact, many slaves in human history were captured as the result of military operations. The first chain gangs were employed in Roman plantations. They were made up of slaves who had been placed in the plantation's *ergastulum*, or prison, for disobedience or attempted escape.

12. There is certainly work on moralists in China, India, the classical world, and their concepts of work and idleness—for instance, the Roman distinction of *otium* and *negotium*—but I am speaking here more of the practical

questions, such as when and where even useless work came to be seen as preferable to no work at all.

13. Writing of sixteenth- and seventeenth-century weavers, E. P. Thompson informs us: "The work pattern was one of alternate bouts of intense labor and of idleness, wherever men were in control of their own working lives. (The pattern persists among some self-employed—artists, writers, small farmers, and perhaps also with students—today, and provokes the question whether it is not a "natural" human work rhythm.) On Monday or Tuesday, according to tradition, the hand-loom went to the slow chant of Plen-ty of Time, Plen-ty of Time: on Thursday and Friday, A day t'lat, A day" (1967:73).

14. When I was in high school there was a kind of macho game among the coolest students, before exams, where they would boast how many hours they'd gone without sleep-cramming beforehand: thirty-six, forty-eight, even sixty hours. It was macho because it implied such students had not done any study at all before, since they had been thinking about more important things. I rapidly figured out that if one reduced oneself to a mindless zombie, the extra hours of study weren't actually going to help. I suspect this is one reason I am now a professor.

15. Hunting versus gathering again being the paradigmatic example. Child-care is probably the most dramatic exception: it's largely a woman's domain, but it is always generating stories.

16. I am ignoring here the managerial functions of running their estates, but it's not clear this was considered labor at the time. I suspect it wasn't.

17. Historically speaking, the institution of wage labor is a sophisticated late-comer. The very idea of wage labor involves two difficult conceptual steps. First, it requires the abstraction of man's labor from both his person and his work. When one purchases an object from an ancient craftsman, one has not bought his labor but the object, which he has produced under his own time and his own conditions of work. But when one purchases an abstraction, labor power, which the purchaser then uses it at a time and under conditions which he, the purchaser, not the "owner" of the labor power, determines (and for which he normally pays after he has consumed it). Second, the wage-labor system requires the establishment of a method of measuring the labor one has purchased, for purposes of payment, commonly by introducing a second abstraction, labor time.) M. I. Finley, *The Ancient Economy* (Berkeley: University of California Press, 1973), 65–66:

"We should not underestimate the magnitude, speaking socially rather than intellectually, of these two conceptual steps; even the Roman jurists found them difficult."

18. An early Christian would have been outright offended, since time, properly speaking, belonged only to God.

19. Though, in fact, Homer represents the fate of the *thes*, or occasional agricultural hireling, who rented himself out in this manner, as actually worse than a slave, since a slave at least is a member of a respectable household (*Odyssey* 11.489–91).

20. The only notable exception to this rule is that free citizens in democracies were often willing to hire themselves out to the government for public works: but this is because the government being seen as a collective of which the citizen was a member, it was essentially seen as working for oneself.

21. See David Graeber, "Turning Modes of Production Inside Out: Or, Why Capitalism Is a Transformation of Slavery (Short Version)," *Critique of Anthropology* 26, no. 1 (March 2006): 61–81.

22. E. E. Evans-Pritchard, *The Nuer: A Description of the Modes of Livelihood and Political Institutes of a Nilotic People* (Oxford: Clarendon Press, 1940), 103. Maurice Bloch, in *Anthropology and the Cognitive Challenge* (Cambridge: Cambridge University Press, 2012), 80–94, argues that Evans-Pritchard overstates things, and is no doubt correct if Evans-Pritchard really is making arguments as radical as is sometimes attributed to him, but I don't think he truly is. Anyway, the counterarguments have to do mainly with a sense of historical time rather than day-to-day activity.

23. E. P. Thompson, "Time, Work Discipline and Industrial Capitalism," *Past & Present* 38 (1967): 56–97.

24. See Jacques LeGoff, *Time, Work and Culture in the Middle Ages* (Chicago: University of Chicago Press, 1982), for classic essays extending E. P. Thompson's insights back to the High Middle Ages.

25. Those who designed modern universal education systems were quite explicit about all this: Thompson himself cites a number of them. I remember reading that someone once surveyed American employers about what it was they actually expected when they specified in a job ad that a worker must have a high school degree: a certain level of literacy? Or numeracy? The vast majority said no, a high school education, they found, did not guarantee such things—they mainly expected the worker would be able to show up on time. Interestingly, the more advanced the level of education,

however, the more autonomous the students and the more the old episodic pattern of work tends to reemerge.

26. The West Indian Marxist Eric Williams (1966) first emphasized the history of plantations in shaping the techniques of worker control later employed in factories; Marcus Rediker, *The Slave Ship: A Human History* (London: Penguin, 2004), adds ships, focusing on merchant vessels active in the slave trade, as the main other experiment-zone for rationalized work discipline during the period of merchant capital. Naval vessels are relevant, too, especially as they often employed unfree labor as well, since many of the sailors were "pressed" into service against their will. All of them involved contexts where in the absence of long traditions of what one could or could not demand of an employee—which were still felt to apply in areas that had emerged more directly from feudal relations—closely supervised work could itself be reorganized around new ideals of clocklike efficiency.

27. One reason all this is not obvious is that we have been conditioned to think, when we think of "wage labor," first of all of factory work, and factory work, in turn, as production-line work where the pace of labor is set by the machines. In fact, only a very small percentage of wage labor has ever been factory work and a relatively small percentage of that based on conveyer-belt-style production lines. I'll be writing more about the effect of such misconceptions in chapter 6.

28. Don't believe me? You can hire them here: www.smashpartyentertainment.com/living-statues-art.

29. I was slightly surprised that someone born around 1900 or 1910 had already internalized such an attitude and asked Wendy if her grandmother had ever been a supervisor or employer. She didn't think so, but later discovered that her grandmother had briefly helped run a chain of groceries many years before.

Chapter 4: What Is It Like to Have a Bullshit Job? (On Spiritual Violence, Part 2)

1. As noted in the last chapter, it's true that the entire class-period structure is really just a way to teach students time discipline for later factory work, and might now be considered redundant on that basis. But that's the system that exists.

2. My translation from the French: Je suis conseiller technique en insolvabilité dans un ministère qui serait l'équivalent de l'Inland Revenue. Environ 5 percent de ma tâche est de donner des conseil techniques. Le reste de la journée j'explique à mes collègues des procédures incompréhensibles, je les aide à trouver des directives qui ne servent à rien, I cheer up the troops, je réattribue des dossiers que "le système" a mal dirigé.

 Curieusement j'aime aller au travail. J'ai l'impression que je suis payé 60 000$/an pour faire l'équivalent d'un Sudoku ou mots croisés.

3. Obviously, such environments are not always nearly as carefree for members of the public who have to interact with such officials.

4. Obviously, the 4 percent figure would only be the case if no workers surveyed felt their work was both useful and unfulfilling, which is unlikely.

5. While it is quite rare for supervisors to tell workers directly they are supposed to pretend to work, it does happen occasionally. One car salesman wrote: "According to my superiors, if I'm being paid a salary, I have to be doing 'something' and 'pretend' to be productive even though there's no real value to the work. So, I spend several hours a day making phone calls to nobody. Does that make any sense?" Too much honesty in such matters appears to be a profound taboo almost anywhere. I remember once in graduate school, I had a gig doing research for a Marxist professor who among many other things specialized in the politics of workplace resistance. I figured if I could be honest with anyone, it would be him, so after he had explained to me how the timesheet worked I asked, "So how much can I lie? How many hours is it okay to just make up?" He looked at me as if I'd just said I was a starseed from another galaxy so I quickly changed the subject and assumed the answer was "a discrete amount."

6. Many workplaces are keenly aware of the dangers of easygoing supervisors and take active measures to head them off. Those who work counters in fast-food chains, which, of course, are in my terms generally shit jobs and not bullshit jobs, often tell me that each branch is carefully wired by closed-circuit TV to ensure that workers with nothing to do are not allowed to just sit around relaxing; if they are observed to do so by those monitoring in some central locations, their supervisor is called up and chewed out.

7. Roy Baumeister, Sara Wotman, and Arlene Stillwell, "Unrequited Love: On Heartbreak, Anger, Guilt, Scriptlessness, and Humiliation," *Journal of Personality and Social Psychology* 64, no. 3 (March 1993): 377–94. One friend of mine who once had a prolonged affair with a married man noted

a similar difficulty—unlike the betrayed wife, there's very little in the way of cultural models telling the "other woman" how she's supposed to feel. She's thinking of writing a book to begin to make up the gap. I hope she does so.

8. Nouri, the software developer, provides an interesting insight, suggesting that the hostility and mutual hatreds in a bullshit office might actually be functional in inspiring workers to act at all. He reports that while working in an obviously doomed banner ad company, an enterprise that made him depressed and sick, "I was so bored that a couple programmers snitched to management (excuse me, Scrum Master) about my productivity. So he hostilely gave me a month to prove myself, trying to accumulate evidence that I was missing doctor's notices. In two weeks, I outperformed the rest of the team combined, and the company's lead architect declared my code 'perfect.' Scrum Master was suddenly all smiles and rainbows again, telling me the doctor's notes were of no concern.

"I advised him to continue insulting me and threatening my job, if he wanted me to remain a high-performer. It was my twisted version of fun. Like an idiot, he refused.

"Lesson: hate is a great motivator, at least when there's no passion and fun. Maybe explains a lot of workplace aggression. Picking fights with someone at least gives you reason to carry on."

9. Erich Fromm, *The Anatomy of Human Destructiveness* (New York: Holt, Rinehart and Winston, 1973). Fromm's prime example of a nonsexual sadist is Joseph Stalin, and of a nonsexual necrophiliac, Adolf Hitler.

10. Lynn Chancer, *Sadomasochism in Everyday Life: The Dynamics of Power and Powerlessness* (New Brunswick, NJ: Rutgers University Press, 1992).

11. Romance novels, for instance, tend to feature attractive men who appear cruel and heartless but are ultimately revealed to be kindhearted and decent instead. One might argue that BDSM practice, from a submissive woman's perspective, encodes the possibility of this transformation as part of the structure of the event and under her own ultimate control.

12. Article 23 of the UN Universal Declaration of Human Rights, for example, states: "Everyone has the right to work, to free choice of employment, to just and favorable conditions of work and to protection against unemployment." It also guarantees equal pay for equal work, compensation adequate to support a family, and the right to form labor unions. It says nothing about the purpose of the work itself.

13. The office was also "rife with bullying and deeply, deeply strange office

politics"—the usual sadomasochistic dynamics one can expect to ensue in hierarchical environments, as usual, too, exacerbated by the shared guilty knowledge that there's nothing really at stake.

14. There is a happy ending to this one, at least temporarily: Rachel reports she was soon after able to find work for a program teaching remedial math to poor children. It is everything her insurance job is not and pays well enough that she should be able to afford grad school.

15. Patrick Butler, "Thousands Have Died After Being Found Fit for Work, DWP Figures Show," *Guardian* (US), last modified August 27, 2015, www .theguardian.com/society/2015/aug/27/thousands-died-after-fit-for-work-assessment-dwp-figures.

16. Mark: "Personally I often used to wish I wasn't aware that my job was bullshit. Kind of like how Neo in the Matrix movies may sometimes have wished he hadn't taken the red pill. I'd despair (and still do) that I'm working in the public sector to help people, but I rarely if ever help anyone. I also feel a sense of guilt that I'm paid by taxpayers to do this."

17. He adds: "Herbert Read's 'To hell with culture' best describes this situation." I checked. It isn't bad.

18. It is important to emphasize that in professional environments, the ability to play the role is generally far more important than the ability to actually do the work. Mathematician Jeff Schmidt in his excellent *Disciplined Minds* (2001) carefully documents how the bourgeois obsession with prioritizing form over content has played havoc with the professions. Why is it, he asks, that *Catch Me If You Can*–style imposters can often successfully pretend to be airline pilots or surgeons without anyone noticing they have no qualifications for the job? The answer he suggests is that it's almost impossible to get fired from a professional job—even pilot or surgeon—for mere incompetence, but very easy to get fired for defiance of accepted standards of external behavior, that is, for not properly playing the part. The imposters have zero competence, but play the part perfectly; hence, they are much less likely to be dismissed from their positions than, say, an accomplished pilot or surgeon who openly defies the unspoken codes of external comportment attendant on the role.

19. Psychological studies have shown that taking part in protests and street actions, at least, tend to have overall health benefits, reducing overall stress and with it rates of heart disease and other ailments: John Drury, "Social Identity as a Source of Strength in Mass Emergencies and Other Crowd

Events," *International Journal of Mental Health* 32, no. 4 (December 1, 2003): 77–93; also M. Klar and T. Kasser, "Some Benefits of Being an Activist," *Political Psychology* 30, no. 5 (2009): 755–77. The study, however, focuses on street actions; it would be interesting to see if this also extends to less embodied forms of protest.

20. Many, of course, then quit in horror and disgust. But we don't know the real numbers. Rachel suggested to me that many young people, unless in expensive metropolises like London, were less inclined to stick it out than their parents had been simply because the cost of housing and life in general is so ridiculously inflated that nowadays even an entry-level corporate job is not going to guarantee stability and security anymore.

Chapter 5: Why Are Bullshit Jobs Proliferating?

1. Louis D. Johnston, "History Lessons: Understanding the Declines in Manufacturing," *MinnPost*, last modified February 22, 2012, www.minnpost .com/macro-micro-minnesota/2012/02/history-lessons-understanding -decline-manufacturing.

2. It would be vain to try to list them all but Reich's book was *The Work of Nations* (1992), and the classic statement on immaterial labor is Maurizio Lazzarato (1996), though it became famous largely through Hardt and Negr's *Empire* (1994, 2000), which predicted the revolt of the computer geeks.

3. There are many such studies. For one example, see Western and Olin Wright 1994.

4. I had a friend who was addicted to heroin and went on a methadone program. Bored of waiting for doctors to decide he was "ready" to begin reducing his dosage, he started pouring off a little of the drug each day until, some months later, he was able to announce triumphantly that he was clean. His doctor was furious, and told him only professionals have the competence to decide when he should have done this. It turns out the program was funded on the basis of the number of patients they served and had no incentive to actually get anyone off drugs.

    One should never underestimate the power of institutions to try to preserve themselves. One explanation for the thirty-year impasse of the Israeli-Palestinian "peace process"—if at this point one can even call it that—is that on both sides, there are now powerful institutional structures which would lose their entire raison d'être if the conflict ended, but also, a vast "peace apparatus" of NGOs and UN bureaucrats whose careers have become entirely dependent on maintaining the fiction that a "peace process" is, in fact, going on.

5. UKIP doesn't count.

6. To head off any possible accusations of essentialism: I am proposing these three levels as modes of analysis, and not suggesting the existence of autonomous levels of social reality that in any sense exist in their own right.

7. I sometimes ask my students, when discussing Marx, "What was the unemployment level in ancient Greece? Or medieval China?" The answer, of course, is zero. Having a large proportion of the population who wish to work, but cannot, appears to be peculiar to what Marx liked to call "the capitalist mode of production." But it appears to be, like public debt, a structural feature of the system which must nonetheless be treated as if it were a problem to be solved.

8. To take a random example, the famous March on Washington in 1963, at which Martin Luther King gave his "I Have a Dream" speech, was officially called the "March on Washington for Jobs and Freedom: demands included not just antidiscrimination measures but also a full-employment economy, jobs programs, and a minimum-wage increase" (Touré F. Reed, "Why Liberals Separate Race from Class," *Jacobin* 8.22.2015, www.jacobinmag .com/2015/08/bernie-sanders-black-lives-matter-civil-rights-movement/), accessed June 10, 2017.

9. David Sirota, "Mr. Obama Goes to Washington," *Nation*, June, 26, 2006.

10. Of course, some might argue that Obama was being disingenuous here, and downplaying the political power of the private health industry, in the same way that politicians justified bank bailouts by claiming it was in the interest of millions of minor bank employees who might otherwise have been laid off—a concern they most certainly do not evince when, say, transit or textile workers are faced with unemployment. But the very fact that he was willing to make the argument is revealing.

11. To those who accuse me of being a paranoid conspiracy theorist for suggesting that government plays any conscious role in creating and maintaining bullshit jobs, I hereby rest my case. Unless you think Obama was lying about his true motives (in which case, who exactly is the conspiracy theorist?), we must allow that those governing us are, in fact, aware that "market solutions" create inefficiencies, and unnecessary jobs in particular, and at least in certain contexts look with favor on them for that very reason.

12. I might note in passing that the same is true of many orthodox Marxists, who argue that since by Marx's definition all labor within the capitalist mode of production must either produce surplus value, or aid in the re-production of the apparatus of value-creation, the appearance that a job is useless must be an illusion based on a false folk theory of social value on the part of the jobholder. This is really just as much a statement of faith as the libertarian insistence that the market can never be responsible for social problems. One might argue whether this position was really held by Marx but even this is basically a theological debate. It ultimately depends on whether one accepts the premise that capitalism is a totalizing system: that is, that within a capitalist system social value is determined only by the market system. I will discuss this further in the next chapter.

13. This is then preemptive. I acknowledge that historically, for an author to head off obvious objections almost never succeeds in stopping future crit-ics from raising those objections anyway; generally, they just pretend their objections were never anticipated and ignore any counterarguments to them that might have been made. But I figured it was worth a try.

14. www.economist.com/blogs/freeexchange/2013/08/labourlabor-markets-0. Accessed April 1, 2017.

15. For instance, it contained glaring flaws in basic logic: the author attempted to refute my argument that giving workers security and leisure time will often result in social unrest by noting unrest by workers who did not have security and leisure time. Even those who have received no training in formal logic, and therefore have never heard of the logical fallacy of affirming the conse-quent, but still have basic common sense, are generally aware that the state-ment "if A then B" is not the same as "if B then A." As Lewis Carroll adroitly put it, "You might as well say 'I see what I eat' is the same as 'I eat what I see'".

16. The piece has no byline.

17. If you ask: "Are you really saying the market is always right?" they will often reply, "Yes, I am saying the market is always right."

18. Instead, it's always assumed the burden of proof is on those who question such assertions.

19. I note in passing—and this will be important later—that while the num-ber of administrators has gone up, the real explosion has been in admin-istrative *staff*. This figure does not, I should emphasize, refer to caterers or cleaners, who were, in fact, being largely outsourced during this period, but to administrative underlings.

20. Most of the changes that did directly affect teaching, such as, say, class chat rooms, were managed by the (proportionally declining numbers of) teachers themselves.

21. Some phrases generated by the random Financial Bullshit Generator, accessed July 4, 2017, www.makebullshit.com/financial-bullshit-generator.php.

22. There are other enterprises, of course, that are basically fraudulent in nature—or, in some cases, are dedicated to providing the means for others to commit fraud. A number of testimonials I received were from college paper writers. There have always been smart students or graduates willing to pick up a little cash writing term papers for lazy classmates, but in America in recent decades, this has coalesced into an entire industry, coordinated on a national level, employing thousands of full-time paper writers. One of them suggested to me that the industry was the predictable result of the convergence of credentialism—the fact that one now needed a degree of some kind to gain access to almost all desirable jobs in America—and business logic.

> Barry: When I first started this work, I imagined I would be constantly learning fascinating, new information about a broad array of subjects. While I have had the opportunity to write the rare, interesting essay on queer theory or the history of Roman blood sport, I've found that I'm largely writing countless papers about business and marketing.
>
> After some consideration, this makes a lot of sense to me. Higher education is constantly justified on the basis that it is an *investment in your future*. The crippling load of student debt is worth it because it is going to allow for a stable six-figure income someday. It's hard for me to imagine that many folks are studying to get a Bachelor of Business Administration because it's their passion—I'm pretty sure they're just jumping through the hoops to get the degree that they see as their path to a high-paying job. As for my clients, I think they see themselves as willing to increase their level of investment in return for a lower workload and guaranteed good marks. The amount I charge for writing a few key term papers is only a tiny fraction of the average tuition cost.

This makes sense to me, too. If you're actually paying attention in business courses when the professor tells you that it's normal and even admirable to attempt to get the greatest benefit for the least amount of investment, and that same professor then assigns you a paper, there's really no reason not to hire someone else to write it if that's the most efficient thing to do.

23. For the record, I don't know which of the four it was.

24. Another reason sometimes cited for the multiplication of unnecessary levels of executive or administrative staff is protection from the threat of lawsuits. Here's the account of one bank employee, Aaron: "It's common to now see 'Chief of Staff' roles in large financial institutions . . . they are simply an ineffectual buffer between senior managers and any potential litigation from regulators or disgruntled employees. This buffer never works because in litigation, the plaintiff will *always* name the senior manager in the court papers as this maximizes the likelihood the case gets settled to avoid embarrassment. So what do the Chiefs of Staff end up doing? Well, they tend to organize meetings with senior managers and their leadership teams and commission lots of pointless management consultant surveys to try and work out why morale is so low (a question that could be answered much more easily by simply asking employees what they think. You often see them organizing charity days and puff pieces in newspapers or journals." According to Aaron, HR staff are now less likely to fulfill such roles, as they, too, fear legal liability. Clearly, the situation varies in different banks.

25. It's probably relevant, admittedly, that the economics department in my college was entirely dominated by Marxists; the phrase goes back at least to Perry Anderson (1974).

26. Much of this argument and several of the examples are taken from the first chapter of Graeber, *Utopia of Rules*, 3–44.

27. Of course, this is not the way things are represented, and, naturally, in any branch of industry defined as "creative," whether software development or graphic design, production is typically outsourced to small groups (the celebrated Silicon Valley start-ups) or individuals (casualized independent contractors) who do work autonomously. But such people are often largely uncompensated. For a good recent critical history of managerialism, see Hanlon, 2016.

28. Definitions of feudalism vary, from any economic system based on tribute-taking, to the specific system prevalent in Northern Europe during the High Middle Ages, in which land was granted in exchange for military service in ostensibly voluntary relations of vassalage—a system which outside Europe is documented mainly in Japan. From this perspective most other

Asian empires and kingdoms operated with, as Weber called them "patrimonial prebendal" systems where lords or important officials collected the income from a certain territory but did not necessarily occupy or directly administer it, an approach European kings also later attempted to impose when they had the power. All this could be endlessly dissected but here I really only want to make the point that in such systems, where there are people who are primary producers, and others whose basic job it is to move those things around, the latter almost invariably end up organized into very elaborate chains of command. The nineteenth-century Ganda kingdom in East Africa might seem a particularly telling example in this regard: all farming and most productive work was done by women; most men, as a result, ended up part of an elaborate hierarchy of titled officials running from the village to the king, or as flunkies or retainers to such officials. When too many idle men accumulated, rulers would start wars or sometimes simply round thousands up and massacre them. (For the best recent synthesis on feudalism from a Marxist perspective, Wood, 2002; on the Ganda, Ray, 1991.)

29. Cited as an anonymous source in Alex Preston, "The War Against Humanities in Britain's Universities," *Guardian*, Education Section, 1, March 29, 2015.

30. One might argue that Marcel Duchamp, by placing a urinal in a gallery and declaring it a work of art, opened the door to the entry of managerialism into the arts. At any rate he eventually became horrified by the door he'd opened up, and spent the last decades of his life playing chess, which, he argued, was also one of the few things he could do that could not possibly be commodified.

31. Many suggest to me one reason for the dishwater mediocrity or even plain incoherence of so many contemporary movie scripts is that each of these supernumeraries will typically insist on changing at least a line or two, just to be able to say they had some influence on the final product. I first heard about this when after seeing the endlessly terrible 2008 remake of *The Day the Earth Stood Still*. The entire plot seemed to be designed to lead up to a moment of realization, where the alien comes to understand the true nature of humanity (that they are not basically evil, just very bad at handling grief). Yet when the moment came, the alien never actually said this. I asked a friend in the industry how this could have happened and he assured me that the line I was expecting was almost certainly in the original

script; some useless executives must have intervened to change it. "You see there are usually dozens of these guys hovering around any production and every one of them will feel they have to jump in and change around at least one line—or else what's the excuse for their even being there?"

32. Joseph Campbell was an historian of religion whose book *The Hero with a Thousand Faces* argued that all hero myths have the same basic plot. The book was an enormous influence on George Lucas in developing the plots for the original Star Wars trilogy. While Campbell's argument for a universal archetypal hero narrative is now considered at best something of an entertaining curio by scholars of epic or heroic myth, the analysis he offers probably would be valid now for Hollywood movies, since almost all screenwriters and producers are familiar with the book and attempt to use it in designing plots.

33. Holly Else, "Billions Lost in Bids to Secure EU Research Funding," Times Higher Education Supplement, October 6, 2016, accessed June 23, 2017. www.timeshighereducation.com/news/billions-lost-in-bids-to-secure -european-union-research-funding#survey-answer.

34. "Of Flying Cars and the Declining Rate of Profit," *Baffler*, no. 19 (Spring 2012): 66–84, with an expanded version in Graeber, *Utopia of Rules*, 105–148.

35. These titles were, in fact, produced by using the random bullshit job title generator at the website BullShit Job, www.bullshitjob.com/title.

36. The argument of this paragraph is a very abbreviated version of the argument of the introductory essay in Graeber, *Utopia of Rules*, 33–44.

Chapter 6: Why Do We as a Society Not Object to the Growth of Pointless Employment?

1. For instance, at the height of the Greek debt crisis, public opinion in Germany was almost unanimous that Greek debt should not be forgiven because Greek workers were entitled and lazy. This was countered by statistics showing Greek workers actually put in longer hours than German ones; which, in turn, was countered by the argument that this might be true on paper but Greek workers slacked off on the job. At no point did anyone suggest that German workers were working *too* hard, creating an overproduction problem that could only be solved by lending foreign countries

money to be able to import their goods, let alone that the Greek ability to enjoy life was in any way admirable or a model for others. To take another example, when, in the 1990s, the French Socialist Party ran on the platform of a thirty-five-hour workweek, I remember being struck by the fact that no American news source I was able to find that deigned to mention this fact suggested that reducing working hours might be seen as, let alone be, good in itself, but only presented it as a tactic for reducing unemployment. In other words, allowing people to work less could only be treated as a social good if it allowed more people to be working.

2. Technically the measure is "marginal utility," the degree to which the consumer finds an additional unit of the good useful in this way; hence, if one already has three bars of soap stockpiled in one's house, or for that matter three houses, how much additional utility is added by a fourth. For the best critique of marginal utility as a theory of consumer preference, see Steve Keen, *Debunking Economics*, 44–47.

3. And I should note just for the sake of clarity that most of those who embrace the labor theory of value do not make this argument; some value comes from nature, as Marx himself, the most famous advocate of the labor theory of value, did occasionally point out.

4. Of course, this is exactly the position also taken by the most radical free market libertarians.

5. Since reproduction is technically "the production of production," then maintaining the physical infrastructure or other elements exploited by capitalism would also count.

6. Similarly, in the domain of values, when market comparisons can be made, they are assumed to be somehow incidental, not a reflection of the object's true worth. No one would actually insist that a Damien Hirst shark is worth, say, two hundred thousand Vipassana meditation retreats, or a Vipassana retreat, one hundred fudge sundaes. It just happens to come out that way.

7. Civil servants in particular would favor the term "help" over "value," though its use was by no means limited to civil servants.

8. See Graeber 2013:84–87.

9. I'm assuming that there is no genre of music, art, etc., that doesn't cause more happiness for some than it annoys others. I could be wrong.

10. Some Belgian friends told me the net effects were extremely beneficial, as almost all major parties were committed to the then European-wide con-

sensus about the need for austerity, but the lack of a government in Belgium at that critical moment meant reforms were not carried out, and the Belgian economy ended up growing substantially faster than its neighbors'. It's also worth noting that Belgium does have seven different regional governments that were unaffected.

11. Caitlin Huston, "Uber IPO Prospects May Be Helped by Resignation of CEO Travis Kalanick," *MarketWatch*, last modified June 22, 2017, www.marketwatch.com/story/uber-ipo-prospects-may-be-helped-by-resignation-of-ceo-travis-kalanick-2017-06-21.

12. Rutger Bregman, *Utopia for Realists: The Case for Universal Basic Income, Open Borders, and a 15-Hour Workweek* (New York: Little, Brown, 2017).

    Even police strikes rarely have the anticipated effects. In December 2015 New York police carried out a work stoppage for all but "urgent" police business; there was no effect on crime rate, but city revenues plummeted owing to the lack of fines for traffic violation and similar infractions. The complete disappearance of police in a major city, either owing to a full strike, or in one documented case in Amsterdam during World War II, mass arrest by German occupiers, tends to lead to a rise in property crime like burglary, but leave violent crime unaffected. In rural areas with some tradition of self-governance, like the part of Madagascar where I lived between 1989 and 1991, the withdrawal of police due to IMF austerity measures made almost no difference at all—when I visited again twenty years later people were almost universally convinced that violent crime had increased sharply since the police had returned.

13. Benjamin B. Lockwood, Charles G. Nathanson, and E. Glen Weyl, "Taxation and the Allocation of Talent," *Journal of Political Economy* 125, no. 5 (October 2017): 1635–82, www.journals.uchicago.edu/doi/full/10.1086/693393. The reference to Marketers is however taken from an earlier (2012) version of the same paper, with the same title, published at https://eighty-thousand-hours-wp-production.s3.amazonaws.com/2014/12/TaxationAndTheAllocationOfTalent_preview.pdf, 16.

14. Eilis Lawlor, Helen Kersley, and Susan Steed, *A Bit Rich: Calculating the Value to Society of Different Professions* (London: New Economics Foundation, 2009), http://b.3cdn.net/nefoundation/8c16eabdbadf83ca79_ojm6b0fzh.pdf. I have standardized and averaged out some of the salaries, which the original report gave sometimes as hourly wages, sometime as yearly salaries, but in the latter case, usually as ranges.

15. See, for instance, Gordon B. Lindsay, Ray M. Merrill, and Riley J. Hedin, "The Contribution of Public Health and Improved Social Conditions to Increased Life Expectancy: An Analysis of Public Awareness," *Journal of Community Medicine & Health Education* 4 (2014): 311–17, which contrasts the received scientific understanding of such matters with popular perception, which assumes improvements are almost entirely due to doctors. https://www.omicsonline.org/open-access/the-contribution-of-public -health-and-improved-social-conditions-to-increased-life-expectancy-an -analysis-of-public-awareness-2161-0711-4-311.php?aid=35861.

16. Another exception would be highly paid athletes or entertainers. Many get paid so much they are often held out as avatars of bullshit, but I would tend to disagree. If such people succeed in bringing happiness or excitement into others' lives, why not? Obviously, questions could be raised about how much more they are responsible for that happiness and excitement than the teams surrounding them, support staff, and the like, most of whom are paid far less.

17. If it had anything to do with the dangers of the job, on the other hand, the highest-paid workers in America would be either loggers or fishermen, and in Britain, farmers.

18. One (in my opinion rather obtuse) economist and blogger named Alex Tabarrok wrote a response to my original bullshit jobs piece that claimed my point about the inverse relation of pay and social benefit was "a great example of faulty economic reasoning," since, he said, I was simply talking about the diamonds-water paradox (which goes back to the Middle Ages, and Adam Smith famously used to propose a distinction between use value and exchange value), that he said had been "solved" a century ago with the introduction of the concept of marginal utility. Actually, my impression was that it had been "solved" at least as far back as Galileo, but the bizarre thing about his claim is that I hadn't engaged in economic reasoning at all, since I didn't propose any explanation for the inverse relation, but just pointed out that it exists (http://marginalrevolution.com/marginalrevolution/2013 /10/bs-jobs-and-bs-economics.html). How can simply pointing out a fact be faulty reasoning? The example of the relative supply of nurses is drawn from Peter Frase's reply to that piece (www.jacobinmag.com/2013/10/the-ethic-of-marginal-value/); for the glut of lawyers, see, for instance, L. M. Sixel, "A Glut of Lawyers Dims Job Prospects for Many," *Houston Chronicle* online, last modified March 25, 2016, http://wtonchronicle.com/business /article/A-glut-of-lawyers-dims-job-prospects-for-many-7099998.php.

I might note that Tabarrok's ploy—take a simple empirical observation and pretend it's an economic argument, and then "refute" it—seems to be common among bad economic bloggers; I once saw a simple observation I had made that kindhearted merchants will sometimes give poor customers a discount on necessities characterized as an attempted "refutation" of economic theory, which the blogger then went on to disprove—as if economists really believed no merchant ever did anything out of kindness!

19. I first encountered the argument in G. A. Cohen, "Back to Socialist Basics," *New Left Review*, no. 207 (1994): 2–16, his critique of the Labour Party manifesto. Various versions of it can be found in his other work, notably in "Incentives, Inequality, and Community: The Tanner Lectures on Human Values" (lecture, Stanford University, Stanford, CA, May 21 and 23, 1991, https://tannerlectures.utah.edu/_documents/a-to-z/c/cohen92.pdf).

20. Back in the 1990s, when I still used to argue with libertarians, I found they would almost invariably justify inequality in terms of work. If I would observe, say, that some disproportionate share of social wealth was being distributed upward, a typical response would be along the lines of "to me this just shows that some people are working harder, or working smarter, than others." This particular formulation always stuck in my head because of the telltale slipperiness. One cannot, of course, really argue that a CEO who makes a thousand times more than a bus driver is working a thousand times harder, so you slip in "smarter"—which implies "more productive" but, in fact, here just seems to be "in a way for which you're paid much more." All that saves this statement from absolutely meaningless circularity (they're smart because they're rich because they're smart, and on and on) is that it emphasizes that (most of) the very rich do have jobs.

21. This is why the books they produce become ever shorter, more simplistic, and less well researched.

22. Geoff Shullenberger, "The Rise of the Voluntariat," *Jacobin* online, last modified May 5, 2014, www.jacobinmag.com/2014/05/the-rise-of-the-voluntariat.

23. Bertrand Russell puts it nicely in his essay "In Praise of Idleness": "What is work? Work is of two kinds: first, altering the position of matter at or near the earth's surface relatively to other such matter; second, telling other people to do so. The first kind is unpleasant and ill paid; the second is pleasant and highly paid." (1935:13).

24. Genesis 3.16. Hannah Arendt in *The Human Condition* (1958:107n53) makes the argument that nowhere in the Bible is it suggested that work

itself is punishment for disobedience; God simply makes the labor more harsh; others are simply reading Genesis through Hesiod. This might be true, but it doesn't really affect my argument; especially since Christians writing and thinking on the subject have assumed that was the meaning of the biblical passage for centuries. For instance, in 1664 Margaret Cavendish argued "neither can tennis be a pastime, for . . . there can be no recreation in sweaty labor; for it is laid as a curse upon man, that they shall live by the sweat of their brows" (in Thomas 1999: 9). For the best discussion of the early Christian debates on Adam and Eve, which argues that it was Saint Augustine who was really responsible for the notion that all humans are tainted, and, hence, cursed, because of original sin, see Pagels (1988).

25. Much of the next section is a summary of an earlier essay of mine, "Manners, Deference, and Private Property" (1997), itself an abbreviated version of my master's thesis, *The Generalization of Avoidance: Manners and Possessive Individualism in Early Modern Europe* (Chicago, 1987). Some of the classic works on traditional Northern European marriage patterns and life-cycle service include Hajnal (1965, 1982), Laslett (1972, 1977, 1983, 1984), Stone (1977), Kassmaul (1981), and Wall (1983); for a more recent survey of the state of the literature, see Cooper (2005). The primary difference between Northern European and Mediterranean marriage patterns from the Middle Ages through the Early Modern period is that in the latter, while men also would often marry late, women married much earlier, and life-cycle service was limited to certain social and professional groups but in no sense a norm.

26. Nowadays, of course, the word "waiter" is used only for those who "wait" tables at restaurants, a mainstay of the "service economy," but the term was still being used primarily for domestic servants—ranking one step below the butler—in Victorian households. The word "dumbwaiter," for example, originally referred to the fact that servants who brought food to the master's table would often gossip about what they overheard people saying around it; mechanical dumbwaiters performed the same function but could not speak.

27. This is inaccurate. Most were apprenticed in early adolescence.

28. I have quoted it myself in the Manners paper (1997:716–17). The translation goes back to: Charlotte A. Sneyd, *A relation, or rather A true account, of the island of England; with sundry particulars of the customs of these people,*

and of the royal revenues under King Henry the Seventh, about the year 1500, by an Italian, Camden Society volume xxxvi, 1847, 14–15.

29. Susan Brigden, "Youth and the English Reformation," *Past & Present* 95 (1982): 37–38.

30. In Renaissance England, for example, one frequent representative of the king was a noble servant entitled the "Groom of the Stool," because he was in charge of emptying the king's chamber pot (Starkey 1977).

31. My father, for example, was for most of his life a plate stripper in offset photo lithography shops. At one point, while first learning my medieval history, I was telling him about the guild system. "Yes," he said, "I served an apprenticeship, too. I retired as a 'journeyman printer.'" When I asked if there were any master printers, he said, "No, we don't have masters anymore. Well, unless you want to say that's the boss."

32. Phillip Stubbes, *Anatomie of Abuses*, 1562. This line of objection, of course, reached its peak with Malthus, who came to argue that the working classes would thus tend to breed everyone into poverty, and famously advocated fostering unsanitary conditions to kill them off. Cazenove, who is cited later, was a disciple of Malthus.

33. K. Thomas 1976:221.

34. Max Weber's (1905) arguments about the relation of Calvinism and the origins of capitalism, I believe, should be understood in this light. That there was some connection between Protestantism, an ethic of self-disciplined work, and economic growth was considered self-evident by many at the time (Tawney 1924) but few examine the confluence of the three factors: Northern European life-cycle service, Protestantism, and emerging capitalism, even though they appear to broadly coincide.

35. Thomas Carlyle, *Past and Present* (London: Chapman and Hall, 1843), 173–74. It is interesting to contrast Carlyle's praise of work for freeing the soul from cares to Nietzsche, who condemned it for that very reason: "In the glorification of 'work' and the never-ceasing talk about the 'blessing of labor' I see ... fear of everything individual. For at the sight of work—that is to say, severe toil from morning till night—we have the feeling that it is the best police, viz., that it holds everyone in check and effectively hinders the development of reason, of greed, and of desire for independence. For work uses up an extraordinary proportion of nervous force, withdrawing it from reflection, meditation, dreams, cares, love, and hatred" (Daybreak, 1881 [1911:176–77]). One wonders if this is a direct response to Carlyle.

36. Carlyle, *Past and Present*, 175. Much of the essay is a condemnation of capitalism, as "Mammonism," and like so many nineteenth-century works sounds vaguely Marxist to the modern ear, even when it comes to conservative conclusions: "Labor is not a devil, even while encased in Mammonism; Labor is ever an imprisoned god, writhing unconsciously or consciously to escape out of Mammonism!" (257).

37. John Cazenove, *Outlines of Political Economy; Being a Plain and Short View of the Laws Relating to the Production, Distribution and Consumption of Wealth* (London: P. Richardson, 1832), 21–22. As far as I know, the first use of the labor theory of value to argue that workers are exploited by their employers is found in a pamphlet called *The Rights of Nature Against the Usurpations of Establishments*, written by the British Jacobin John Thelwall in 1796.

38. From Edward Pessen, *Most Uncommon Jacksonians: The Radical Leaders of the Early Labor Movement* (Albany, NY: SUNY Press, 1967), 174: Faler's (1981) study of the town of Lynn in Massachusetts from 1780 to 1860 documents at length the degree to which the labor theory of value formed the framework of public debate for almost a century after the Revolution.

39. Marx's own works, for example, were little known in the US at the time, though not completely unknown, since Marx himself was working as a freelance newspaper opinion writer and would often publish columns in US papers. Marx, in his capacity as head of the Workingmen's Association, also wrote directly to Lincoln with his own analysis of the American situation a few years later, in 1865, and while Lincoln seems to have read the letter, he had one of his adjuncts respond.

40. Already in 1845, New York state assemblyman Mike Walsh was arguing along explicitly anticapitalist lines: "What is capital, but that all-grasping power which has been wrung, by fraud, avarice, and malice from the labor of this and all ages past." In Noel Ignatiev, *How the Irish Became White* (New York: Routledge, 2008), 149.

41. E. P. Goodwin, *Home Missionary Sermon*, 1880, in Josiah Strong, *Our Country: Its Possible Future and Its Present Crisis* (New York: Baker & Taylor, 1891), 159. Denis Kearney was a California labor leader of the time, now remembered largely for his campaigning against Chinese immigration, and Robert Ingersoll, the author of well-known refutations of the Bible, is now mainly known secondhand through Clarence Darrow's arguments against the literal interpretation of Genesis in the play *Inherit*

the Wind, which appear to be taken directly from Ingersoll's writings. I can add a personal testimony here: my own grandfather Gustavus Adolphus ("Dolly") Graeber, who, owing to my family's peculiarly long generations, was born before the US Civil War and worked as a musician for many years along the Western frontier at exactly the time Goodwin was writing—he is reputed to be the man who introduced the mandolin into American music—was, my father once told me, "an Ingersoll man" and, hence, a fervent atheist. He was never a Marxist, but my father became one later.

42. The movie *Treasure of the Sierra Madre* is based on a novel of the same name by B. Traven, the pseudonym for a German anarchist novelist who fled his own country and lived most of the years of his life in southern Mexico. His real identity remains the object of speculation to this day.

43. Thus, for instance, when in 1837 the group of businessmen from Amherst, Massachusetts, proposed to create a limited-liability carriage company, the proposal was opposed by a petition by journeymen on the grounds that "as journeymen, they looked forward to being their own masters when they would not have to relinquish to others the value they created," stating "'incorporations put means into the hands of inexperienced capitalists, to take from us the profits of our art, which has cost us years of labor to obtain, and which we consider to be our exclusive privilege to enjoy'" (Hanlon 2016:57). Ordinarily such requests were only approved if the company was dedicated to creating and maintaining public works of an obviously useful nature such as a railroad or canal.

44. Durrenberger and Doukas 2008:216–17.

45. 1974:246.

46. There is some debate over the relative weight, in medieval Christian theology, of the degree to which work was seen as an imitation of divine creation, and as a means of perfecting the self (see the discussion in Ehmer and Lis 2009:10–15), but both principles appear to have been present from the very beginning.

47. Classic studies include Kraus, Côté, and Keltner 2010, and Stellar, Manzo, Kraus, and Keltner 2011.

48. As a result underlings will also tend to care more about their superiors than their superiors will care about them, and this extends to almost any relation of structural inequality: men and women, rich and poor, black and white, and so on. It has always seemed to me this is one of the main forces that

allows such inequalities to continue. (I've discussed this in various places, but the curious reader might consult the second chapter of Graeber, *Utopia of Rules*, 68–72.)

49. From this perspective, for instance, money, markets, finance are just ways of strangers alerting us to what they care about, because we care that caring is directed appropriately; which implies, in turn, that contemporary banking is simply a bad form of caring labor, insofar as it aims it in the wrong direction.

50. The book was eventually renamed *Crack Capitalism* (2010), which I've always felt was a far inferior title.

51. One oft-quoted passage from Studs Terkel's *Working*: "Unless a guy's a nut, he never thinks about work or talks about it. Maybe about baseball or about getting drunk the other night or he got laid or he didn't get laid. I'd say one out of a hundred really get excited about work" (1972:xxxiv); but at the same time, from the same testimony, "somebody has to do this work. If my kid ever goes to college, I just want him to have a little respect" (1972:xxxv).

52. Gini and Sullivan 1987:649, 651, 654.

53. Noel Ignatiev's *How the Irish Became White* (1995) is the classic study of this phenomenon.

54. The formula was later reduced to "the greatest good for the greatest number," but Bentham's original theory was based on hedonistic calculation and that's what Carlyle was responding to.

55. Carlyle 1843:134.

56. *Ibid.*

Chapter 7: What Are the Political Effects of Bullshit Jobs, and Is There Anything That Can Be Done About This Situation?

1. Matthew Kopka, "Bailing Out Wall Street While the Ship of State is Sinking? (Part 2)," *The Gleaner*, January 25, 2010, http://jamaica-gleaner.com /gleaner/20100125/news/news5.html, accessed July 22, 2017. At the time, one frequently circulated claim was that autoworkers were making as much as $75 an hour, but this was based on an industry PR statement that took the total costs of all wages, benefits, and pensions for all workers, and divided them by the total number of hours worked. Obviously, if one calculated by

these means, almost any worker in any industry could be represented as getting two or three times his or her actual hourly wage.

2. The second reason was that as factory workers they were all concentrated in the same place, which made it easy to organize together. This meant that they could threaten strikes that would have a serious effect on the economy.

3. Eli Horowitz, "No Offense Meant to Individuals Who Work With Bovine Feces," http://rustbeltphilosophy.blogspot.co.uk/2013/08/no-offense-meant-to-individuals-who.html, accessed August 31, 2013.

4. What follows is drawn largely from an essay that appeared in long format as "Introduction: The Political Metaphysics of Stupidity." In *The Commoner* (www.thecommoner.org.uk), Spring 2005, and shorter format in *Harper's* as "Army of Altruists: On the Alienated Right to Do Good," *Harper's*, January 2007, 31–38.

5. Insofar as there are not quite enough children of privilege to go around—since elites almost never give birth to enough offspring to reproduce themselves demographically—the jobs are likely to go to the most remarkable children of immigrants. Executives with Bank of America, or Enron, when facing a similar demographic problem, are much more likely to recruit from poorer white folk like themselves. This is partly because of racism; partly, too, because corporations tend to encourage a broadly anti-intellectual climate themselves. It is well known at Yale, where I once worked, that executive recruiters tend to prefer to hire Yale's "B" students, since they are more likely to be people "they'll feel comfortable with."

6. There has been a great deal of effort to normalize the idea that caring tasks can or should be carried out by machines, but I don't think it has been or really could be successful in the long run.

7. It is interesting to note in this context that Vonnegut had, in fact, been enrolled for a master's degree in anthropology at the University of Chicago immediately after the war, though he never completed his dissertation. This no doubt explains why one of the main characters in the book is an anthropologist. Perhaps if he'd studied harder, he'd have realized that his premise—that workers would not be able to handle too much leisure—was profoundly flawed. (Ray Fogelson, who was there at the time, told me he returned many years later with a thesis so obviously dashed together it left the department in a quandary, so they decided to grant him a degree, instead, for *Cat's Cradle*.)

8. The most likely at #702 is Telemarketer; the least, at #1, Recreational Thera-

pist; Anthropologists such as myself are fairly safe at #32. See Frey and Osborne (2017)—the original, online version of the paper appeared in 2013, and received a good deal of news coverage at the time.

9. Stanislaw Lem, *Memoirs of a Space Traveler: The Further Reminiscences of Ijon Tichy* (Evanston, IL: Northwestern University Press), 1981 [1971] 19–20.

10. Lem was writing in still-Socialist Poland in the 1970s; but for what it's worth, his satire of Stalinism is just as merciless. On another journey, Ijon Tichy finds himself in a planet governed by a vast irrigation bureaucracy that has become so caught up in their mission that they have developed the ideology that humans are naturally evolving into fish. The inhabitants are forced to practice "breathing water" for increasing numbers of hours every day.

11. Bear in mind that, averaged over a year, even medieval serfs did not work even close to a forty-hour week.

12. I'm not going to dignify here arguments put forward in some quarters that reducing hours of employment will lead to an increase in crime, unhealthy practices, or other negative social effects. I'm sure identical arguments could have been made against freeing slaves, and likely were. I see them as having an equivalent moral standing. How is arguing that people should be forced to work forty hours a week they would not otherwise have to work because they might otherwise drink, smoke, or commit crimes any different from arguing that the entire population should be placed in prison for an equivalent amount of time as a form of preventative detention?

13. One might call it "human production," and I have done so elsewhere; but in this context, even that seems to hit the wrong note.

14. No doubt one could quibble over who received the most money from whom in what circumstances, but it was Bill Clinton who presided over the repeal of Glass-Steagall, thus "liberalizing" finance and opening the way to the 2008–09 crisis, and Tony Blair in the UK who first introduced tuition in the British universities.

15. Frank 2016.

16. Brown 1983.

17. Gorz's actual words: "The search for higher productivity would lead to the standardization and industrialization of such activities, particularly those involving the feeding, minding, raising and education of children. The last enclave of individual or communal autonomy would disappear; socializa-

tion, 'commodification' and preprogramming would be extended to the last vestiges of self-determined and self-regulated life. The industrialization, through home computers, of physical and psychical care and hygiene, children's education, cooking or sexual technique is precisely designed to generate capitalist profits from activities still left to individual fantasy" (Gorz 1997:84, originally published in French in 1980, which makes it really quite prophetic). The more specific engagement with the Wages for Housework movement is in *Critique of Economic Reason* 2010:126, 161–64, 222).

18. The details can be found in Sarath Davala, etc. *Basic Income: A Transformative Policy for India* (London: Bloomsbury Academic Press, 2015).

19. For the most thorough recent exploration of the current arguments for basic income, see Standing (2017).

20. In fact, in some ways, they might have to be expanded. One could make the argument UBI wouldn't work with a rent-based economy because, say, if most homes were rented, landlords would just double rents to grab the additional income. At the very least controls would have to be imposed.

21. This is also why conditional versions of the same program, or guaranteed jobs programs, are in no sense variations on—let alone "improved versions of"—the same thing. The key to UBI is the unconditional element, which allows for a massive reduction of the role of government intrusion in citizens' lives. These supposedly "modified" or "improved" versions either will not do this, or will have the opposite effect.

22. Obviously, moral philosophy tends to assume that the "free rider" problem is a fundamental question of social justice, outweighing considerations of human freedom, and therefore usually concludes that it would be justifiable to set up a system of surveillance and coercion so as to ensure that not even a small number of people live off of others' work (unless they're rich, in which case that's usually somehow totally okay). My own position, which is the typical Libertarian Socialist position, is, "So what if they do?"

23. I never met Foucault, but I base my descriptions on some of those who did.

24. It is sometimes said that Foucault never defines "power" and it's true that he was often slightly coy about the matter, but when he did, he defined power as "a set of actions on other actions," and its exercise as "acting on another's actions" (1982:789). This is, surprisingly, closer to the Parsonian tradition than anything else.

25. Foucault 1988:18–19.

Bibliography

Ackroyd, Stephen, and Paul Thompson. *Organizational Misbehaviour*. London: Sage, 1999.

Anderson, Perry. *Passages from Antiquity to Feudalism*. London: Verso Press, 1974.

Applebaum, Herbert. *The Concept of Work: Ancient, Medieval, and Modern* (SUNY Series in the Anthropology of Work). Albany, NY: SUNY Press, 1992.

Arendt, Hannah. *The Human Condition*. Chicago: University of Chicago Press, 1958.

Baumeister, Roy, Sara Wotman, and Arlene Stillwell. "Unrequited Love: On Heartbreak, Anger, Guilt, Scriptlessness, and Humiliation." *Journal of Personality and Social Psychology* 64, no. 3 (1993): 377–94.

Beder, Sharon. *Selling the Work Ethic: From Puritan Pulpit to Corporate PR*. London: Zed Books, 2000.

Black, Bob. "The Abolition of Work." *The Abolition of Work and Other Essays*. Port Townsend, WA: Loompanics, 1986.

Bloch, Maurice. *Anthropology and the Cognitive Challenge*. Cambridge: Cambridge University Press, 2012.

Braverman, Harry. *Labor and Monopoly Capital: The Degradation of Work in the Twentieth Century*. New York: Monthly Review Press, 1974.

Bregman, Rutger. *Utopia for Realists: The Case for Universal Basic Income, Open Borders, and a 15-Hour Workweek*. Amsterdam: The Correspondent, 2016.

Brigden, Susan. "Youth and the English Reformation." *Past & Present* 95 (1982): 37–67.

Broucek, Francis. "The Sense of Self." *Bulletin of the Menninger Clinic* 41 (1977): 85–90.

_____. "Efficacy in Infancy: A Review of Some Experimental Studies and Their Possible Implications for Clinical Theory." *International Journal of Psycho-Analysis* 60 (January 1, 1979): 311–16.

Brown, Wilmette. *Black Women and the Peace Movement*. Bristol, UK: Falling Wall Press, 1983.

Brygo, Julien, and Olivier Cyran. *Boulots de Merde! Enquête sur l'utilité et la nuisance sociales des métiers*. Paris: La Découverte, 2016.

Budd, John W. *The Thought of Work*. Ithaca, NY: Cornell University Press, 2011.

Carlyle, Thomas. *Past and Present*. London: Chapman and Hall, 1843.

Chancer, Lynn. *Sadomasochism in Everyday Life: The Dynamics of Power and Powerlessness*. New Brunswick, NJ: Rutgers University Press, 1992.

Clark, Alice. *Working Life of Women in the Seventeenth Century*. London: George Routledge and Sons, 1919.

Cooper, Sheila McIsaac. "Service to Servitude? The Decline and Demise of Life-Cycle Service in England." *History of the Family* 10 (2005): 367–86.

Davala, Sarath, Renana Jhabrala, Soumya Kapor, et al. *Basic Income: A Transformative Policy for India*. London: Bloomsbury Academic Press, 2015.

Doukas, Dimitra. *Worked Over: The Corporate Sabotage of an American Community*. Ithaca, NY: Cornell University Press, 2003.

Durrenberger, E. Paul, and Dimitra Doukas. "Gospel of Wealth, Gospel of Work: Counterhegemony in the U.S. Working Class." *American Anthropologist* (new series) 110, no. 2 (2008): 214–24.

Ehmer, Josef, and Catharina Lis. "Introduction: Historical Studies in Perception of Work." In *The Idea of Work in Europe from Antiquity to Modern Times*, edited by Ehmer and Lis, 33–70. Farnham, UK: Ashgate, 2009.

Ehrenreich, Barbara. *Fear of Falling: The Inner Life of the Middle Class*. New York: Pantheon, 1989.

Ehrenreich, Barbara, and John Ehrenreich. "The Professional-Managerial Class." In *Between Labor and Capital*, edited by Paul Walker. Boston: South End Press, 1979, 5–45.

Evans-Pritchard, E. E. *The Nuer: A Description of the Modes of Livelihood and Political Institutes of a Nilotic People*. Oxford: Clarendon Press, 1940.

Faler, Paul G. *Mechanics and Manufacturers in the Early Industrial Revolution:*

Lynn, Massachusetts, 1780–1860. Albany, NY: State University of New York Press, 1981.

Finley, Moses I. *The Ancient Economy.* Berkeley: University of California Press, 1973.

Fleming, Peter. *The Mythology of Work: How Capitalism Persists Despite Itself.* London: Pluto Press, 2015.

Ford, Martin. *The Rise of the Robots: Technology and the Threat of Mass Unemployment.* London: Oneworld, 2015.

Foucault, Michel. "The Subject and Power." *Critical Inquiry* 8, no. 4 (1982): 777–95.

_____. *The Final Foucault.* Cambridge, MA: MIT Press, 1988.

Frank, Thomas. *Listen Liberal, Or What Ever Happened to the Party of the People?* New York: Henry Holt, 2016.

Frayne, David. *The Refusal of Work: The Theory and Practice of Resistance to Work.* London: Zed Books, 2015.

Frey, Carl B., and Michael A. Osborne. "The Future of Employment: How Susceptible Are Jobs to Computerisation?" *Technological Forecasting and Social Change* 114 (2017): 254–80.

Fromm, Erich. *The Anatomy of Human Destructiveness.* New York: Henry Holt, 1973.

Galbraith, John Kenneth. *American Capitalism: The Concept of Countervailing Power.* Harmondsworth, UK: Penguin, 1963.

_____. *The New Industrial State.* Harmondsworth, UK: Penguin, 1967.

_____. *The Affluent Society.* Harmondsworth, UK: Penguin, 1969.

_____. "On Post-Keynesian Economics." *Journal of Post-Keynesian Economics* 1, no. 1 (1978): 8–11.

Gini, Al. "Work, Identity and Self: How We Are Formed by the Work We Do." *Journal of Business Ethics* 17 (1998): 707–14.

_____. *My Job, My Self: Work and the Creation of the Modern Individual.* London: Routledge, 2012.

Gini, Al, and Terry Sullivan. "Work: The Process and the Person." *Journal of Business Ethics* 6 (1987): 649–55.

Ginsberg, Benjamin. *The Fall of the Faculty.* New York: Oxford University Press, 2013.

Glenn, Joshua, and Mark Kingwell. *The Wage Slave's Glossary.* Windsor, Can.: Biblioasis, 2011.

Gorz, Andre. *Farewell to the Working Class: An Essay on Post-industrial Socialism.* London: Pluto, 1997.

_____. *Critique of Economic Reason*. London: Verso, 2010.

Graeber, David. "Manners, Deference, and Private Property." *Comparative Studies in Society and History* 39, no. 4 (1997): 694–728.

_____. *Debt: The First 5,000 Years*. Brooklyn, NY: Melville House, 2011.

_____. "Of Flying Cars and the Declining Rate of Profit." *Baffler*, no. 19 (Spring 2012): 66–84.

_____. *The Utopia of Rules: Technology, Stupidity, and the Secret Joys of Bureaucracy*. Brooklyn, NY: Melville House, 2015.

Gutman, Herbert G. "Protestantism and the American Labor Movement: The Christian Spirit in the Gilded Age." *American Historical Review* 72, no.1 (1966): 74–101.

Hajnal, John. "European Marriage Patterns in Perspective." In *Population in History: Essays in Historical Demography*, edited by D. V. Glass and D. E. C. Eversley, 101–43. London: Edward Arnold, 1965.

_____. "Two Kinds of Preindustrial Household Formation System." *Population and Development Review* 8, no. 3 (September 1982): 449–94.

Hanlon, Gerard. *The Dark Side of Management: A Secret History of Management Theory*. London: Routledge, 2016.

Hardt, Michael, and Antonio Negri. *Labor of Dionysus: A Critique of the State Form*. Minneapolis: University of Minnesota Press, 1994.

_____. *Empire*. Cambridge, MA: Harvard University Press, 2000.

Hayes, Robert M. "A Simplified Model for the Fine Structure of National Information Economies." In *Proceedings of NIT 1992: The Fifth International Conference on New Information Technology*, 175–94. W. Newton, MA. MicroUse Information, 1992.

Hochschild, Arlie Russell. *The Managed Heart: Commercialization of Human Feeling*. Berkeley: University of California Press, 2012.

Holloway, John. *Crack Capitalism*. London: Pluto Press, 2010.

Ignatiev, Noel. *How the Irish Became White*. New York: Routledge, 1995.

Kazin, Michael. *The Populist Persuasion: An American History*. New York: Basic Books, 1995.

Keen, Steve. *Debunking Economics: The Naked Emperor Dethroned?* London: Zed, 2011.

Klein, G. S. "The Vital Pleasures." In *Psychoanalytic Theory: An Exploration of Essentials*, edited by M. M. Gill and Leo Roseberger, 210–38. New York: International Universities Press, 1967.

Kraus, M .W., S. Côté, and D. Keltner. "Social Class, Contextualism, and Empathic Accuracy." *Psychological Science* 21, no. 11 (2010): 1716–23.

Kussmaul, Anne. *Servants in Husbandry in Early-Modern England.* Cambridge: Cambridge University Press, 1981.

Laslett, Peter. "Characteristics of the Western Family Considered over Time." In *Household and Family in Past Time,* edited by P. Laslett and R. Wall. Cambridge: Cambridge University Press, 1972.

_____. *Family Life and Illicit Love in Earlier Generations.* Cambridge: Cambridge University Press, 1977.

_____. "Family and Household as Work Group and Kin Group." In *Family Forms in Historic Europe,* edited by R. Wall. Cambridge: Cambridge University Press, 1983.

_____. *The World We Have Lost, Further Explored: England Before the Industrial Revolution.* New York: Charles Scribner's Sons, 1984.

Lazerow, Jama. *Religion and the Working Class in Antebellum America.* Washington, DC: Smithsonian Institution Press, 1995.

Lazzarato, Maurizio. "Immaterial Labor." In *Radical Thought in Italy,* edited by Paolo Virno and Michael Hardt, 133–47. Minneapolis: University of Minnesota Press, 1996.

Le Goff, Jacques. *Time, Work and Culture in the Middle Ages.* Chicago: University of Chicago Press, 1982.

Lockwood, Benjamin B., Charles G. Nathanson, and E. Glen Weyl, "Taxation and the Allocation of Talent." *Journal of Political Economy* 125, no. 5 (October 2017): 1635–82, www.journals.uchicago.edu/doi/full/10.1086/693393.

Maier, Corinne. *Bonjour Paresse: De l'art et la nécessité d'en faire le moins possible en entreprise.* Paris: Editions Michalan, 2004.

Mills, C. Wright. *White Collar: The American Middle Classes.* New York: Galaxy Books, 1951.

Morse, Nancy, and Robert Weiss. "The Function and Meaning of Work and the Job." *American Sociological Review* 20, no. 2 (1966): 191–98.

Nietzsche, Friedrich. *Dawn of the Day.* 1911). New York: Macmillan, 1911.

Orr, Yancey, and Raymond Orr. "The Death of Socrates: Managerialism, Metrics and Bureaucratization in Universities." *Australian Universities' Review* 58, no. 2 (2016): 15–25.

Pagels, Elaine. *Adam, Eve and the Serpent.* New York: Vintage Books, 1988.

Paulsen, Roland. *Empty Labor: Idleness and Workplace Resistance.* Cambridge: Cambridge University Press, 2014.

Pessen, Edward. *Most Uncommon Jacksonians: The Radical Leaders of the Early Labor Movement.* Albany, NY: SUNY Press, 1967.

Bibliography

Ray, Benjamin C. *Myth, Ritual and Kingship in Buganda*. London: Oxford University Press, 1991.

Rediker, Marcus. *The Slave Ship: A Human History*. London: Penguin, 2004.

Reich, Robert. *The Work of Nations: Preparing Ourselves for 21st Century Capitalism*. New York: Alfred A. Knopf, 1992.

Russell, Bertrand. *In Praise of Idleness*. London: Unwin Hyman, 1935.

Schmidt, Jeff. *Disciplined Minds: A Critical Look at Salaried Professionals and the Soul-Battering System That Shapes Their Lives*. London: Rowman & Littlefield, 2001.

Sennett, Richard. *The Fall of Public Man*. London: Penguin, 2003.

_____. *Respect: The Formation of Character in an Age of Inequality*. London: Penguin, 2004.

_____. *The Corrosion of Character: The Personal Consequences of Work in the New Capitalism*. New York: Norton, 2008.

_____. *The Craftsman*. New York: Penguin, 2009.

Standing, Guy. *The Precariat: The New Dangerous Class* (Bloomsbury Revelations). London: Bloomsbury Academic Press, 2016.

_____. *Basic Income: And How We Can Make It Happen*. London: Pelican, 2017.

Starkey, David. "Representation Through Intimacy: A Study in the Symbolism of Monarchy and Court Office in Early Modern England." In *Symbols and Sentiments: Cross-Cultural Studies in Symbolism*, edited by Ioan Lewis, 187–224. London: Academic Press, 1977.

Stellar, Jennifer, Vida Manzo, Michael Kraus, and Dacher Keltner. "Class and Compassion: Socioeconomic Factors Predict Responses to Suffering." *Emotion* 12, no. 3 (2011): 1–11.

Stone, Lawrence. *The Family, Sex and Marriage in England, 1500–1800*. London: Weidenfeld and Nicolson, 1977.

Summers, John. *The Politics of Truth: Selected Writings of C. Wright Mills*. Oxford: Oxford University Press, 2008.

Tawney, R. H. *Religion and the Rise of Capitalism*. New York: Harcourt, Brace & World, 1924.

Terkel, Studs. *Working: People Talk About What They Do All Day and How They Feel About What They Do*. New York: New Press, 1972.

Thomas, Keith. *Religion and the Decline of Magic*. New York: Scribner Press, 1971.

_____. "Age and Authority in Early Modern England." *Proceedings of the British Academy* 62 (1976): 1–46.

_____. *The Oxford Book of Work*. Oxford: Oxford University Press, 1999.

Thompson, E. P. *The Making of the English Working Class*. London: Victor Gollancz, 1963.

_____. "Time, Work-Discipline and Industrial Capitalism." *Past & Present* 38 (1967): 56–97.

Thompson, Paul. *The Nature of Work: An Introduction to Debates on the Labour Process*. London: Macmillan, 1983.

Veltman, Andrea. *Meaningful Work*. Oxford: Oxford University Press, 2016.

Wall, Richard. *Family Forms in Historic Europe*. Cambridge: Cambridge University Press, 1983.

Weber, Max. *The Protestant Ethic and the Spirit of Capitalism*. London: Unwin Press, 1930.

Weeks, Kathi. *The Problem with Work: Feminism, Marxism, Antiwork Politics, and Postwork Imaginaries*. Durham, NC: Duke University Press, 2011.

Western, Mark, and Erik Olin Wright. "The Permeability of Class Boundaries to Intergenerational Mobility Among Men in the United States, Canada, Norway, and Sweden." *American Sociological Review* 59, no. 4 (August 1994): 606–29.

White, R. "Motivation Reconsidered: The Concept of Competence." *Psychological Review* 66 (1959): 297–333.

Williams, Eric. *Capitalism and Slavery*. New York: Capricorn Books, 1966.

Wood, Ellen Meiksins. *The Origins of Capitalism: A Longer View*. London: Verso, 2002.